To John Burleigh

With love & thanks

for your support of

the arts.

Hansonia

Caldwell

3/97

FIRST EDITION

AFRICAN AMERICAN MUSIC - A CHRONOLOGY 1619 - 1995

BY DR. HANSONIA L. CALDWELL

IKORO COMMUNICATIONS, INC.
LOS ANGELES, CA

First printing 1996.

ISBN 0-9650441-0-6
ISBN 0-9650441-1-4 *(hardback)*

ATTENTION COLLEGES AND UNIVERSITIES, CORPORATIONS, AND PROFESSIONAL ORGANIZATIONS. Quantity discounts are available on bulk purchases of this book for educational training purposes, fund raising or gift giving. Special books, booklets, or book excerpts can also be created to fit your specific needs. For information contact: IKORO Communications, Inc. P.O. Box 7390, Culver City, CA 90233 (310) 649-0372.

TO MY MOTHER, BEULAH HALL CALDWELL

CONTENTS

ACKNOWLEDGMENTS

I want to express my gratitude for the support of my husband, Charles Harriford, whose enthusiasm inspired this book, whose tenacity kept us on task, and whose skills helped to create the index. I am thankful to those who helped in the preparation of the final copy, including Diane Trotter Nelson and Dion Riley. I am also particularly grateful to Reid Freeman for his excellent editing and Linda Clegg for her proofreading.

A very special acknowledgment goes to a number of people for reading and commenting upon the text, including David Baker, Nicola Fowles, Joyce Johnson, Maulana Karenga, Ora Williams, Dean Selase Williams and the students of the African American music course I teach at California State University, Dominguez Hills. I am also indebted to a number of people for providing insightful comments, suggestions and materials, including Diedre Badejo, Trish Brys-Overeem, Rosemarie Cook-Glover, Jester Hairston, Danellen Joseph, and William A. Little. Of course, the book could not have been written without the assistance of the librarians at the Library of Congress and the New York Public Library (Schomburg Collection and Lincoln Center Americana Collection).

The book is dedicated to my mother, Beulah Hall Caldwell, whose newspaper clipping collection provided an important view of the musical life of Baltimore, Maryland. She always supported my love of music and throughout my life consistently affirmed the value of black culture. Her vision emerges in a poem she wrote in 1988:

The History of The Music of The Black Man

If you open your eyes, ears and heart
You will, through history, learn how black music did start.
It includes a great, wonderful lesson for all mankind....

That should be shared and relished down through the years,
For your heart will let you hear the black man's moans,
groans and tears...
While teaching mankind in this world of all races
The trials, tribulations and struggles that Black History
traces
The imported black man's cries were ignored,
While his value as a stud and field worker were gloried.
The black man worked and gave praises to God.
Who in His good time, used His chastening rod
For the black man's love was certain and sound.
Our history grew, and became renowned.
In our hearts, we give love and caring
While, with your history.....we are sharing
Let us give God thanks for His sincere love,
Until we meet with Him and reign above. Hallelujah!

INTRODUCTION

African American Music - A Chronology has been developed to provide the reader with a different way of looking at the evolution of African American music and musicians. As public interest in African American history has grown, numerous chronologies have been published. Many include limited amounts of information in a generic arts category; but none provide an inclusive overview of African American accomplishments in music. And, too many texts that purport to present a history of music in the United States ignore the breadth of the contributions of African Americans. This book presents a chronological record of the music and musicians of African American culture from 1619 to the present day.

Historians will note that the first Africans arrived in the Western Hemisphere in 1492 with Christopher Columbus. Subsequently, numerous Spanish explorers and conquerors were accompanied to the Americas by Africans (e.g. with the Vasco Nunez de Balboa expedition to the Pacific Ocean in 1513, with the Hernando Cortes expedition to Mexico in 1519, with Lucas Vasquez de Aylions expedition to the Florida Peninsula in 1526). Furthermore, throughout the 14th and 15th centuries, thousands of Africans were brought into Latin America as slaves. However, the study of the manifestation of African musical culture in the United States begins with the development of slavery in the English colonies, as African musical practices respond to the new circumstance. Consequently, this study begins in 1619.

All genres of African American music are represented (Spirituals, Gospel Music, Ragtime, Minstrelsy, The Blues, Jazz, R&B, Soul, Disco, Reggae and Rap), as well as the work of African American musicians who specialize in the Americanized European Classical tradition of the concert stage, the Broadway tradition of Musical Theatre, and the Country tradition of the Grand Ole Opry. Additionally, some of the significant accomplishments in theatre, dance, visual arts (particularly works that reflect a connection to music), religion, film, and sports are presented to provide a context for viewing the musical history. Certain technological, economic, sociological and intellectual developments that affect the evolution of black music are also cited.

The study presents a systematic chronicle of the total musical experience of African Americans, placed in the context of overall intellectual and cultural history. In so doing, it is divided into eight chapters, denoting significant eras, including:

1619 - 1865	**The Music of Enslavement and Struggle**
1866 - 1900	**The Music of Emancipation**
1901 - 1920	**The New Secular Voice**
1921 - 1945	**The Music of the Renaissance**
1946 - 1959	**The Music of International Communication**
1960 - 1969	**The Music of Civil Rights and Cultural Revolution**
1970 - 1980	**The Music of Commercialism and Fusion**
1981 - 1995	**The Music of New Media and Contemporary Griots**

These dates span frames of time in which there are innovations in the individual genres of African American music, usually in response to sociological, economic, political, religious and philosophical developments. The innovations emerge as individual musicians achieve unique and significant accomplishments that make an impact upon the community. Within each period the individual years open with a review of significant births, a celebration of our elders (agba) that gives an overview of the people who have become our musical national treasures. The dateline continues with a presentation of the creativity of the year (kuumba) and a recognition of the concluding life passage (iku). This factual picture of African American music and musicians reveals a continuity of creativity that is truly impressive.

The data is derived from records that have been reviewed in various archives in Los Angeles, New York, Memphis and Baltimore, and in the Library of Congress. Additionally, personal interviews of musicians and scholars have been conducted by the author, and information developed by numerous scholars in the field has been synthesized. The book concludes with a full bibliography and index.

A particular effort has been made to include documentation of the creation of individual musical compositions, recordings and other works of art, while recognizing the problems connected with achieving precision in the process of dating. The book also documents compositions by white composers that reflect the influence of African American music.

One volume cannot possibly cover every aspect of almost four centuries of African American music and musicians. The author also recognizes that there is a special challenge that emerges from the typical research tendency to present historical information that has a regional bias. For example, most of the activity of Swing bands is placed within the context of life in New York, Chicago, Kansas City and Los Angeles. A complete picture of the Swing years needs to embrace the musicians of the other forty-six states. This, then is a beginning, and it is an ongoing project. Therefore, the book begins a conversation between the author and the reader. For dialogue, the author can be reached via e-mail - aamme@ikoro.com or via fax, 310-649-2758.

AFRICAN AMERICAN MUSIC -
A CHRONOLOGY
1619 - 1995

1

1619 - 1865
THE MUSIC OF ENSLAVEMENT
AND STRUGGLE

This is the period of the Atlantic Slave Trade portion of the global African Holocaust. A population of Africans is stolen from the continent of Africa and legally and illegally imported to the United States over a span of 250 years. As they arrive, the institution of slavery is formed and an African American musical heritage is established.

While whites import the formal "written" music of England, France, Germany and Italy, enslavement becomes the driving force in the creation of the musical culture of the country. Africans create music (spirituals) that speaks to various aspects of enslavement, and the music they craft becomes the foundation for all other music types created by blacks in America.

Africans and whites create music for the churches and religious movements of this period, some of which serves the purpose of providing a Christian focus for living within this unpardonable situation, and some of which serves the purpose of articulating protest. In America, the Africans enter a strange world where their language, religion, traditions, music and overall culture are denigrated and suppressed. Since, among other things, the practice of African religion becomes punishable by death throughout the south, Africans have to find new approaches to religious expression. Christianity is all that is legally available, and the Africans turn to it. Particularly, these gifted artists adapt themselves to the new religion through music by taking familiar African melodies and changing the words to fit the English Christian mold, by adapting denominational hymns of the United States, and by creating new, compelling melodies set to imaginative lyrics that dramatically chronicle the episodes and imagery of the Bible.

The rhythms, harmonies, and vocal cadence always remain African. And the adaptation of this music to the work environment as rowing songs, work songs, and during breaks, as social songs, is also African in practice. This is functional music, appropriate for almost every situation—music to be used much as the African ancestors would have used it, present in every aspect of the new culture. More importantly, this is music that helped create a new sense of community.

The musical metamorphosis resulted in the universally appealing spiritual, a folk music of many forms and styles, from the slow, exquisitely melodic spirituals to the rhythmically organizing work song to the quick, driving and ecstatic "shout spirituals" often used in the camp meetings. From the spiritual sprang the holler, gospel music, creole songs, ragtime, the blues, rhythm and blues, rock and roll, soul music, and the various phases of jazz.

Additionally, during this era, whites and Africans create music (abolitionist songs) to inspire the political movement that is fighting against enslavement. Whites create the popular music industry of the United States with the music of minstrelsy, a genre that imitates and denigrates slave culture. Africans create and perform music in the style of the music of European culture, as slaves who are given the responsibility of providing entertainment for the slave owners, and as free Blacks who make an effort to assimilate into the culture of this country. The time span ends with the end of the Civil War.

TRENDS
1619 - 1865

1620s

◊ The African Holocaust generates an enslaved population that begins to establish the African foundation for musical practice in the United States.

1640s

◊ Individual states begin to pass slave codes to establish a legal framework for slavery.

◊ White colonialists begin to put into place the European foundation for musical practice in the United States.

1670s

◊ Various court records and census reports reveal that blacks are reported with only a first name (no surname), establishing the foundation for the evolution of the Sambo image, a focal image subsequently used on the minstrelsy stage and on the covers of Tin Pan Alley sheet music publications.

1680s

◊ Laws restricting the use of instruments by enslaved Africans begin to emerge in the West Indies. And, in the next century, throughout the Southern United States. This legal approach to controlling the musical performance of African Americans continues up to 1995 (noting the legal attacks on Rap).

1690s

◊ Captured slaves are urged to dance on the Dutch, English and French slave ships in order to diminish the mortality rate and preserve their health. This practice continues until the end of international slave trading. Ethnomusicologist Dena J. Epstein reports an example of this specific activity on the slave ship *Hannibal,* documented in her book *Sinful Tunes and Spirituals.*

1700s

♭ Numerous accounts of the singing, dancing and instruments of Africans in Africa, in the West Indies, and in the United States appear throughout the century in the diaries and journals of English, French, Spanish and Portuguese observers.

♭ Missionaries begin to proselytize Christianity to blacks, thus helping to create a shared vocabulary for Africans who arrived in America speaking many different languages, and helping to create a theology that helped Africans survive within the institution of slavery—a theology that was articulated within the texts of spirituals.

1730s

♭ The "Great Awakening" - a religious movement of Presbyterians, Baptists and Methodists lasting until about 1790. Described as an "ecclesiastical declaration of independence from the Old World," the movement establishes the foundation for evangelical theology. During this time, hymn singing is popularized (particularly the use of hymns by Dr. Isaac Watts and Charles Wesley), extending until about 1790.

1740s

♭ Blacks begin to provide social entertainment as fiddlers and dance musicians on the plantations in the South.

1750s

♭ Letters from white enslavers and visitors document the use of work songs performed by enslaved Africans to control the rhythm of work in the fields, on boats and at other work sites—a continuation of an African cultural practice.

1760s

♭ Blacks living in enslavement give musical expression to their sorrow with the development of the Spiritual.

1770s

◊ Letters from white visitors to the West Indies and the South describe the singing and dancing that occurs at the funerals of enslaved Africans, a continuation of an African practice. These letters provide the earliest documentation of the musical practices of Africans.

1780s

◊ A number of Europeans of African descent begin achieving acclaim for their abilities to perform and compose music of the European classical tradition. This includes The Chevalier de Saint-George and George Polgreen Bridgetower. Ultimately, in the first decade of the twentieth century an Afro-English composer (Samuel Coleridge-Taylor) becomes very influential upon African Americans, inspiring them to study and perform the music of this tradition.

1820s

◊ The concept of Sunday School begins in the United States, an outgrowth of the Second Awakening's camp meeting movement. The Sunday School movement eventually leads to the development of the Temperance movement, leading to the establishment of Prohibition, a legal situation that generates the commercial foundation for jazz.

1830s

◊ The Negro Philharmonic Society is established in New Orleans, performing symphony concerts throughout the decade.

◊ A concentration of African American composers and performers of the European classical genre begin to emerge in Philadelphia and in New England.

◊ Minstrel Thomas "Daddy" Rice performs comic representations of Jim Crow, Corn Meal and other blacks in an act that tours the United States and London.

◊ The abolitionist movement begins to flourish.

1840s

- In a period known as the Golden Age of Minstrelsy (lasting until about 1875), full-scale minstrelsy shows/Ethiopian Concerts are popularized as a burlesque of black culture,

- Antislavery organizations flourish, using music to generate excitement and unity—music that could be viewed as the precursor to 1960s civil rights freedom songs.

- The Underground Railroad flourishes, using spirituals as "Map" songs, such as *Follow the Drinking Gourd* and as "signal songs," such as *Steal Away, Good News, The Chariot's Comin', Swing Low, Sweet Chariot* and *Wade in the Water.*

- Santeria - "worship of the saints," a religion that mixes Yoruba culture with Catholicism, emerges in Cuba, including the use of drumming and dancing to create spirit possession. It is eventually imported to the United States as a result of the 1959 Cuban Revolution and finds some musical expression in the free jazz movement of the 1960s.

1850s

- Visitors to the South write letters and journals that document the performance of street cries, used by black street vendors to sell their wares.

- Blackface minstrel shows become extremely popular. Blacks begin to form touring minstrel companies.

- The abolitionist movement flourishes, with singing family ensembles providing entertainment at the various meetings.

1860s

- Minstrelsy continues to be popular. Increasing numbers of blacks begin to appear (in blackface) on the minstrelsy stage because of the shortage of actors caused by the war - and eventually black troupes begin to perform.

- Black marching bands begin to appear in New Orleans parades (the precursors of the jazz band).

- The decade of the Civil War.

ACHIEVEMENT DATELINE
1619 - 1865

 **1619**

The Atlantic Slave Trade portion of the global African Holocaust begins a population flow of Africans into the United States. The first twenty Africans are captured and brought to the English colonies, arriving in Jamestown, Virginia as indentured servants. Through the next century the structure of enslavement emerges and grows. One aspect of the cultural response of blacks to this enslavement is the creation of Spirituals.

 **1640**

Kuumba:

Psalm singing constitutes the primary musical practice in the white churches of much of the North and some of the South (through 1720), subsequently with blacks joining whites in the churches and often providing leadership. Spirituals begin to emerge when African musical practice interacts with the musical expression of the white church.

 **1641**

The peculiar institution of slavery begins to acquire a legal foundation with the state-by-state establishment of slave codes. Massachusetts becomes the first colony to legalize slavery.

1648

Kuumba:

Slavery begins to acquire a theological foundation. For example, Massachusetts requires its families to provide religious instruction to both their children and their slaves. This has the unforeseen affect of providing a shared language for African peoples who arrive in the United

States from many different tribes, speaking many different languages. Eventually, in all the enslavement territory of the country the language of religion becomes the primary language of spirituals. For example, the miraculous story told in Daniel 6: 19-23 - *At the first light of dawn, the king got up and hurried to the lions' den. When he came near the den, he called to Daniel in an anguished voice, "Daniel, servant of the living God, has your God, whom you serve continually, been able to rescue you from the lions?" Daniel answered, "O king, live forever! My God sent his angel, and he shut the mouths of the lions. They have not hurt me, because I was found innocent in his sight. Nor have I ever done any wrong before you, O king." The king was overjoyed and gave orders to lift Daniel out of the den. And when Daniel was lifted from the den, no wound was found on him because he had trusted in his God...* becomes:

> *Didn't my Lord deliver Daniel,*
> *Deliver Daniel? Deliver Daniel?*
> *Didn't my Lord deliver Daniel?*
> *And why not every man?*
>
> *He delivered Daniel from the lions' den*
> *And Jonah from the belly of the whale,*
> *He delivered children from the fiery furnace,*
> *And why not every man?*
>
> *Didn't my Lord deliver Daniel,*
> *Deliver Daniel? Deliver Daniel?*
> *Didn't my Lord deliver Daniel?*
> *And why not every man?*

 **1650**

Approximately 300 blacks live in the colonies.

 **1651**

Kuumba:

The revised edition of the *Bay Psalm Book* is published and used by whites throughout the colonies via the hymn singing practice of "lining out," a style of recitative-like chanting. The song leader sings one or two lines of text, ending on a pitch that is picked up immediately by the congregation as it comes in to repeat the line. This lining tradition is incorporated into the church of the African American.

1652

Rhode Island establishes laws to recognize and regulate slavery.

1661

Virginia establishes laws to recognize and regulate slavery.

1663

Maryland establishes laws to recognize and regulate slavery.

1665

New York establishes laws to recognize and regulate slavery.

1682

South Carolina establishes laws to recognize and regulate slavery.

1700

Pennsylvania establishes laws to recognize and regulate slavery. At this point, slavery has been fully established in all of the original colonies.

1701

The Society for the Propagation of the Gospel in Foreign Parts is established by the Church of England.

1702

The Society for the Propagation of the Gospel in Foreign Parts begins to send missionaries to proselytize black slaves (working at this task until 1785), followed by the work of numerous others intent upon converting blacks throughout the United States.

 **1704**

Kuumba:

The *Boston News-Letter* becomes the first permanent colonial newspaper. It includes the typical practice of providing advertisements for the sale of slaves. Many of the ads reflect the fact that musical talent in slaves has become a priority qualification. Slaves who could lead the "call and response" of work songs are in special demand.

 **1705**

Kuumba:

Minister/physician Isaac Watts publishes a collection of religious poems, *Hymns and Spiritual Songs*, which becomes popular throughout the colonies—performed by blacks and whites.

 **1715**

North Carolina establishes laws to recognize and regulate slavery.

North American slave population reaches 58,000.

 **1718**

The city of New Orleans is established as a French colony, and builds its wealth as a major seaport for the slave trade. Its culture blends French, Spanish and African influences.

 **1719**

The black population of New Orleans is established with 147 slaves.

 **1720**

The first African slaves are brought into Mississippi.

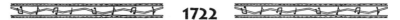 **1722**

The free black population of New Orleans begins to emerge.

 **1725**

The North American slave population reaches 75,000.

 **1735**

John and Charles Wesley come to America to preach, bringing with them the emotional hymn style that became the hallmark of the Great Awakening.

 **1739**

Agba:

Black classical composer Chevalier de Saint-Georges (Joseph Boulogne) is born in the West Indies.

Kuumba:

A violent slave revolt, the Stono Rebellion, takes place in Stono, South Carolina. The insurrection is triggered when African slaves drum-beat a message of revolt to alert slaves at neighboring plantations. Eventually, throughout the South, blacks reflect their unwillingness to accept enslavement through both music (e.g. *Didn't My Lord Deliver Daniel*) and action.

 **1740**

Kuumba:

Fearing that music would be used to communicate and camouflage insurrections, South Carolina passes a Slave Code that prohibits the use of "drums, horns or other loud instruments" by enslaved Africans. Instead, slaves continue the African tradition of using the human body as a percussion instrument, with hand claps, knee slaps and foot beats used to substitute for musical instruments.

The North American slave population reaches 150,000.

 **1741**

Kuumba:

Blacks in the New England colonies begin the practice of celebrating the "Negro election day," during which time a "Negro governor" would be elected. They accompanied the celebrations with music and dance. The festivities reflect strong similarities with those that were celebrated in the Caribbean, in the black areas of Latin America, and in Africa.

North Carolina's legislature passes the Act of 1741, requiring children born to life servants to assume the status of the mother.

 **1742**

Rev. John Wesley and his brother Rev. Charles Wesley publish the forerunner of the Methodist Hymnal, *Collection of Psalms and Hymns*, a collection that was very popular during the Great Awakening.

 **1746**

Agba:

Composer/Singing-school master Newport Gardner (Occramer Marycoo) is born in Africa.

 **1750**

Kuumba:

New England slaves continue the tradition of celebrating the "Lection Day," holiday and include various musical performances in their festivities. Slaves typically accompany their festivities with the instruments such as banjo, fiddle, quills, tambourine, bones, and when available, drums or pots and pans, that are struck like drums.

The North American slave population reaches 236,000.

 **1751**

Kuumba:

Presbyterian minister Samuel Davies becomes an active evangelist, proselytizing to blacks throughout Virginia and other parts of the South distributing Bibles and the psalms and hymns of Isaac Watts. He and numerous other ministers wrote in reports and journals about the singing abilities of blacks.

 **1752**

Kuumba:

Blacks are reported to be providing fiddle music to accompany the dances of the colonialists.

 **1755**

Georgia establishes laws to recognize and regulate slavery.

 **1760**

Kuumba:

Musicologist John Lovell, Jr., identifies this as the year of the earliest appearance of the Spiritual, a repertoire of music identified as the first authentic American folk song. Eventually between 1000 and 6000 songs are created, expressing both the pain of enslavement and the path to freedom. Examples include *Go Down Moses, Nobody Knows The Trouble I've Seen, Ain't Goin' To Study War No Mo', Behold That Star, Couldn't Hear Nobody Pray, De Gospel Train, Deep River, Didn't My Lord Deliver Daniel, Don't Be Weary Traveler, Ev'ry Time I Feel The Spirit, Go Down In The Lonesome Valley, Go Tell It On De Mountains,*

I Don't Feel No-Ways Tired, I Got A Home In-a Dat Rock, I Stood On De Ribber Ob Jerdon, I've Been In De Storm So Long, I Want To Be Ready, Joshua Fit De Battle Ob Jericho, Let Us Cheer the Weary Traveler, Little David Play On Your Harp, Oh Didn't It Rain, Oh Wasn't Dat a Wide Ribber, Oh Peter Go Ring Dem Bells, Sinner Please Doan Let Dis Harves' Pass, Sometimes I Feel Like a Motherless Child, Stan' Still Jordan, Swing Low, Sweet Chariot, Tis Me, O Lord, Wade In De Water, Were You There.

Newport Gardner is sold into slavery (to Caleb Gardner of Newport, Rhode Island). In spite of his enslavement, he teaches himself to read, write, sing and compose.

A Narrative of the Uncommon Sufferings, and Surprising Deliverance of Briton Hammon, A Negro Man Servant to General Winslow, of Marshfield is published—one of the earliest examples of a slave narrative, many of which contain descriptions of the musical part of life on a plantation.

 **1764**

Kuumba:

Promise Anthem, a composition by Newport Gardner, is published.

 **1767**

Kuumba:

Andrew Barton, a white composer, writes and publishes *The Disappointment, or the Force of Credulity,* a satirical ballad comic opera that has been identified as containing the first published lyrics of "Yankee Doodle" and the first role in American drama depicting a black character, a Jamaican given the name Raccoon. The opera is given its world premiere by musicians from the University of Rochester's Eastman School of Music at the Library of Congress as part of the 1976 Bicentennial celebration. The original premiere is scheduled to be performed by the American Company of Comedians in Philadelphia in 1769, but the event is canceled because the text presents characters who are perceived to be "unfit for the stage."

Phillis Peters Wheatley, a former slave, writes the poem *A Poem by Phillis, A Negro Girl, on the Death of Reverend George Whitefield.*

 **1769**

Kuumba:

The Pad Lock is performed in New York, a comic opera that contained a black character, Mungo, who sang a "Negro Song." This play is a precursor of the 19th century minstrelsy.

 **1770**

Runaway slave Crispus Attucks becomes one of the first to die in the Boston Massacre.

The North American slave population reaches 462,000.

 **1772**

The first black Baptist Church is founded at Silver Bluff, South Carolina.

 **1773**

Kuumba:

A group of blacks petition the Governor of Massachusetts for their freedom.

Phillis Peters Wheatley becomes the first black to write a book that is published in the United States. *Poems on Various Subjects, Religious and Moral.*

 **1774**

Kuumba:

Records show that blacks entertain at plantation parties, including performances on the fiddle and the banjo.

 **1775**

Kuumba:

The first Abolitionist society is formed in Philadelphia, Pennsylvania, beginning the Abolitionist movement, with its accompanying musical response (signal/code songs used by Underground Railroad conductors and Abolitionist songs performed at rallies).

The Revolutionary War begins.

 **1776**

The Declaration of Independence is signed in Philadelphia.

The black population of the U.S. consists of 500,000 slaves and 40,000 free blacks.

A slave rebellion led by Toussaint L'Ouverture occurs in Haiti.

 **1777**

Vermont becomes the first territory to abolish slavery.

 **1778**

Kuumba:

Composer/violinist Chevalier de Saint-Georges composes a set of six string quartets.

 **1779**

Jean Baptiste Pointe DuSable becomes the father of the city of Chicago.

1780

Agba:

Concert violinist George Polgreen Bridgetower is born in Baila, Poland.

Kuumba:

The era of the "Second Awakening" (1780-1835). This is a period of interracial camp meeting revivals noted for spontaneous praying and singing, the prolonged altar call, the invitation to conversion, and the performance of camp meeting congregational hymns, with their repetitious refrains. After the completion of the general session, there are performances of a number of musical items by African Americans in their own tent (including spirituals and the emergence of the "Ring Shout"—a music/dance form derived from African traditional practices that is often performed in a circle by blacks.)

Massachusetts declares all men to be born free and equal.

Slavery is abolished in Pennsylvania.

1781

Kuumba:

Composer/violinist Chevalier de Saint-Georges composes a group of three sonatas for violin and piano.

Twenty-six Africans are part of the group that become the founders of the city of Los Angeles.

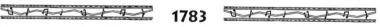 **1783**

The Revolutionary War ends.

 **1784**

Kuumba:

Thomas Jefferson makes observations about the musical creativity of blacks in his *Notes on the State of Virginia: In music they are more generally gifted than the whites, with accurate ears for tune and time, and they have been found capable of imagining a small catch. Whether they will be equal to the composition of a more extensive run of melody, or of complicated harmony, is yet to be proved.* He also provides documentation of the use of the banjo by Africans: *The instrument proper to them is the Banjar, which they brought hither from Africa, and which is the original of the guitar....*

Slavery is abolished in Rhode Island.

Richard Allen is licensed to preach at Philadelphia's St. George's Methodist Episcopal Church.

 **1787**

Kuumba:

Richard Allen purchases a parcel of real estate in Philadelphia (that ultimately becomes the home of the African Methodist Episcopal (AME) church). The property is the oldest land to be continuously owned by blacks in the U. S.

Allen and Absalom Jones organize the Free African Society in Philadelphia, Pennsylvania to promote self-reliance and the abolition of slavery.

The African Free School opens in New York City.

The Free African Society is established in Philadelphia. It assisted its members with their funeral and burial needs, thus continuing the African practices that includes the performance of appropriate music.

Prince Hall establishes African Lodge No. 1 in Boston, Massachusetts, the first Black Masonic lodge.

The country of Sierra Leone is established by England to serve as a resettlement site for emancipated blacks from Canada and England.

The U.S. Constitution is adopted.

The Marriage Act of 1787 passes into law in North Carolina, stipulating that *if a free Negro marries a slave without the written permission of the master, he shall be liable and held to pay the masters of such slave the sum of ten pounds and on failing to pay such sum, shall be held to service the master or mistress for and during the term of one year.*

 **1788**

The first African Baptist Church is established by Andrew Bryan in Savannah, Georgia.

 **1789**

Kuumba:

Violinist George Bridgetower, the son of a West Indian father and a polish mother, makes his debut as a soloist in the Concert Spiritual of Paris, France.

The Sons of the African Society is organized in Boston to assist its members with their funeral and burial needs, continuing the elaborate African "Going Home" practices.

Benjamin Franklin publicly denounces slavery, and becomes president of the Pennsylvania Society for Promoting the Abolition of Slavery.

George Washington becomes president of the United States.

 **1790**

Kuumba:

Violinist George Bridgetower makes his London debut.

The Brown Fellowship Society is established in Charleston, South Carolina, to assist its members with their funeral and burial needs.

750,000 blacks are reported in the first U.S. Census.

 **1791**

Kuumba:

Composer/teacher Newport Gardner purchases his freedom, and establishes a singing school in Newport, Massachusetts. He becomes the first African American publicly acknowledged to be a professional musician.

Benjamin Banneker is appointed to help survey and lay out the Federal Territory, an area that becomes the District of Columbia.

St. Thomas Episcopal Church is established in Philadelphia as the first Black Episcopal church of the United States.

 **1792**

Agba:

Composer/band leader Frank Johnson is born in Martinique, West Indies.

Kuumba:

The painting by Samuel Jennings, *Liberty Displaying the Arts and Sciences,* includes the portrait of a black playing the Banjo, further documentation of the use of this instrument by blacks.

Congress passes laws to establish military bands - ensembles that will soon include blacks.

 **1793**

Congress passes the first Fugitive Slave Law, making it easier for slaveholders to capture escaped slaves.

Canada passes the Upper Canada Abolition Act permitting any slave *newly entering the province, whether with his or her master or in flight from bondage* to be deemed legally free. Canada subsequently becomes a destination for slave escapees.

 **1794**

Kuumba:

Bethel African Methodist Episcopal Church is founded in Philadelphia, Pennsylvania, and helps establish the tradition of African American church music rooted in the free black community, a development that parallels the evolution of the spiritual on the plantations of the South. The church becomes a haven for runaway slaves.

Eli Whitney patents a device to separate cotton fiber from the seed, revolutionizing the cotton industry in the United States.

 **1795**

Italian composer Muzio Clementi (active in England) composes a piano sonata with variations on an *Arietta alla Negra*.

 **1796**

John Adams becomes president of the United States.

 **1797**

Kuumba:

The enslaved African continues to adapt the text of the Bible into the lyrics of spirituals. The Book of Revelations is a favorite, as seen in the spiritual *My Lord, What A Mornin'*. Revelations 8, 10: *The third angel sounded his trumpet, and a great star, blazing like a torch, fell from the sky on a third of the rivers and on the springs of water—* becomes:

> *My Lord what a mornin',*
> *My Lord what a mornin',*
> *Oh, my Lord what a mornin',*
> *When de stars begin to fall*
> *When de stars begin to fall.*

 **1798**

Kuumba:

Biblical verses that describe the possibility of being saved from a desperate situation also provide lyrics for spirituals. For example, Mark 10, verse 46 - *Then they came to Jericho. As Jesus and his disciples, together with a large crowd, were leaving the city, a blind man, Bartimaeus (that is, the Son of Timaeus), was sitting by the roadside begging, etc.,* through verse 52, provides the inspiration for the spiritual *De Blin' Man Stood On De Road An' Cried:*

> *O de blin' man stood on' de road an' cried*
> *O de blin' man stood on de road an' cried*
> *Cryin' O my Lord, save me,*
>
> *De blin' man stood on de road an' cried.*
> *Cryin' dat he might receib his sight,*
> *Cryin' dat he might receib his sight,*
> *Cryin' O my Lord, save me,*
> *De blin' man stood on de road an' cried. etc.*

Visual artist Joshua Johnston advertises his services in Baltimore, becoming the first recognized African American portrait painter.

 **1799**

Iku:

Composer Chevalier de Saint Georges dies in Paris, France.

 **1800**

Agba:

Composer/dance bandleader James Hemmenway is born in Philadelphia.

Kuumba:

Camp meetings of the "Second Awakening" are held in Logan County, Kentucky.

Free blacks in Philadelphia, Pennsylvania present an antislavery petition to Congress.

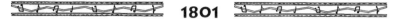 **1801**

Kuumba:

Richard Allen publishes a hymnal *A Collection of Hymns and Spiritual Songs Selected from Various Authors by Richard Allen, African Minister* (text only). This is a collection of fifty-four hymns, including music from the oral tradition of the South - the first hymnal compiled by a black man for a black congregation.

 **1802**

Kuumba:

Slaves continue the African tradition of call and response singing. In this musical structure, the performance of phrases or parts of melodies alternate between the group and the group leader. The group leader is often telling a story, in the tradition of the African griot. An example of this can be found in the spiritual *Great Gettin' Up Mornin':*

Call:	*In that great gettin' up mornin'*
Response:	*Fare thee well, fare thee well.*
Call:	*In that great gettin' up mornin'*
Response:	*Fare thee well, fare thee well.*
Call:	*I'm goin' to tell you 'bout the comin' of the judgment,*
Response:	*Fare thee well, fare thee well,*
Call:	*I'm goin' to tell you 'bout the comin' of the judgment*
Response:	*Fare thee well, fare thee well*
Call:	*In that great gettin' up mornin', etc.*

 **1803**

Kuumba:

Teacher/composer Newport Gardner writes a composition, "Crooked Shanks," that is published in the book *A Number of Original Airs, Duettos and Tirros.*

Napoleon sells Louisiana to the United States (The Louisiana Purchase) bringing New Orleans, the birthplace of Jazz, into the U.S.

 **1804**

Haiti, the first independent black republic in the Western Hemisphere, is established.

Slavery is abolished in New Jersey. The state of Ohio combats the issue of runaway slaves by passing the Black Laws, prohibiting blacks from settling in the state unless they carry proof of freedom.

 **1805**

Agba:

Abolitionist singer Alexander C. Luca (and father of the Luca family) is born in Milford, Connecticut.

Kuumba:

The African Baptist Church is established in Boston and lead by Thomas Paul.

 **1806**

Kuumba:

The quest for freedom permeates the lyrics of the spirituals that are sung by enslaved Africans:

> *O freedom! O freedom!*
> *O freedom over me!*
> *An' befo' I'd be a slave,*
> *I'll be buried in my grave,*
> *An' go home to my Lord an' be free.*

 **1807**

Agba:

Actor Ira Frederick Aldrige is born in New York City.

Kuumba:

The African slave trade is outlawed, but illegal slave trade continues until the Civil War. Anthropologist Melville Herskovits estimates the number of African slaves brought into this country between 1808 and 1860 to be two and one-half million.

The New Jersey State Legislature passes a law restricting the right to vote to "free white male citizens, 21-years of age, worth 50 pounds."

The First African Presbyterian Church is established in Philadelphia.

 **1808**

Agba:

French hornist/composer/conductor William Appo is born in Philadelphia, Pennsylvania.

Kuumba:

Abyssinian Baptist Church is established in New York.

James Madison becomes president of the United States.

The North American slave population reaches one million.

 **1809**

Agba:

Organist Ann Appo is born in Philadelphia.

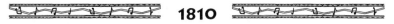 **1810**

Kuumba:

The free black (mostly Creole) population of New Orleans grows to 5,000, increasing because of the flow of free blacks from Haiti and Cuba. A significant community of musicians emerges from within this population.

The Afro-American Insurance Company opens in Philadelphia, Pennsylvania, the first insurance company to be owned by African-Americans.

 **1811**

Kuumba:

Enslaved Africans create spirituals with texts that give them hope. For example, the question that is asked in Jeremiah 8, 21-22: *Since my people are crushed, I am crushed; I mourn, and horror grips me. Is there no balm in Gilead? Is there no physician there? Why then is there no healing for the wound of my people?* is answered in the spiritual *Balm in Gilead:*

>*There is a Balm in Gilead*
>*To make the wounded whole*
>*There is a Balm in Gilead*
>*to heal the sin-sick soul.*
>
>*Sometimes I feel discouraged*
>*And think my work's in vain,*
>*But then the Holy Spirit,*
>*Revives my soul again.*
>
>*There is a Balm in Gilead, etc.*

 **1812**

Kuumba:

Spirituals migrate all over the south as blacks are sold from plantation to plantation/state to state. Using the African oral tradition, they carry their musical memories with them. Some of the songs are lost to history because they are never written down. However, many have been retained through the process of oral history, becoming the repertoire for choirs and concert singers, and the freedom songs of the twentieth century.

 **1813**

Agba:

Composer Henry F. Williams is born in Boston, Massachusetts.

 **1814**

Kuumba:

Francis Scott Key writes the poem "The Star-Spangled Banner," after witnessing the British bombardment of Fort McHenry in Maryland. The words are subsequently set to the tune of an English drinking song, and becomes the national anthem of the United States. The performance of the anthem eventually is standardized until the era of Soul music arrives in the 1960s, when performers like Aretha Franklin, Jimi Hendrix and others begin expressing the Black aesthetic through the song.

 **1815**

Kuumba:

Conductor/trumpeter Frank Johnson organizes his first band.

Shape-note singing teachers begin to migrate to the South.

The War of 1812 ends.

 **1816**

Kuumba:

Africans continue to express their sorrow through song. This is evident in the classic sorrow songs, *When I Get Home:*

> *I'm goin' to tell God all of my troubles,*
> *When I get home,*
> *I'm goin' to tell God all of my troubles,*
> *When I get home.* and:
>
> *Sometimes I Feel Like A Motherless Child:*
> *Sometimes I feel like a motherless child,*
> *Sometimes I feel like a motherless child,*
> *Sometimes I feel like a motherless child,*
> *A long way from home, A long way from home.*

The African Methodist Episcopal Zion Church is organized in New York.

James Monroe becomes president of the United States.

 **1817**

Kuumba:

Slaves continue Sunday performances of African music in an area of New Orleans known as Congo Square. Playing drums and other instruments of African ancestry, they participate in dances that are part of voodoo ceremonies.

 **1818**

Agba:

Frederick Douglass is born in Maryland.

Kuumba:

The African Methodist Episcopal (AME) church begins leading camp meetings of the Second Awakening.

 **1819**

Agba:

Singer Elizabeth Taylor Greenfield, "The Black Swan," is born in Natchez, Mississippi.

Guitarist/teacher/composer Justin Holland is born in Virginia.

Kuumba:

John F. Watson writes *Methodist Error or Friendly Christian Advice to Those Methodists Who Indulge in Extravagant Religious Emotions and Bodily Exercises*, describing the performance of music by blacks (expressing particular concern about the Ring Shout).

 **1820**

Kuumba:

Rev. Thomas Cooper compiles and composes hymns in *The African Pil-*

grim's Hymns, including anti-slavery words for "The Doxology," with the new name, "The Negro's Complaint."

White actors perform songs that imitate "black" dialogue, such as found in *The Bonja Song:*

> *Me sing all day, me sleep all night*
> *Me have no care, me sleep is light*
> *Me tink, no what tomorrow bring*
> *Me happy so me sing.*

Trumpeter Frank Johnson performs with white bands throughout Philadelphia.

 **1821**

Agba:

Harriet Ross (Tubman) is born in Maryland.

Singer/composer Eugene V. Macarty is born in New Orleans, Louisiana.

Kuumba:

The African Grove Theater is organized in an area of New York City known as the Five Points, a cultural center for free blacks. The Theater featured the African Company, the first black theatrical company, and it provides the only exception to blackface performance in this era. Ira Aldridge is among its members.

White novelist James Fenimore Cooper writes *The Spy,* which includes a black servant character for comic relief.

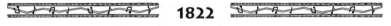 **1822**

Kuumba:

Peter Spencer publishes the *Union African Hymn Book* to use at the Ezion Union African Church of Wilmington, Delaware.

Teacher/composer Newport Gardner moves to Africa to become a missionary.

Denmark Vesey slave revolt breaks out in Charleston, South Carolina. It results in the imposition of extreme legal, physical and psychological controls on the remaining enslaved population. This includes a prohibition from singing the spiritual *Go down, Moses.*

As a result of the 19th century Back-to-Africa Movement, the nation of Liberia is founded in West Africa as a colony for freed slaves from the United States.

 **1823**

Agba:

Concert tenor Thomas Bowers, "The Colored Mario," is born in Philadelphia, Pennsylvania. The nickname emerges from public comparisons that are made between his voice and that of the great Italian tenor Giovanni Mateo Mario.

Kuumba:

The African Company of New York performs Henry Brown's *The Drama of King Shotaway,* the first play written by a black man. Thereafter, a group of whites destroy the theatre.

The Monroe Doctrine is established.

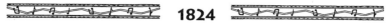 **1824**

Kuumba:

Trumpeter/bandleader Frank Johnson organizes an all black military band in Philadelphia.

John Quincy Adams is elected president of the United States.

 **1825**

Agba:

Minstrel/Dancer William Henry "Juba" Lane is born in New York.

Minstrel banjoist Horace Weston is born in Derby, Connecticut.

Kuumba:

Trumpeter/bandleader Frank Johnson composes *Recognition March on the Independence of Hayte.* Throughout his career he composes more than two hundred compositions.

 **1826**

The North Carolina legislature passes into law the Act of 1826, declaring it to be unlawful for a free Negro or mulatto to migrate to North Carolina.

Iku:

Music teacher/composer Newport Gardner dies in Monrovia, Liberia.

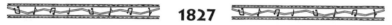 **1827**

Agba:

Classical composer Edmund Dede is born in New Orleans, Louisiana.

Kuumba:

The nation's first black newspaper, *Freedom's Journal,* is published in New York by Samuel Cornish, a clergyman, and John Russwurm, the first black to receive a college degree in the United States.

Slavery is abolished in New York State.

 **1828**

Kuumba:

Philadelphia's St. Thomas Episcopal Church becomes the first black church to own an organ, with Ann Appo serving as organist.

Andrew Jackson is elected president of the United States.

 **1829**

Agba:

Creole composer/pianist Louis Moreau Gottschalk is born in New Orleans.

Kuumba:

Thomas Dartmouth "Daddy" Rice, the "Father of American Minstrelsy," performs the song *Jump Jim Crow,* based on his observation of the performance of a deformed stable-groom in Louisville, Kentucky, which he incorporates into his act—*Wheel about, turn about, Do just so; Everytime I wheel about, I jump Jim Crow.* Jim Crow becomes a central stereotypical character of the Minstrelsy stage.

 **1830**

Kuumba:

Minstrelsy enters its golden age with white actors imitating the black song and dance of the plantation and presenting stereotyped images of Africans as laughing, lazy, pompose, irresponsible, chicken-stealing, child-like, empty-headed, "edjumkated," crap-shooting cake-walkers.

Minstrel Daniel D. Emmett composes *Old Dan Tucker.*

From 1830-1860 more than thirty thousand fugitive slaves are helped by the Underground Railroad, a movement that is centered in Pennsylvania, with Ohio, Massachusetts and Connecticut as active participants.

The Manumission Society of North Carolina publishes *An Address to the People of North Carolina on the Evils of Slavery,* a pamphlet that asserts that there is no justification for the enslavement of Africans.

The free black population of Pennsylvania reaches thirty-eight thousand, with almost fifteen thousand residing in Philadelphia County.

 **1831**

Kuumba:

The Nat Turner rebellion occurs in Southhampton County, Virginia. *Steal Away*, a double-meaning spiritual, serves as the signal song for the participants in the rebellion:

> *Steal away, steal away,*
> *Steal away to Jesus.*
> *Steal away, steal away home,*
> *I ain't got long to stay here.*

Slaves continue the African tradition of using the rhythm and tempo of work songs to coordinate the rhythm of work. Some ethnomusicologists have placed these songs into categories identified by the type of work, e.g. corn husking songs:

> *Master's slaves are slick and fat,*
> *Oh! Oh! Oh!*
> *Shine just like a beaver hat,*
> *Oh! Oh! Oh!*
> *Turn out here and shuck this corn,*
> *Oh! Oh! Oh!*
> *Biggest pile seen since I was born,*
> *Oh! Oh! Oh!*

Webster's Dictionary is published with the term "Samboe" defined as "The offspring of a black person and a mulatto."

A group of free Negroes (from seven states) hold their first convention in Philadelphia, Pennsylvania to air grievances, establishing the National Negro Convention, and naming Bishop Richard Allen as the leader of the group.

White abolitionist leader William Lloyd Garrison begins publication of the anti-slavery newspaper, the *Liberator.*

Iku:

Bishop Richard Allen dies.

 **1832**

Kuumba:

Minstrel Thomas Dartmouth Rice introduces the *Jump Jim Crow* song and dance, with blackface costume, to a New York City audience.

 **1833**

Kuumba:

The Philadelphia Library Company of Colored Persons is organized, becoming an organization that also sponsored concerts and lectures.

Visual artist Robert M. Douglass, Jr. creates a lithograph of abolitionist William Lloyd Garrison, copies of which are sold to raise money for the abolitionist cause.

Oberlin College is founded in Oberlin, Ohio.

Ira Aldridge appears in Othello in London.

 **1834**

Agba:

Pianist/composer Samuel Snaer is born in New Orleans, Louisiana.

Kuumba:

Black musicians begin performing on Mississippi River showboats.

The first African American Lutheran congregation is organized in Philadelphia.

 **1835**

Kuumba:

A black congregation worships at Sharp Street Methodist Church in Baltimore. Services in this and other black churches are described by visitors as incorporating musical performance practices that are unique to African Americans.

Oberlin College becomes one of the first colleges in the U.S. to admit black students. The city of Oberlin is later called the city that starts the Civil War because of the large number of abolitionists coming out of Oberlin College.

 **1836**

Kuumba:

Africans continue to tell the stories of the Bible through the spiritual. For example, the story of the healing abilities of Jesus, as articulated in Luke 4:40 - *When the sun was setting, the people brought to Jesus all who had various kinds of sickness, and laying his hands on each one, he healed them,* is turned into the spiritual *I Know the Lord Laid His Hands On Me.*

Robert Benjamin Lewis publishes *Light and Truth*, the first history book written by a black.

Martin Van Buren is elected president of the United States.

 **1837**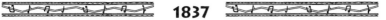

Kuumba:

Mr. Cornmeal, a street vendor and one of the first black minstrels, appears at the St. Charles Theatre in New Orleans and his performances were subsequently copied by Thomas "Daddy" Rice.

Bandmaster Frank Johnson takes his band to England and performs a series of concerts, leading the first U.S. musical ensemble to give a command performance before Queen Victoria.

The Colored American newspaper begins publication.

More than 200 women from ten states attend the first Anti-Slavery Convention of American Women in New York City.

 **1838**

Kuumba:

Bishop Christopher Rush (with Rev. Samuel M. Giles and Rev. Joseph P. Thompson) publishes *Hymns for the Use of the African Methodist Episcopal Zion Church in America.*

British actress Fanny Kemble writes in her *Journal of a Residence on a Georgia Plantation in 1838-1839* of her travels in the U.S., describing the musical abilities of slaves on a Georgia plantation: *They always keep exquisite time and tune, and no words seem too hard for them to adapt to their tunes, so that they can sing a long-metre hymn to a short-metre tune without any difficulty...with the most perfect time and rarely with any discord....*and she reports *that I have heard that many of the masters and overseers on these plantations prohibit melancholy tunes or words, and encourage nothing but cheerful music and senseless words....* (127-129)

Frederick Douglass successfully escapes from slavery and goes on to become an important orator and active abolitionist.

Pennsylvania passes a new constitution taking the right to vote away from free blacks.

 **1839**

A successful slave-ship revolt occurs aboard the Amistad, led by Cinque.

The first anti-slavery party, the Liberty Party, is organized in Warsaw, New York.

 **1840**

Agba:

Minstrel Sam Lucas is born in Washington, Ohio.

Kuumba:

Composer/Band leader/trumpeter Frank Johnson writes *Voice Quadrille,* a typical social-dance composition.

The cakewalk originates on plantations—developed by slaves who adapt the fashions and mimic the dancing (the minuet grand march) of whites. A prize of a cake is given to the slave who performs the fanciest walk.

The Theatre de la Renaissance opens in New Orleans. This is a theatre for the free colored population featuring a black music director and black orchestra members and presenting dramas, opera-comiques, and vaudeville.

William Henry Harrison is elected president of the United States.

 **1841**

Kuumba:

The instrumentation that accompanies minstrels is adapted from the instruments used by slaves on southern plantations: the banjo, the fiddle, the bones (the jawbone of an ass or horse).

Abolitionist William Lloyd Garrison writes abolitionist words to the tune of *Auld Lang Syne:*

> *I am an abolitionist! I glory in the name; Though now by Slavery's minions hiss'd; And covered o'er with shame; It is a spell of light and power; The watchword of the free; Who spurns it in this trial-hour; A craven soul is he!*

> *I am an abolitionist! Then urge me not to pause; For joyfully do I enlist; In Freedom's sacred cause; A nobler strife the world ne'er saw; Th' enslaved to disenthral; I am a soldier for the war; Whatever may befall!*

The use of choirs and choral singing is started at Philadelphia's Bethel AME church, causing an immediate split in the congregation, many of whom identified the choir as "instruments of the devil."

Composer/trumpeter/bandleader Francis "Frank" Johnson and Choir Director Morris Brown, Jr., conduct a performance of the *Creation* (Haydn) at Philadelphia's First African Presbyterian Church.

Several churches are established for the free black population. The First African Baptist Church opens in Richmond, Virginia. The First Colored Presbyterian Church opens on 15th street in Washington, D.C. (subsequently becoming the Fifteenth Street Presbyterian Church, the site at which the public school system for black students was established in 1870).

 **1842**

Agba:

Minstrel William "Billy" Kersands is born in New York.

Kuumba:

The Hutchinson Family, (a white ensemble beginning with Abby, Judson, John and Asa Hutchinson in a quartet), performs concerts throughout the U.S. and Great Britain in support of the antislavery movement, temperance, and women's suffrage.

English author Charles Dickens cites the exciting dance abilities of minstrel William Henry "Juba" Lane in *American Notes for General Circulation*, describing him as "the greatest dancer known": *Single shuffle, double shuffle, cut and cross-cut; snapping his fingers, rolling his eyes, turning in his knees, presenting the backs of his legs in front, spinning about on his toes and heels like nothing but the manm's fingers on the tambourine; dancing with two left legs, two right legs, two wooden legs, two wire legs, two spring legs—all sorts of legs and no legs—what is this to him? And in what walk of life, or dance of life, does man ever get such stimulating applause as thunders about him, when, having danced his partner off her feet, and himself too, he finishes by leaping gloriously on the bar-counter, and calling for something to drink, with the chuckle of a million of counterfeit Jim Crows, in one inimitable sound!* (138-139).

The New York Philharmonic Society is founded, becoming the oldest symphony orchestra in the U.S.

Composer/conductor Richard Lambert is active with the New Orleans Philharmonic Society Orchestra.

The first black convent, the Convent of the Holy Name, is established in New Orleans.

 **1843**

Kuumba:

The Frank Johnson Band performs throughout Philadelphia.

Daniel Decatur Emmett and the Virginia Minstrels establish the standard full-length minstrelsy concert. It consists of two acts filled with an overture, songs, jokes (performed by characters known as Mr. Tambo, Mr. Bones and the master of ceremonies - the interlocutor), comic skits, dancing, and the "walk-around" as the plantation festival finale performed by the full cast at the end of both parts of the show (later replaced by the cakewalk). This white ensemble begins the practice of using blackface makeup in order to affirm the authenticity of their performance. All of the songs and dances purported to show how happy slaves were with life on the plantation.

The Christy Minstrels are founded by Edwin P. Christy.

The City officials of New Orleans prohibit the Sunday afternoon festivals in Congo Square, forcing the blacks to take the activities underground.

 **1844**

Kuumba:

The Hutchinson Family continues combining music and abolitionist politics, composing such songs as *The Bereaved Slave Mother, The Slave's Appeal,* and *Clear the Track.*

Dan Emmett and The Virginia Minstrels tour Great Britain.

Numerous minstrelsy groups are created because of the popular response to the Virginia Minstrels and the Christy Minstrels. They include the Alabama Minstrels, Bryant's Minstrels, the Columbia Minstrels, the Congo Minstrels, the Ethiopian Serenaders, among others. The minstrelsy show is refined with "Northern Darkies" or "Northern Dandies" being the focus of part one of the show and "Southern Darkies" being the focus of part two of the show.

Adolphe Sax unveils his new invention in France, the saxophone, a revolutionary new instrument that captures the emotional inflections of the human voice better than any other instrument.

 **1845**

Agba:

Basile Bares is born in New Orleans, Louisiana.

Kuumba:

William Brady composes the solo song *Leila, Leila Cease Thy Lay.*

William Henry "Juba" Lane, the first black dance star, wins the title "King of All Dancers" in a challenge contest.

Frederick Douglass publishes his autobiography *Narrative of the Life of Frederick Douglass, an American Slave,* (published originally by The Anti-Slavery Office of Boston and republished in 1995 by Dover Publications)—containing the following description of the place of music in the life of the slave:

> *The slaves selected to go to the Great House Farm, for the monthly allowance for themselves and their fellow-slaves, were peculiarly enthusiastic. While on their way, they would make the dense old woods, for miles around, reverberate with their wild songs, revealing at once the highest joy and the deepest sadness. They would compose and sing as they went along, consulting neither time nor tune. The thought that came up, came out—if not in the word, in the sound;—and as frequently in the one as in the other. They would sometimes sing the most pathetic sentiment in the most rapturous tone, and the most rapturous sentiment in the most pathetic tone. Into all of their songs they would manage to weave something of the Great House Farm. Especially would they do this, when leaving home. They would then sing most exultingly the following words: "I am going away to the Great House Farm! O, yea! O, yea! O, yea!" This they would sing, as a chorus, to words which to many would seem unmeaning jargon, but which, nevertheless, were full of meaning to themselves. I have sometimes thought that the mere hearing of those songs would do more to impress some minds with the horrible character of slavery, than the reading of whole volumes of philosophy on the subject could do.*
>
> *I did not, when a slave, understand the deep meaning of those rude*

and apparently incoherent songs. I was myself within the circle; so that I neither saw nor heard as those without might see and hear. They told a tale of woe which was then altogether beyond my feeble comprehension; they were tones loud, long, and deep; they breathed the prayer and complaint of souls boiling over with the bitterest anguish. Every tone was a testimony against slavery, and a prayer to God for deliverance from chains. The hearing of those wild notes always depressed my spirit, and filled me with ineffable sadness. I have frequently found myself in tears while hearing them. The mere recurrence to those songs, even now, afflicts me; and while I am writing these lines, an expression of feeling has already found its way down my cheek. To those songs I trace my first glimmering conception of the dehumanizing character of slavery. I can never get rid of that conception. Those songs still follow me, to deepen my hatred of slavery, and quicken my sympathies for my brethren in bonds. If any one wishes to be impressed with the soul-killing effects of slavery, let him go to Colonel Lloyd's plantation, and, on allowance-day, place himself in the deep pine woods, and there let him, in silence, analyze the sounds that shall pass through the chambers of his soul,—and if he is not thus impressed, it will only be because "there is no flesh in his obdurate heart."

I have often been utterly astonished, since I came to the north, to find persons who could speak of the singing, among slaves, as evidence of their contentment and happiness. It is impossible to conceive of a greater mistake. Slaves sing most when they are most unhappy. The songs of the slave represent the sorrows of his heart; and he is relieved by them, only as an aching heart is relieved by its tears. At least, such is my experience. I have often sung to drown my sorrow, but seldom to express my happiness. Crying for joy, and singing for joy, were alike uncommon to me while in the jaws of slavery. The singing of a man cast away upon a desolate island might be as appropriately considered as evidence of contentment and happiness, as the singing of a slave; the songs of the one and of the other are prompted by the same emotion. (8-9)

Louis Moreau Gottschalk writes "Bamboula: Danse des Negres" based upon his memories of dancing in Congo Square.

Sculptor Mary Edmonia Lewis becomes the first black woman to study in Europe.

 **1846**

Kuumba:

William Henry "Juba" Lane becomes a banjoist and tambourine player with Charley White's Serenaders.

Music on the plantation is described by a plantation owner in *Plantation Life in the Florida Parishes of Louisiana, 1836-1846, as Reflected in the Diary of Bennet H. Barrow* (edited by Edwin Adams Davis and published in 1943 by Columbia University Press): *finding no cotton to trash out....I sent out for the Fiddle and made them Dance from 12 till dark.*

Iowa becomes a state.

Iku:

Trumpeter/band leader Frank Johnson dies.

 **1847**

Kuumba:

The Christy Minstrels start a ten-year Broadway engagement.

Frederick Douglass cofounds and serves as editor of the abolitionist newspaper, *The North Star*, in Rochester, New York.

John Wesley AME Church is established in Washington, D.C.

 **1848**

Kuumba:

Instrumental music is performed for the first time in a Baltimore AME church, conducted by James Fleet.

Minstrel/dancer William Henry "Juba" Lane moves to England.

White minstrel Stephen Foster composes *Oh Susanna*.

The California Gold Rush begins.

Zachary Taylor is elected president of the United States.

1849

Agba:

Child prodigy Thomas Greene (Bethune), "Blind Tom", is born near Columbus, Georgia.

Kuumba:

Minstrel/dancer William "Juba" Lane tours England with Richard Pell's Ethiopian Serenaders.

William Wells Brown publishes *The Anti-Slavery Harp*, a collection of anti-slavery song texts.

Harriet Tubman escapes from slavery and becomes one of the most famous of the conductors of the Underground Railroad, leading 300 slaves to freedom. Her favorite spiritual is said to have been *Go down Moses Way down in Egypt Land and tell old Pharaoh to let my people go.*

Creole concert pianist Louis Moreau Gottschalk performs the first public concert of music that is identified with African American folk themes.

Narrative of the Life and Adventures of Henry Bibb, An American Slave, is published—a very strong example of a slave narrative.

Iku:

Composer James Hemmenway dies.

1850

Kuumba:

Child prodigy "Blind Tom" is purchased by Colonel Bethune.

The Luca Family, a black singing family ensemble, consisting of Alexander Luca, Cleveland Luca, Alexander C. Luca, Jr., and John W. Luca, performs at a New York abolitionist convention.

The minstrelsy band expands, incorporating the use of orchestral instruments.

Lucy Sessions graduates from Oberlin College, possibly becoming the first black woman in the U.S. to receive a college degree.

Millard Fillmore becomes president of the United States.

 **1851**

Agba:

Gospel composer Rev. Charles Albert Tindley is born in Berlin, Maryland.

Kuumba:

White minstrel Stephen Foster composes *Old Folks At Home.*

Soprano Elizabeth Taylor Greenfield makes her debut in concert for the Buffalo Musical Association, and is described as the "Black Swan" in a review of the concert.

Author William Wells Brown publishes the first novel by a black American, *Clotel.*

Former slave Sojourner Truth makes her classic *Ain't I A Woman* speech at a women's rights convention.

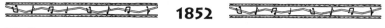 **1852**

Agba:

Classical singer Madame Marie Selika is born in Natchez, Mississippi.

Kuumba:

Minstrel Stephen Foster composes *My Old Kentucky Home.* He goes on to become one of the most prominent of the minstrel composers.

William Steffe composes the melody for the camp-meeting song, *Glory, glory, hallelujah,* a melody that is then adapted to the words *John Brown's Body lies a-mouldering in the grave.* This melody is adapted by Julia Ward Howe into *The Battle Hymn of the Republic* in 1862.

White abolitionist Harriet Beecher Stowe publishes *Uncle Tom's Cabin*—the great abolitionist work, written as a passionate indictment of slavery.

Frederick Douglass makes a speech at Corinthian Hall in Rochester, New York, on July 5th:

> *What, to the American Slave, is your Fourth of July? I answer: a day that reveals to him, more than all other days in the year, the gross injustice and cruelty to which he is the constant victim. To him, your celebration is a sham, your boasted liberty, an unholy license, your national greatness, swelling vanity, your sounds of rejoicing are empty and heartless, your denunciations of tyrants, brass fronted imprudence, your shouts of liberty and equality, hollow mockery, your prayers and hymns, your sermons and thanksgivings, with all your religious parade, and solemnity, are to him, mere bombast, fraud, deception, impiety and hypocrisy, a thin veil to cover up crimes which would disgrace a nation of savages. There is not a nation on the earth guilty of practices, more shocking and bloody, than are the people of these United States, at this very hour.* (published in *The Negro Almanac*, a compilation edited by Harry A. Ploski and Ernest Kaiser, The Bellwether Company, 1971, pages 121-124).

Franklin Pierce is elected president of the United States.

Iku:

William Henry "Juba" Lane dies.

 **1853**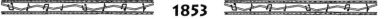

Agba:

Singer Anna Madah Hyers is born in Sacramento, California.

Kuumba:

Elizabeth Taylor Greenfield makes her New York City debut at Metropolitan Hall for an audience of white patrons only.

The Luca Family performs at Antislavery Society meetings, receiving critical and public acclaim in Boston and other New England states.

Thomas Dilworth (a black dwarf minstrel known as Japanese Tommy) joins the Christy Minstrels.

Frederick Douglass publishes his second autobiographical study, *My Bondage and My Freedom*, including descriptions of the performance of spirituals.

Creole composer/pianist Louis Moreau Gottschalk undertakes a United States concert tour, performing many of his African American-inspired compositions, such as *Bamboula,* and *La Savane.*

The Western Colored Baptist Convention is established.

Visual artist Robert S. Duncanson depicts a southern landscape in *Uncle Tom and Little Eva* (the two primary characters in Harriet Beecher Stowe's book *Uncle Tom's Cabin*).

 **1854**

Agba:

Composer/minstrel James Bland is born in Flushing, New York.

Violinist/bandleader Walter Craig is born in Princeton, New Jersey.

Kuumba:

Elizabeth Taylor-Greenfield gives a command performance for Queen Victoria in London's Buckingham Palace.

Ashmum Institute is established in Chester County, Pennsylvania, as the first college for African-Americans (renamed Lincoln University in 1866).

 **1855**

Agba:

Singer Emma Louise Hyers is born in Sacramento, California.

Concert pianist Samuel Jamieson is born in Washington, D.C.

Kuumba:

Richard Milburn composes the popular *Listen To The Mocking Bird,* a song that is identified as "A Sentimental Ethiopian Ballad" selling it for 20 copies of the music and receiving nothing for the 20 million copies that sold between 1855 and 1905.

Creole composer Louis Moreau Gottschalk writes *The Banjo,* imitating the banjo playing of blacks.

Leon Scott invents the "phonautograph," the precursor of the phonograph.

Dwight's Journal of Music, a weekly Boston journal, publishes a number of articles on the theme "Musical Talent of the Americans," analyzing the status of congregational singing and concluding that *the Americans are not a musical people...do not delight in song, appreciate it or feel strongly about it.*

Mt. Zion AME Church is founded in Long Green, Maryland.

 **1856**

Agba:

Booker T. Washington is born.

Kuumba:

Wilberforce University is founded in Ohio by the African Methodist Episcopal Church, becoming America's first autonomous black institution.

James Buchanan is elected president of the United States.

 **1857**

Kuumba:

Pianist Thomas Greene "Blind Tom" Bethune makes his formal debut at Temperance Hall in Columbus, Georgia.

John "Picayune" Butler, a black minstrel, competes in a New York Banjo competition. He is identified as the creator of the "Zip Coon" character.

Rev. Elisha Weaver is rejected by his Chicago congregation because he brought choral and instrumental music into the church.

The Institute for Colored Youth is founded (later to become Cheney State College).

The Supreme Court issues the "Dred Scott" decision, declaring that blacks *were beings of an inferior order, and altogether unfit to associate with the white race either in social or political relations; and so far inferior that they had no rights which the white man was bound to respect.*

 **1858**

Kuumba:

Author William Wells Brown writes *Escape, or A Leap for Freedom*, the oldest extant published play by an African American.

Visual artist Robert Stuart Duncanson paints the portrait of Richard Sutton Rust, the first president of Wilberforce University.

 **1859**

Kuumba:

The Luca Family joins the Hutchinson Family in performing concerts throughout Ohio.

White minstrel Daniel Decatur Emmett composes *Dixie* as a minstrelsy "walk-around," a song that gained popularity in all parts of the country. Note that the song is performed at the inauguration of Jefferson Davis in 1861.

James Hungerford writes *The Old Plantation and What I Gathered There in an Autumn Month,* the first book to record the music and text of spirituals.

The Negro (or Creole) Dramatic Company begins to give annual performances in New Orleans.

Abolitionist John Brown leads the Harper's Ferry (West Virginia) raid on the Federal Armory.

 **1860**

Agba:

Concert singer Sidney Woodward is born in Stockbridge, Georgia.

Kuumba:

Minstrel Stephen Foster composes *Old Black Joe,* and goes on to build a career through the appropriation of black culture.

Abolitionist musician Cleveland Luca leaves this country to settle in Liberia, where he composes the national anthem.

The U. S. Census reports the black population as 4,441,830.

The *Slave Code of the District of Columbia, 1860,* provides a definition of a slave: *A slave is a human being, who is by law deprived of his or her liberty for life, and is the property of another. A slave has no political rights and generally has no civil rights.*

Abraham Lincoln is elected president of the United States.

South Carolina secedes from the Union.

 **1861**

Kuumba:

The spiritual *Go Down Moses* is published in an arrangement titled "Oh Let My People Go" by Englishman Thomas Baker.

The minstrel song *Dixie* remains popular in the North, and therefore anti-Southern words are adapted:

> *Away down south in the land of traitors; Rattlesnakes and alligators;*
> *Right away, come away, right away, come away.*

Where cotton's king and men are chattles; Union-Boys will win the battles; Right away, come away, right away, come away.

Julia Ward Howe writes the popular words to *The Battle Hymn of the Republic: Mine eyes have seen the Glory of the coming of the Lord; etc.*

The U.S. Civil War begins.

 **1862**

Kuumba:

Soprano Elizabeth Taylor Greenfield organizes the Black Swan Opera Troupe.

The city of Nashville surrenders to Northern invaders.

Iku:

Minstrel/dancer William Henry "Juba" Lane dies.

 **1863**

Agba:

Minstrel Gussie Davis is born in Dayton, Ohio.

Kuumba:

President Lincoln signs the Emancipation Proclamation: *all persons held as slaves within any State, or any designated part of a State, the people whereof shall then be in rebellion against the United States, shall be then, thence forward and forever free.* January 1, becomes "The Day of Jubilee."

The War Department approves and encourages the use of black men as Union Army soldiers, ultimately resulting in 186,000 enlistments and 38,000 deaths by the end of the war.

 **1864**

Agba:

Soprano Flora Batson is born in Washington, D.C.

Kuumba:

Edmonia Lewis, the first acknowledged black woman sculptor, exhibits her work in Boston, Massachusetts.

Rebecca Lee Crumpler becomes the first black woman to receive a medical degree from the New England Female Medical College in Boston, Massachusetts.

Abraham Lincoln is reelected president of the United States.

The first black daily newspaper, *The New Orleans Tribune* begins publication.

 **1865**

Agba:

Composer/showman Ernest Hogan is born in Bowling Green, Kentucky.

Kuumba:

Showman Charles "Barney" Hicks organizes the Georgia Minstrels, the first permanent black minstrel company - a successful group that is quickly taken over by a white manager, Charles Callender, and thereafter tours the U. S. and Europe. The members of the company perform in blackface, providing the anomaly of imitating whites who are imitating blacks. Their success leads to the development of numerous other black companies. The outstanding quality of the work of the black groups causes the white groups to expand and redirect the focus of their shows, contributing to the emergence of vaudeville.

Atlanta University is founded in Georgia.

Shaw University is founded in Raleigh, North Carolina.

Virginia Union University is founded in Richmond.

Bowie State College is founded in Maryland.

Congress creates the Bureau of Refugees, Freedmen, and Abandoned Lands.

The Juneteenth celebration starts in Texas, when news of the Emancipation Proclamation finally reaches that state (June 19).

The Thirteenth Amendment to the United States Constitution is ratified *(Neither slavery nor involuntary servitude, except as a punishment for crime whereof the party shall have been duly convicted, shall exist within the United States, or any place subject to their jurisdiction).*

Abraham Lincoln is assassinated by white actor John Wilkes Booth.

The Civil War ends.

New York Emancipation Celebration March

Photos courtesy of the Library of Congress

2

1866 - 1900
THE MUSIC OF EMANCIPATION

The music of Emancipation reflects the search for adjustment to a new status. African Americans affirm their freedom with the creation of new musical forms. Blacks begin migrating from plantations and anonymous musicians continue the development of a folk music culture as they serve on railroad and prison chain gangs, work the cotton fields of the South, and meet the musical heritage of New Orleans. Specifically, the earliest folk-forms of ragtime and jazz emerge in urban areas and the earliest folk-forms of the blues emerge in the fields of the rural South.

In this era the institutions that are fundamental to the community of free blacks are established, including the historically black colleges and the black church. These institutions become a source for musical expression. African Americans begin to treat the spiritual as a cultural treasure, developing college choirs that actively perform arrangements of this repertoire throughout the United States and Europe. Gospel music develops for the newly emerging Pentecostal churches.

During this period, whites involved with music of the European classical tradition begin to establish the major music and music education institutions of the country. White America begins the search for a separate musical identity for this country. Eventually a "nationalism" emerges, partially based upon spirituals and other black folk music styles. Additionally, whites expand their involvement in popular music- to vaudeville and musical theatre. African Americans become essential contributors first to blackface minstrelsy and then to the Broadway musical.

The time span ends with the birth of jazz great Daniel Louis Satchmo Armstrong, and with the development of the player piano, the music reproduction device that contributes so directly to the national awareness of Ragtime.

TRENDS
1866 - 1900

1860s

◊ The primary musical form of this decade continues to be minstrelsy, a genre that increasingly enjoys the participation of blacks who, unfortunately, are in the position of having to perform in blackface makeup. They therefore become black entertainers imitating whites who are imitating blacks.

1870s

◊ In response to emancipation, blacks begin migrating to the North and to Southern cities, and creating new social, educational, economic and cultural structures.

◊ The Jubilee Singer tradition is born, including the concert performance of spirituals by choirs that emerge at historically black colleges.

◊ African Americans continue the folk practice of communal singing, as exemplified in the work songs performed at the docks, at railroad building sites, and in prisons.

◊ African Americans who were previously enslaved begin to migrate to New Orleans from the plantations, contributing to the creation of the instrumentally sophisticated population that creates jazz.

◊ A black bourgeoisie seeks to separate itself from black folk culture, joining the churches of the middle-class white community (Congregational, Catholic, Episcopalian and Presbyterian), and establishing social, artistic and literary organizations devoted to the expression of the cultural practices of the white community.

◊ African American music clubs emerge, devoted to the performance of the classical music of European culture.

◊ Jooks (known as Honky-Tonks, Jook Houses and After-hours joints) emerge.

- Secret societies flourish in the black communities, e.g., Elks, Eastern Star, Masons, Odd Fellows, The True Reformers, often providing sickness benefits and burial services for its membership. The burial services are distinguished by the music that accompanied them.

- Emancipation Day celebrations emerge throughout the South, filled with singing, drumming and dancing.

- The U.S. undergoes an urban religious revival movement led by Dwight Moody and Ira Sankey, composers of popular hymns.

- AME church leadership seeks to eliminate from the church service the performance of slave spirituals and the ring shout.

- The Reconstruction period ends and formal segregation policies and terrorist vigilante violence begins.

1880s

- Country Blues begins to emerge in the folk practices of the rural South.

- Increasing numbers of blacks perform on the minstrelsy stage, in blackface. At the same time, the Golden Age of minstrelsy comes to an end, losing its large national audience, while the minstrel/coon songs emerge in a separate setting. A number of the black minstrels open their own clubs, and after-hours jooks and honky-tonks.

- New York's Tin Pan Alley "coon song" craze begins - sheet music that presents negative caricatures of black culture in the music, texts, titles and illustrated covers. This song type becomes a staple of the Broadway show, of vaudeville, and of the white rural South's twentieth century country music.

1890s

- Minstrelsy dies out in this decade, and is replaced by vaudeville, the Broadway musical and the Creole Show.

- The decade is known as The Gay Nineties. It is the heyday of Tin Pan Alley and its commercially successful Coon Songs with their "darky" sheet music covers filled with racist symbolism. Tin Pan

Alley provides a cultural expression that parallels the escalation of legal racism in the United States. Much of the music that is published is performed by the various stars of the Vaudeville stage, including the increasingly popular Barbershop Quartets.

◊ This is also the decade of the Creole show - Broadway musical shows that showcase beautifully dressed black women performing a variety of original music and opera arias. These works are eventually written, produced and directed by African Americans.

◊ New Orleans traditional jazz continues to evolve, as performed by the black brass bands that often accompany funeral processions and perform at parades, park concerts, and at the activities of various fraternal groups.

◊ Military marches gain in national popularity, as in the music of white composer/conductor John Philip Sousa - a contributor to the evolution of jazz.

◊ Ragtime musicians emerge in the tenderloin districts of Baltimore, Boston, Chicago, Kansas City, Memphis, New Orleans, New York and Philadelphia. The folk ragtime tradition (syncopated piano music) evolves into a written, structured music form and becomes the national ragtime craze.

◊ The cakewalk dance craze sweeps the country.

◊ Black Holiness/Pentecostal churches begin to originate, becoming the home of the new style of sacred music - gospel music, with its expanded instrumentation, e.g., drums, guitars and tambourines.

◊ The legal and philosophical foundation for separate but equal discrimination is established.

◊ The era of the Black Womens Club Movement, generated partially by the constant attacks on the morality of the African American woman and the attacks on the black family.

◊ A small group of black entrepreneurs and professionals begin to create a middle class in the urban areas.

ACHIEVEMENT DATELINE
1866 - 1900

 **1866**

Agba:

Singer/composer Harry T. Burleigh is born in Erie, Pennsylvania.

Kuumba:

Child prodigy/composer/pianist Thomas Greene "Blind Tom" Bethune tours Europe; and his piano composition is published—*The Battle of Manassas.*

A white ensemble performs *The Black Crook*, the first musical comedy. It runs for four hundred and seventy-five performances in a Broadway theatre. African Americans become major contributors to the Broadway musical repertoire in the 1890s.

Southern states pass laws known as *black codes.* They are intended to legalize discrimination against blacks.

Race riots occur in Memphis, Tennessee

Fisk University is founded in Tennessee by the American Missionary Association.

Lincoln University is founded in Missouri.

The Buffalo Soldiers–black cavalry/infantry units–are established.

The Ku Klux Klan is founded in Pulaski, Tennessee.

 **1867**

Agba:

Singer/guitarist/harmonica player Johnny "Daddy Stovepipe" Watson is born in Alabama.

Concert singer E. Azalia (Emma Azalia Smith) Hackley is born in Murfreesboro, Tennessee.

Kuumba:

The first collection of Negro spirituals (and work songs) is published, *Slave Songs of The United States* (collected by William Allen, Charles Ware, and Lucy McKim Garrison), including this explanation in the introduction: *The musical capacity of the negro race has been recognized for so many years...It is hard to explain why no systematic effort has hitherto been made to collect and preserve their melodies.*

Singers Anna and Emmie Louise Hyers make their concert debut in Sacramento, California.

Visual artist Mary Edmonia Lewis creates the dramatic sculpture *Forever Free,* an artistic response to the Emancipation Proclamation.

Howard University is established in Washington, D.C.

Augusta Institute is founded in Georgia (later to become Morehouse College).

Talladega College is founded in Alabama.

Biddle University is founded (later to become Johnson C. Smith University).

Blacks in the District of Columbia are given the right to vote.

The Reconstruction Era begins in the South with the passage of the First Reconstruction Act.

The National Holiness Convention convenes, and the white community establishes the holiness movement.

The National Association of Baseball Players votes to exclude black players and teams from membership.

Iku:

Actor Ira Aldridge dies.

 **1868**

Agba:

Broadway composer Robert Allen "Bob" Cole is born in Athens, Georgia.

Ragtime pianist/composer Scott Joplin is born in eastern Texas.

Kuumba:

Edmond Dede becomes conductor of the L'Alcazar Theatre Orchestra on Bordeaux, France.

Congress passes the Fourteenth Amendment, granting blacks citizenship and equal protection under the law: *No State shall deprive any person of life, liberty, or property, without due process of law; nor deny to any person within its jurisdiction the equal protection of the laws.* This effectively abolishes the black codes.

Hampton Institute is established in Hampton, Virginia.

Tougaloo College is founded in Mississippi.

Historically black college, St. Augustines College, is founded in North Carolina.

Ulysses S. Grant is elected president of the United States.

North Carolina, South Carolina, Louisiana, Georgia, Alabama and Florida are readmitted to the Union, provided each state gives all citizens the right to vote.

 **1869**

Agba:

Composer Will Marion Cook is born in Washington, D.C.

Classical composer Harry Lawrence Freeman is born in Cleveland, Ohio.

Singer Matilda Sissieretta Joyner-Jones (The Black Patti) is born in Portsmouth, Virginia.

Kuumba:

Dillard University is chartered in New Orleans, Louisiana.

Clark College is founded in Atlanta, Georgia.

The National Woman Suffrage Association is established.

Iku:

Composer Louis Moreau Gottschalk dies.

 **1870**

Kuumba:

Abolitionist/army officer Thomas Wentworth Higginson publishes *Army Life in a Black Regiment*, including texts and descriptions of the spirituals performed by the ex-slaves of his Civil War regiment.

The Colored Methodist Episcopal Church (CME) of America is established in Jackson, Tennessee by blacks who leave the predominantly white Methodist Church.

Allen University is founded in Columbia, South Carolina.

LeMoyne-Owen College is founded in Memphis, Tennessee.

4,880,009 African Americans are reported in the United States.

 **1871**

Agba:

Violinist Joseph Douglass (grandson of Frederick Douglass) is born in Washington, D.C.

Kuumba:

The Fisk Jubilee Singers tour America (with stops at Wilberforce University, Oberlin, and Brooklyn), bringing national recognition to the spirituals they perform.

Circus man P. T. Barnum establishes "The Greatest Show on Earth" in Brooklyn, including performances by two blacks—Jo-Jo the Dogface Boy and Zip the Pin-Headed Man.

Sculptor Mary Edmonia Lewis becomes the first black artist to exhibit in Rome.

Alcorn A & M College opens in Lorman, Mississippi.

   **1872**

Agba:

Composer/educator John Wesley Work II is born in Nashville, Tennessee.

Kuumba:

The Fisk Jubilee Singers perform at the World Peace Jubilee in Boston. Theodore F. Seward publishes a collection of 24 spirituals, the repertoire of the Fisk Jubilee Singers, *Jubilee Songs.*

The Hampton Jubilee Singers group is established at Hampton College.

Walter Crain organizes Craig's Celebrated Orchestra in New York. The group plays for society balls on the east coast.

Twelve African Americans are reported lynched.

Ulysses S. Grant is reelected president of the United States.

First African Methodist Episcopal Church is founded in Los Angeles.

Iku:

Pianist/abolitionist performer Cleveland Luca dies in Liberia.

 **1873**

Agba:

"The Father of the Blues," composer William Christopher (W. C.) Handy is born in Florence, Alabama.

Ragtime pianist/composer Tom Turpin is born in Savannah, Georgia.

Pianist/composer John Rosamond Johnson is born in Jacksonville, Florida.

Kuumba:

The Fisk Jubilee Singers tour Europe for the first time, sponsored by the American Missionary Association. They perform for Queen Victoria, and raise one hundred and fifty thousand dollars to build Jubilee Hall.

African Americans build the Big Bend Tunnel of the Chesapeake and Ohio Railroad. One of the workers, John Henry, is immortalized in the work song of the same name:

> *Well early in the morning,*
> *When the bluebirds begin to sing,*
> *You can see John Henry out on the line,*
> *You can hear John Henrys hammer ring,*
> *Lord, Lord, You can hear John Henry's hammer ring.*
> *...They took John Henry to the graveyard*
> *And they buried him in the sand.*
> *And every locomotive comes a-roaring by says,*
> *There lies a steel-driving man...*

This song is popularized in the twentieth century by Paul Robeson who often includes it in his many concerts.

The Colored American Opera Company is established in Washington, D.C.

Bennett College is founded in Greensboro, North Carolina.

University of Arkansas, Pine Bluff, is founded.

Wiley College is founded in Marshall, Texas.

 **1874**

Agba:

Pianist/musicologist Maude Cuney Hare is born in Galveston, Texas.

Symphony conductor Edward Gilbert Anderson is born in Still Pond, Maryland.

Minstrel Egbert Austin "Bert" Williams is born in Antigua, British West Indies.

Kuumba:

The Hampton Jubilee Singers of Hampton College tour the North, and a collection of their songs is published, *Cabin and Plantation Songs.*

Composer/guitarist Justin Holland publishes an instructional method book, *Comprehensive Method for the Guitar.*

 **1875**

Agba:

Classical composer Samuel Coleridge-Taylor is born in London, England.

Archivist/folklorist John Avery Lomax is born in Goodman, Mississippi.

Kuumba:

The Fisk Jubilee Singers begin their second European tour. Jubilee Hall is dedicated at Fisk University, having been funded with the monies raised by Jubilee Singers concerts. J.B.T. Marsh publishes their story in *The Story of The Jubilee Singers, With Their Songs.*

James Bland begins his professional career as a minstrel, appearing with the successful all-black troupe, Callender's Original Georgia Minstrels. Over the span of his career, he composes over six hundred minstrel songs.

P. P. Bliss and Ira Sankey publish *Gospel Hymns and Sacred Songs*.

Knoxville College is founded in Tennessee.

The nation's white women organize the Women's Christian Temperance Union, starting a campaign against what was perceived to be a national alcoholism problem—a movement that eventually culminates with Prohibition, the legal status that creates the commercial foundation for jazz.

 **1876**

Kuumba:

The Hyers Sisters Comic Opera Company is founded, with members that included the Hyers Sisters, Samuel Lucas and William "Billy" Kersands.

The AME church publishes *The Hymn Book of the African Methodist Episcopal Church*, compiled by Rev. Henry McNeal Turner - containing 1,115 hymns, including a setting of the melody of "My Country Tis of Thee" to a new text, Freedoms Morn:

> *All hail! fair Freedoms morn,*
> *When Africa's sons were born,*
> *We bless this day.*
> *From slavery we are freed,*
> *No more our hearts will bleed—*
> *Lord, make us free indeed.*
> *To thee we pray.*

Religious music historian Jon Michael Spencer reports that Rev. Turner is the AME bishop who *prevented his congregations from singing Wash me and I shall be <u>whiter</u> than snow. Washing, he explained, is meant to make one clean, not white.* (Page 201 of *Black Hymnody–A Hymnological History of the African American Church*, published by the University of Tennessee Press in 1992.)

Visual artist Edward Mitchell Bannister receives a bronze medal at the Centennial Exhibition in Philadelphia, Pennsylvania, for his painting *Under the Oaks*.

Custer's last stand at Little Big Horn.

The National Baseball League is established.

Prairie View A&M University is founded in Texas.

Stillman College is founded in Tuscaloosa, Alabama.

Meharry Medical College is founded in Nashville, Tennessee.

Rutherford B. Hayes becomes president of the United States.

Alexander Graham Bell patents the telephone.

Iku:

Soprano Elizabeth Taylor Greenfield dies in Philadelphia, Pennsylvania.

 **1877**

Agba:

Jazz trumpeter Charles (Buddy) Bolden is born in New Orleans, Louisiana.

Kuumba:

Two California-based singers, Anna Madah and Emma Louise Hyers, produce and perform in two shows: *The Underground Railroad*, and *Princess Orelia of Madagascar*. Minstrel/composer James Bland's *Oh Dem Golden Slippers* is featured in another of the sisters shows, *Out of Bondage* - a song that he later claims sold over 100,000 copies of sheet music.

Thomas Edison invents the mechanical phonograph.

Ex-slave George Washington Johnson becomes one of the first performers to record on tinfoil disks, singing *The Laughing Song* and *The Whistling Coon*.

The Colored Literary Society is active in Mercer, Pennsylvania.

Philander Smith College is founded in Little Rock, Arkansas.

Jackson State University is founded in Jackson, Mississippi.

Fayetteville State University is founded in Fayetteville, North Carolina.

The period of Reconstruction ends.

 **1878**

Agba:

Minstrel/composer James Bland writes *Carry Me Back to Ole Virginny*, a song that portrays a happy slave as the first person protagonist in the lyrics:

> *Carry me back to old Virginny; There's where the cotton and the corn and tatoes grow; There's where the birds warble sweet in the springtime; There's where the old darkey's heart am longd to go.*

> *There's where I labored so hard for old massa; Day after day in the field of yellow corn; No place on earth do I love more sincerely; Than old Virginny, the state where I was born.*

> *Carry me back to old Virginny; There let me live till I wither and decay; Long by the old Dismal Swamp have I wandered; There's where this old darkey's life will pass away.*

> *Massa and missis have long gone before me; Soon we will meet on that bright and golden shore; There well be happy and free from all sorrow; There's where we'll meet and we'll never part no more.*

Jack Haverly purchases the Callender's Minstrels, and presents them in New York City, advertised as "The Minstrel Carnival of Genuine Colored Minstrels."

Frederick J. Loudin becomes the director of the Fisk Jubilee Singers, and the group separates from the University, becoming the Loudin Jubilee Singers.

Minstrel Sam Lucas becomes the first black to play the role of Uncle Tom in a touring version of *Uncle Tom's Cabin*.

James Monroe Trotter becomes the first African American music historian, publishing *Music and Some Highly Musical People* to document the achievements of black musicians and to inspire racial pride.

Selma University is founded in Alabama.

 **1879**

Agba:

Jazz trumpeter William Bunk Geary Johnson is born in New Orleans.

Composer Frederick Jerome Work is born in Nashville, Tennessee.

Kuumba:

Florida Memorial College is founded.

Thomas Edison demonstrates the light bulb.

 **1880**

Agba:

Composer/violinist Clarence Cameron White is born in Clarksville, Tennessee.

Musical theater star Ada Overton Walker is born in New York City.

Kuumba:

Minstrel songs by James Bland are published—*De Golden Wedding* and *Keep Dem Golden Gates Wide Open.*

Country blues begins to emerge as a popular folk music style.

William Wells Brown documents the performance of street cries by African street vendors who use the uniquely identifying cry to arouse the attention needed to sell their wares.

Artist Henry Ossawa Tanner is accepted into the Pennsylvania Academy of Fine Arts in Philadelphia, studying with Thomas Eakins.

Chandler Harris publishes *Uncle Remus: His Songs and Sayings,* providing documentation of the oral tradition of black culture.

Writer/journalist Pauline Elizabeth Hopkins has a play produced in Boston by the Hopkins Colored Troubadors, *Slaves' Escape; or The Underground Railroad.*

James A. Garfield is elected president of the United States.

The Baptist Foreign Mission Convention is created for the purpose of sending black missionaries to Africa.

 **1881**

Agba:

James Reese Europe is born in Mobile, Alabama.

Kuumba:

The Louisville (Kentucky) Colored Musical Association produces a Sangerfest, involving 200 singers in a choral festival.

The song *John Gilbert* becomes an example of a popular riverboat work song, performed by blacks who worked loading cargo.

P.T. Barnum continues the practice of blacking up black performers for minstrelsy show performances.

Jack Haverly's Colored Minstrels tour Europe, with James Bland as a featured performer. Their debut performance is described thus:

> *When the curtain went up on opening night it disclosed on the stage about 65 real Negroes, both male and female, ranging in shades of complexions from the coal black Negro to the light brown mulatto or octoroon. They were of all ages, from the ancient Uncle Toms and Aunt Chloes, down to the little Picanniny a few months old nestling in its mothers lap. Their costumes were of the plantation, somewhat reminiscent of the Jubilee Festival Scene from Uncle Tom's Cabin. There were 16 corner men in all: 8 bones and 8 tambourines arranged in two rows on the stage....Jubilee quartettes and spirituals were interspersed with comic ditties and witticisms by the comedians. The best of the vocalists were Richard Little, a deep bass singer, and Wallace King, a gentleman with a very dark complexion and a long black beard to match, who in addition to his song in the first part introduced in the second part that old favorite ballad, "My Sweetheart When a Boy." He possessed a powerful tenor voice of excellent quality in the upper register, but rather guttural in the bottom notes, a characteristic of many colored vocalists.*

Tony Pastor opens a vaudeville theatre in New York to provide a forum for family entertainment.

The Boston Symphony Orchestra is founded.

Tuskegee Normal and Industrial Institute is founded by Booker T. Washington in Alabama.

The Gunfight at the O.K. Corral.

President James A. Garfield is assassinated; Vice President Chester A. Arthur becomes president.

Frederick Douglass publishes his third autobiography, *The Life and Times of Frederick Douglass.* President James Garfield appoints Frederick Douglass the Recorder of Deeds for the District of Columbia.

Allen University is founded in Columbia, South Carolina.

Morris Brown College is founded in Tennessee.

Spelman College is founded in Atlanta, Georgia.

Bishop College is founded in Marshall, Texas.

The Bethel Literary and Historical Association is founded.

 **1882**

Kuumba:

George Washington Williams writes a two-volume work, *History of the Negro Race in America from 1619 to 1880.*

Forty-eight African Americans are lynched.

Virginia State University is founded in Petersburg, Virginia.

Lane College is founded in Jackson, Tennessee.

Paine Institute (renamed Paine College) is founded in Augusta, Georgia.

 **1883**

Agba:

Ragtime pianist/composer Eubie Blake is born in Baltimore, Maryland.

Concert pianist Hazel Harrison is born in La Porte, Indiana.

Blues singer Mamie Smith is born in Cincinnati, Ohio.

Kuumba:

Various southern penitentiary systems "lease" convicts to private contractors, to help build the railroad system. Those convicts often used work songs to help organize the rhythm of the work, such as *Swannanoa Tunnel*, a tunnel that was built through the Blue Ridge Mountains of North Carolina (near Asheville).

A Collection of Revival Hymns and Plantation Melodies is compiled by Marsall Taylor.

The Metropolitan Opera House opens in New York.

Fifty-two African Americans are lynched.

 **1884**

Agba:

Arranger/music director William Henry Bennet Vodery is born in Philadelphia, Pennsylvania.

Music publisher/record producer Harry Pace is born in Covington, Georgia.

Kuumba:

Minstrel Gussie Davis writes *When Nellie Was Raking the Hay* and becomes the first black songwriter to succeed on Tin Pan Alley.

Boston organist/music teacher Rachel Washington publishes *Musical Truth: The Rudiments of Music.*

Fifty African Americans are lynched.

Grover Cleveland is elected president of the United States.

The *Philadelphia Tribune* newspaper is founded by Christopher Perry, Sr. - the oldest continuing black newspaper in the country.

 **1885**

Agba:

Blues artist Leadbelly (Huddie Ledbetter) is born in Mooringsport, Louisiana.

Music critic Nora Holt is born in Kansas City, Kansas.

Gospel music composer Lucie Eddie Campbell Williams is born in Kansas City, Kansas.

Jazz cornetist/bandleader Joseph (King) Oliver is born in New Orleans, Louisiana.

Jazz pianist/composer Jelly Roll Morton (Ferdinand Joseph La Menthe) is born in New Orleans, Louisiana.

Kuumba:

The National Conservatory of Music is established in New York.

Bert William's and his family settle in Riverside, California, where he graduates from Riverside High School.

Seventy-four African Americans are lynched.

The Cuban Giants are established as the first African American professional baseball team.

Iku:

Tenor Thomas Bowers, "The Colored Mario" dies.

 **1886**

Agba:

Blues singer Gertrude Pridgett, (Ma) Rainey, is born in Columbus, Georgia.

Jazz trombonist Edward (Kid) Ory is born in LaPlace, Louisiana.

Concert pianist/singer Carl Rossini Diton is born in Philadelphia, Pennsylvania.

Songwriter Shelton Brooks is born in Amesburg, Ontario - Canada.

Gospel composer/performer Charles Henry Pace is born.

Kuumba:

Walter Craig performs throughout New York, coming to be called "The Prince of Negro Violinists."

The American National Baptist convention is founded as the organizing forum for the historic black Baptist denomination.

Seventy-four African Americans are lynched.

Livingstone College is founded in Salisbury, North Carolina.

Kentucky State University is founded in Frankfort, Kentucky.

University of Maryland, Eastern Shore, is founded.

 **1887**

Agba:

Blues singer Charley Patton is born in Bolton, Mississippi.

Roland Hayes is born in Curryville, Georgia.

Jazz pianist Charles Luckey Roberts is born in Philadelphia, Pennsylvania.

Kuumba:

Emile Berliner patents the gramophone.

Seventy African Americans are lynched.

Central State University is founded in Wilberforce, Ohio.

Florida Agriculture & Mechanical (A&M) University is founded in Tallahassee, Florida.

Iku:

Composer/guitarist Justin Holland dies.

 **1888**

Agba:

Concert singer Camille Nickerson is born in New Orleans, Louisiana.

Composer Florence Price is born in Little Rock, Arkansas

Conductor/arranger (Francis) Hall Johnson is born in Athens, Georgia.

Songwriter/bandleader Armand Piron was born in New Orleans, Louisiana.

Kuumba:

Singer Sissieretta Joyner Jones ("The Black Patti") makes her New York City debut, performing with the Georgia Minstrels.

Sixty-Nine African Americans are lynched.

Benjamin Harrison is elected president of the United States.

The phonograph begins to be manufactured in quantity for home entertainment.

Kodak introduces the box camera.

 **1889**

Agba:

Ragtime/Broadway artist Noble Sissle is born in Indianapolis, Indiana.

Pop singer/guitarist John Mills (of the Mills Brothers) is born in Piqua, Ohio.

Composer Asadata Dafora Horton is born in Freetown, Sierra Leone, West Africa.

Kuumba:

A black opera company, Theodore Drury Colored Opera Company, is established in Brooklyn, New York.

John Philip Sousa composes *The Washington Post March.*

Ninety-two African Americans are lynched.

The Church of the Living God is established by William Christian.

President Benjamin Harrison appoints Frederick Douglass Minister Resident and Consul General to Haiti.

 **1890**

Agba:

Opera Singer Lillian Evanti is born in Washington, D.C.

New Orleans Traditional Jazz pianist/bandleader Fate Marable is born in Paducah, Kentucky.

Kuumba:

Entrepreneur Sam T. Jack produces a hybrid minstrel/burlesque show, the *Creole Burlesque Show.* Using the minstrel show format with black women as the minstrel group for the first time, it tours Massachussets, New York, and other eastern, and midwestern states and Canada.

Jazz trumpeter Buddy Bolden leads a band that performs throughout New Orleans.

Eighty-five African Americans are lynched.

Mississippi amends its constitution, creating a "literacy clause," requiring individuals to read and interpret any part of the constitution in order to be eligible to vote.....giving the state the ability to disenfranchise blacks.

Savannah State College is established in Georgia.

Iku:

Minstrel banjoist Horace Weston dies.

 **1891**

Kuumba:

Dancer Bill Robinson makes his stage musical debut in *The South Before the War.*

To avoid racism, visual artist Henry O. Tanner leaves America to live in Paris, France.

One hundred and twelve African Americans are lynched.

West Virginia State College is founded in Institute, West Virginia.

Delaware State College is founded in Dover, Delaware.

North Carolina Agriculture and Technical (A&T) State University is founded in Greensboro, North Carolina.

James Naismith invents basketball.

 **1892**

Kuumba:

Sissieretta Joyner Jones ("The Black Patti") performs for President Benjamin Harrison at the White House.

Singer/art-song-composer Harry T. Burleigh begins his studies at the National Conservatory of Music where he works with the director of the Conservatory, Czech composer Antonin Dvorak.

Cakewalk competitions are held across the country.

The Afro-American newspaper is founded by Rev. William M. Alexander in Baltimore, Maryland.

Grover Cleveland is elected president of the United States.

One hundred and sixty African Americans are lynched.

The Ellis Island Immigration Station opens in New York.

Feminist lecturer/poet Frances Harper publishes the novel *Iola Leroy Shadows Uplifted.*

 **1893**

Agba:

Blues artist William Lee Conley "Big Bill" Broonzy is born in Scott, Mississippi.

Blues singer Mississippi John Hurt is born in Teoc, Mississippi.

Blues/jazz pianist/composer Perry Bradford is born in Montgomery, Alabama.

Pianist/accompanist Lawrence Brown is born in Jacksonville, Florida.

Kuumba:

Antonin Dvorak composes the symphony *From the New World*, incorporating the sound of the Negro spiritual, a precedent-setting work that articulates a pathway for American classical musical nationalism. Dvorak writes a letter to the New York *Herald* explaining his perception of the indigenous music of the U.S.: *The country is full of melody, original, sympathetic and varying in mood, colour and character to suit every phase of composition. It is a rich field. America can have great and noble music of her own, growing out of the very soil and partaking of its nature—the natural voice of a free and vigorous race* (May 25th). Ethnomusicologists of the 1990s have described this as the "Blacking Up" of concert music, recognizing an effort to construct American "high culture" on an Africanist base.

Singer Sissieretta Joyner Jones "The Back Patti" tours Europe.

The Harp of Zion is published. The book is the first to include gospel music by an African American composer.

Chicago World's Fair is the performance venue for Ragtime piano players as well as for violinist Joseph Douglass.

The Excelsior Brass Band becomes a popular African American dance band in New Orleans.

Bert Williams and George Walker become a musical comedy duo in San Francisco, California.

An integrated theater company, The Forty Whites and Thirty Blacks minstrel company is established in New York by Primrose and West.

The Martyr, an opera by Harry Lawrence Freeman, is produced in Denver, Colorado.

One hundred and seventeen African Americans are lynched.

The Panic of 1893 begins a four-year economic depression.

The first silent motion pictures are produced.

Dr. Daniel Hale Williams performs the world's first successful heart operation at the Provident Hospital of Chicago.

Paul Laurence Dunbar publishes his first book of poetry, *Oak and Ivy.*

Visual artist Henry O. Tanner completes *The Banjo Lesson*, portraying an elderly black musician giving a small child a banjo lesson.

The Baptist National Educational Convention is established with the mission to reach young African-Americans and educate future ministers.

 **1894**

Agba:

Blues singer Bessie Smith is born in Chattanooga, Tennessee.

Jazz pianist James Price Johnson is born in New Brunswick, New Jersey.

Opera director Mary Cardwell Dawson is born in Meridian, North Carolina.

Kuumba:

Robert Cole forms the All-Star Stock Company in New York, to train future professional show people. Members include composer-performers Gussie Davis and Will Marion Cook.

Billboard Magazine is established as a music industry publication.

Concert singer Harry T. Burleigh is appointed to the position of soloist at St. Georges Church in New York City, a position he held until 1949.

The Church of Christ Holiness is founded by Rev. C. P. Jones in Selma, Alabama. It is subsequently organized into the national denomination, the Church of Christ (Holiness), USA, at its first Holiness Convention in 1897.

One hundred and thirty-five African Americans are lynched.

Visual artist Henry Ossawa Tanner paints two of his most important works, *The Thankful Poor,* and *The Bagpipe Lesson.*

 **1895**

Agba:

Classical composer William Grant Still is born in Woodville, Mississippi.

Choral Conductor Eva Jessye is born in Coffeyville, Kansas.

Gospel singer Alberta Hunter is born in Memphis, Tennessee.

Gospel singer/composer Sallie Martin, the mother of gospel music, is born in Pittfield, Georgia.

Blues pianist Perry Bradford is born in Montgomery, Alabama.

Blues singer Trixie Smith is born in Atlanta, Georgia.

Blues guitarist Mance Lipscomb is born in Navasota, Texas.

Kuumba:

Ragtime artist Scott Joplin tours with his quartet, The Texas Medley Quartette.

John W. Isham organizes a black production company that performs a "musical farce," *The Octoroons.*

Ernest Hogan composes the hit song, *All Coons Look Alike to Me*, an example of the stereotypical "coon songs."

W. C. Handy reports hearing an early version of country blues, performed in Tutwiler, Mississippi.

English composer Samuel Coleridge-Taylor writes *Ballade in D Minor* for violin and piano.

White composer Antonin Dvorak writes an article for Harpers *New Monthly* Magazine (XC), "Music in America," in which he asserts: *The most potent as well as the most beautiful (among American songs)...according to my estimation are certain of the so-called plantation melodies and slave songs.*

The Church of God in Christ is founded by C. H. Mason in Mississippi, a denomination known for its exuberant performance of gospel music, including the use of a variety of instruments as accompaniment (guitar, piano, trumpet, drums, etc.).

The National Baptist Convention of the United States of America is established through the merger of The Foreign Mission Convention, The American National Baptist Convention, and the National Education Convention.

Visual artist Henry Ossawa Tanner wins honorable mention in the Paris salon with his painting, *Daniel in the Lion's Den*, subsequently receiving the silver medal at the Universal Exposition in Paris, France, and the silver medal at the Pan American exhibition in Buffalo, New York.

Black women from twenty black womens clubs form the National Federation of Afro-American Women.

One hundred and twelve African Americans are lynched.

Scholars identify this year as "the beginning of African American modernism," marked by the famous Atlanta Compromise speech given by Booker T. Washington at the Negro exhibit of the Atlanta Cotton States and International Exposition. It is a speech that calls upon African Americans to become willing to accommodate segregation and to respond to the situation through the development of economic self-reliance.

Iku:

Frederick Douglass dies in Washington, D.C.

 **1896**

Agba:

Blues singer Ida Cox is born in Toccoa, Georgia.

Blues/Gospel artist Rev. "Blind" Gary Davis is born in Lawrence County, South Carolina.

Composer Shirley Graham DuBois is born near Evansville, Indiana.

Singer Ethel Waters is born in Philadelphia, Pennsylvania.

Musical theatre singer Florence Mills is born in Washington, D.C.

Blues singer Minnie (Memphis Minnie) Douglas is born in Algiers, Louisiana.

Kuumba:

Black Patti's Troubadours, written by Bob Cole opens on Broadway, with an all-black cast, including Sissieretta Joyner Jones ("The Black

Patti"). In the same year, Sissieretta Joyner Jones formally establishes the Black Patti Troubadours, a group of over 40 black performers organized because of the frustration created by the racism of this country. The group's repertoire includes ragtime and grand opera.

Composer/pianist J. Rosamund Johnson becomes supervisor of music in Jacksonville, Florida.

Oriental America becomes the first operatic-type musical produced on Broadway by John W. Isham with an all-black cast, including J. Rosamond Johnson and Sidney Woodward, performing a finale that includes selections from *Faust, Rigoletto,Carmen* and *Il Trovatore*.

Composer Will Marion Cook writes the art song *Love Is the Tendrest of Themes.*

The Cakewalk dance craze begins.

Seventy-seven African Americans are lynched.

The U.S. Supreme Court upholds the doctrine of "separate but equal" in Plessy vs. Ferguson: *Our constitution is color-blind, and neither knows nor tolerates classes among citizens. In respect of civil rights, all citizens are equal before the law. The humblest is the peer of the most powerful. The law regards man as man, and takes no account of his color when his civil rights guaranteed by the supreme law of the land are involved.*

William McKinley is elected president of the United States.

Scientist George Washington Carver joins the faculty at Tuskegee Institute as director of agricultural research.

The National Baptist Publishing Board is established - the organization that publishes the hymnals of the Baptist church.

South Carolina State College is established at Orangeburg, South Carolina.

1897

Agba:

Blues singer Blind Lemon Jefferson is born in Wortham, Texas.

Jazz conductor/arranger Fletcher Henderson is born in Cuthbert, Georgia.

Jazz saxophonist/clarinetist Sidney Bechet is born in New Orleans, Louisiana.

Jazz pianist William Henry Joseph Berthol Bonaparte Berthloff Smith (Willie "The Lion" Smith) is born.

Kuumba:

The national Ragtime era begins.

Tom Turpin's *Harlem Rag* becomes the first published rag.

Ragtime pianist/composer Scott Joplin moves to Sedalia, Missouri.

The National Gramophone Company begins manufacturing disc records.

Jazz trumpeter Buddy Bolden performs in New Orleans with a group consisting of cornet, clarinet, trombone, guitar, violin, string bass and drums.

Storyville is created in New Orleans, Louisiana, becoming the the French Quarter's home of prostitution and jazz.

W. C. Handy tours California with Mahara's Colored Minstrels.

The National Baptist Publishing Board publishes the quarterly, *The Sunday School Teacher*, and churches begin to purchase almost all church literature from the Publishing Board (ultimately including gospel music).

The American Negro Historical Society is founded.

Blacks are featured in the silent motion picture *Dancing Darkey Boy.*

One hundred and twenty-three African Americans are lynched.

Solomon Carter Fuller graduates from the Boston University School of Medicine, and goes on to become the first African American psychiatrist and the husband of sculptor Meta Vaux Warrick Fuller.

 **1898**

Agba:

Blues singer Beulah "Sippie" Wallace is born in Houston, Texas.

Jazz pianist/composer/band leader Lillian (Lil) Hardin (Armstrong) is born in Memphis, Tennessee.

Band leader/arranger Fletcher Hamilton Henderson is born in Cuthbert, Georgia.

Concert pianist Lorenza Jordan Cole is born.

Singer Paul Robeson is born in Princeton, New Jersey.

Singer Jules Bledsoe is born in Waco, Texas.

Composer/publisher Clarence Williams is born in Plaquermine, Louisiana.

Composer Edward H. Boatner is born in New Orleans, Louisiana.

Organist/choral director/composer/conductor Frederick Douglass Hall is born in Atlanta, Georgia.

Kuumba:

A Trip to Coontown, the first true black Broadway musical comedy, breaks away from the minstrel tradition by creating a cast of characters that combines music with plotline. Composed and produced by Bob Cole and Billy Johnson, and starring Sam Lucas, the comedy is produced as a declaration of independence to separate black actors from the financial domination of white managers.

A Broadway show by composer Will Marion Cook with lyrics by Paul Laurence Dunbar, *Clorindy, The Origin Of The Cake-Walk,* opens. Starring Ernest Hogan, it is the first show to introduce ragtime music to the New York theatre.

A cakewalk finale is included in the white Broadway show *Yankee Doodle Dandy.*

The Maple Leaf Club is founded in Sedalia, Missouri.

Samuel Coleridge-Taylor composes *Hiawatha Trilogy* (based upon the Longfellow poem) and the opera *Dream Lovers* (with poet Paul Laurence Dunbar as librettist).

Pianist Thomas Greene "Blind Tom" Bethune retires from the concert stage.

John Wesley Work II becomes a faculty member at Fisk University, and the conductor of the Fisk Jubilee Singers.

One hundred and one African Americans are lynched.

The Spanish-American War begins.

Helen Bannerman writes *The Story of Little Black Sambo.*

Paul Laurence Dunbar publishes *Lyrics of Lowly Life.*

 **1899**

Agba:

Gospel composer William Herbert Brewster is born in Somerville, Tennessee.

Jazz pianist/composer/conductor Edward Kennedy "Duke" Ellington is born in Washington, D.C.

Blues singer/guitarist Sleepy John Estes is born in Ripley, Tennessee.

Blues Harmonica-player Sonny Boy No. 2 Williamson (Willie Rice Miller) is born in Glendora, Mississippi.

Blues/Gospel pianist/composer Thomas A. Dorsey (Georgia Tom) is born in Villa Rica, Georgia.

Country music singer/harmonica player Deford Bailey is born near Nashville, Tennessee.

Classical composer William Levi Dawson is born in Anniston, Alabama.

Kuumba:

Scott Joplin's first rag, *Original Rags*, is published in March. In September his *Maple Leaf Rag* is published by John Stark. The international craze begins.

Eubie Blake composes his first rag, *Charleston Rag*.

Will Marion Cook composes the Broadway show, *Jes Lak White Fo'ks*.

Bert Williams and George Walker star in the Broadway musical comedy, *The Policy Players*.

The Columbia Record Company is established, and exclusively records white performers until after World War I.

The Fisk Jubilee Singers perform in London in a concert attended by the Afro-English composer Samuel Coleridge-Taylor, inspiring him to write and arrange concert music based upon the melodies of spirituals.

New Orleans Traditional Jazz flourishes (as performed by an instrumental ensemble that includes cornet, clarinet and trombone) in the Storyville area. When performed by whites it is known as Dixieland.

The Church of Christ (Holiness), USA publishes its first songbook, *Jesus Only,* a collection that is expanded into *Jesus Only Nos 1 and 2* in 1901. The second publication contains an essay by C. P. Jones "Inductive Lessons in Vocal Music," providing fifteen pointers for amateur church musicians, including the admonition to *Sing full round tones. Do not blare like a file against a saw. If the voice at first be not sweet and musical, practice will bring it to be so. To this end, sing much when by yourself. Practice the scale; practice correct pronunciation. Yet so practice it as to let your heart be on what you sing, not how. Avoid any sort of "put on."* Jon Michael Spencer publishes the full list of fifteen in his *Black Hymnody,* p. 108-110.

The Church of the Living God is founded by Rev. William Christian in Wrightsville, Arkansas.

Novelist Charles Waddell Chesnutt publishes *The Conjure Woman.*

The Philadelphia Museum buys the Henry O. Tanner painting, *The Annunciation.*

Eighty-five African Americans are lynched.

W.E.B. DuBois publishes a social, economic and political study—*The Philadelphia Negro.*

Iku:

Minstrel Gussie Davis dies.

1900

Agba:

Jazz trumpeter Daniel Louis "Satchmo" Armstrong is born in New Orleans, Louisiana.

Jazz bassist Walter Sylvester Page is born in Gallatin, Missouri.

Jazz saxophonist/band arranger Don Redman is born in Piedmont, West Virginia.

Kuumba:

Charles Tindley composes *I'll Overcome Some Day*, the textual precursor of the freedom song, *We Shall Overcome.*

J. Rosamond Johnson and James Weldon Johnson compose the song *Lift Every Voice and Sing: National Hymn For the Colored People of America*–the song that ultimately becomes known as the Negro National Anthem.

John Stark and Scott Joplin move from Sedalia, Missouri to St. Louis, Missouri.

Tom Turpin opens his Rosebud Cafe, a gathering place for ragtime pianists.

The player piano is marketed as a pianola, with piano rolls that reproduce the sounds of ragtime.

Clarence Cameron White begins to tour the country as a concert violinist.

Harry T. Burleigh becomes the baritone soloist at New York's Temple Emanu-El.

Blacks are featured in the silent motion picture *Watermelon Contest.*

W. E. B.DuBois delivers the speech that contains the famous line: *The problem of the twentieth century is the problem of the color line.*

One hundred and fifteen African Americans are lynched.

William McKinely is reelected president of the United States.

Coppin State College is founded in Baltimore, Maryland.

77.5% of the black population live in rural areas 22.6% live in urban areas.

Madam C. J. Walker introduces the straightening comb to the market for the care of the hair of African American women.

Booker T. Washington establishes the National Negro Business League.

3

1901 - 1920
THE NEW SECULAR VOICE

The primary black music of this era is secular—Ragtime, Blues and Jazz. Performed by soloists, ensembles, and vaudeville troupes, it emerges in New Orleans, Missouri, New York, Baltimore, in the rural sections of the south, and in the World War I bands of the U. S. Army. The creators of this music are no longer anonymous. Through their work, the secular music of African American culture evolves from folk status into formal status. It is written down, and published by white-owned and black-owned publishing houses. It is recorded. It is performed in the black theatres throughout the country, and it finds its way to the audiences of Europe and Australia.

At the same time, black composers, producers and performers are creating a sensation in Harlem, on Broadway and in Europe with the creation of dynamic musicals. Some African American popular musicians are performing with and creating music for white artists such as the Ziegfield Follies, Sophie Tucker and Irene and Vernon Castle. Increasing numbers of African Americans are becoming composers and performers of music from the European cultural tradition, establishing a national structure, The National Association of Negro Musicians, to support their work. In many instances, these musicians incorporate the folk music styles of ragtime and spirituals into their work, and some provide important interpretations of their work in the introductions of their publications.

The time span ends after the demise of Ragtime and with the achievement of high profile status for Blues and Jazz as symbolized by the start of the Jazz Age and the beginning of the era of Classic Blues.

TRENDS
1901 - 1920

1900s

ʕ Ragtime flourishes as a national craze.

ʕ Country blues and ragtime are performed in the jook joints/honky-tonks of the black community, accompanying dances such as the Slow Drag, the Shimmy, the Grind, and the Funky Butt.

ʕ The pre-gospel music era begins with the composed hymns of Charles Albert Tindley.

ʕ Over one million African Americans migrate to the urban industrial centers.

ʕ Lynchings continue to flourish.

1910s

ʕ Public dance halls proliferate around the United States, usually with a "whites-only" restriction for all but one night a week, despite the fact that the live music emerges primarily from black culture and is most often performed by black musicians. This level of segregation continues until after World War II.

ʕ Country blues, a vocal style that is usually performed by males accompanied with acoustic guitar, continues to flourish - centered in the Mississippi Delta (between the Yazoo River and the Mississippi River, including towns such as Clarksdale, Greenville and Greenwood, Mississippi). This is an area with a large concentration of African Americans. A similar style emerges in Texas. The evolution moves the blues form from its folk style into a more formal structure that eventually becomes Classic Blues. The lyrics of both Country and Classic Blues provide the musical response to post reconstruction discrimination.

- The East Coast/Piedmont style of the country blues emerges, created by agricultural workers and street musicians in the Virginia's, North Carolina, South Carolina, Kentucky and Georgia. The singers accompany themselves on guitar, using a ragtime-influenced finger-picking style. It is sometimes performed with guitar and harmonica. Blind Blake has been identified as the father of this style.

- African American entrepreneurs establish publishing companies and open vaudeville theatres.

- Homes across the United States begin to acquire phonographs.

- Collections of spirituals are published.

- Ragtime retains its popularity for a while and then fades.

- The period of Traditional New Orleans jazz continues.

- The NAACP begins an anti-lynching campaign and organizes branches across the U.S.

ACHIEVEMENT DATELINE
1901 - 1920

 **1901**

Agba:

Composer John Wesley Work III, is born in Tullahoma, Tennessee.

Blues singer William Samuel "Blind Willie" McTell is born in Thomson, Georgia.

Composer/arranger/conductor/actor Jester Hairston is born in Belew's Creek, North Carolina.

Singer Adelaide Hall is born in Brooklyn, New York.

Gospel singer Gertrude Mae Murphy Ward is born in Anderson, South Carolina.

Kuumba:

Scott Joplin, The King of Ragtime, composes the piano piece *The Easy Winners*. It reflects the typical ragtime format, with a percussive left hand playing a regular duple meter and a right hand playing a melody that is continuously syncopated.

Williams & Walker become the first African American artists to be recorded on disc for the Victor Talking Machine Company.

James Weldon Johnson, J. Rosamond Johnson and Bob Cole become the first black songwriters to have a signed contract with a Broadway music company–the Joseph W. Stern & Co.

Concert artist Emma Azalia Smith Hackley has a debut recital in Denver.

The Coleridge-Taylor Society is established in Washington, D.C., devoted to the performance of the music of a very distinguished Afro-English composer.

Singer/composer Harry T. Burleigh composes *Six Plantation Melodies for Violin and Piano.*

Minstrel James Bland returns to America from England, destitute and penniless.

One hundred and thirty African Americans are lynched.

Ex-slave Booker T. Washington publishes his autobiography *Up from Slavery.*

William Monroe Trotter begins publishing a militant newspaper, *The Boston Gardian.*

Joe Walcott becomes the welterweight boxing champion.

Grambling State University is founded in Grambling, Louisiana.

Oil is discovered in Texas.

President William McKinley is assassinated and succeeded by Theodore Roosevelt.

 **1902**

Agba:

Jazz bandleader Blanche Calloway is born in Baltimore, Maryland.

Jazz bandleader James (Jimmie) Lunceford is born in Fulton, Missouri.

Contralto Marian Anderson is born in Philadelphia, Pennsylvania.

Author/poet/librettist Langston Hughes is born in Joplin, Missouri.

Singer/dancer John Bubbles is born in Louisville, Kentucky.

Jazz/blues singer Jimmy Rushing is born in Oklahoma City.

Blues singer Eddie "Son" House is born in Riverton, Mississippi.

Kuumba:

Ragtime composer Scott Joplin's *The Entertainer* is published. It becomes a hit once again in 1974 as part of the movie soundtrack for *The Sting*.

Jelly Roll Morton claims to have "invented" jazz.

The Victor Talking Machine Company becomes a pioneer in the field of sound recording. Its first records by actors, music-hall entertainers and after-dinner speakers on wax cylinder technology includes six songs by the Dinwiddie Colored Quartet - the first black barbershop quartet.

Tin Pan Alley flourishes as the center of music publishing, with a focus upon Ragtime music.

Iku:

Composer Basile Bares dies.

 **1903**

Agba:

Opera singer Caterina Jarboro is born in Wilmington, North Carolina.

Opera singer Robert Todd Duncan is born in Danville, Kentucky.

Opera singer Zelma Watson George is born in Hearne, Texas.

White jazz artist Bix Beiderbecke is born in Davenport, Iowa.

Kuumba:

W. C. Handy observes a Mississippi guitarist performing in a style that incorporates the bottleneck technique of sliding on the strings (creating a blue tonality).

The Broadway hit musical *In Dahomey*, composed by Will Marion Cook with lyrics by poet Paul Laurence Dunbar. With comedian Bert Williams as the featured performer, it becomes the first all-black show to play in a major Broadway theater. It is also the first black musical to be performed abroad, giving a command performance for King Edward VII in London.

W. E. B. DuBois' collection of essays, *The Souls of Black Folk*, is published, espousing a philosophy that differs from that of Booker T. Washington. It includes an essay about the Sorrow Songs of slave days: *Through all the sorrow of the Sorrow Songs there breathes a hope—a faith in the ultimate justice of things. The minor cadences of despair change often to triumph and calm confidence. Sometimes it is faith in life, sometimes a faith in death, sometimes assurance of boundless justice in some fair world beyond. But whichever it is, the meaning is always clear: that sometime, somewhere, men will judge men by their souls and not by their skins.*

A Guest of Honor, ragtime opera by Scott Joplin, is presented in St. Louis, Missouri.

The Washington Conservatory of Music is established in the District of Columbia.

The 200-voice Samuel Coleridge-Taylor Choral Society performs his *Hiawatha* at Washington, D.C.'s Metropolitan African Methodist Episcopal Church. In this same year Samuel Coleridge-Taylor becomes a professor of music at the Trinity College of Music in London, England.

Composer Will Marion Cook composes a ragtime piece, *Emancipation Day.*

Maggie Lena Walker of Richmond, Virginia becomes the first woman bank president for the St. Luke Penny Savings Bank.

Ninety-nine African Americans are lynched.

The automobile industry begins.

The Wright Brothers have their first flight.

Iku:

Composer Henry F. Williams dies.

Composer Edmond Dede dies in Bordeaux, France.

 **1904**

Agba:

Classical composer Undine Smith Moore is born in Jarratt, Virginia.

Jazz saxophonist Coleman Hawkins is born in St. Louis, Missouri.

Gospel singer Willie Mae Ford is born in Rolling Fork, Mississippi.

Jazz pianist/bandleader William (Count) Basie is born in Red Bank, New Jersey.

Jazz pianist/composer Thomas Wright "Fats" Waller is born in New York City.

Boogie-woogie pianist Clarence "Pine Top" Smith is born in Troy, Alabama.

Kuumba:

Classical pianist Hazel Harrison gives her European debut performance in Berlin.

Edward Gilbert Anderson begins conducting the Philadelphia Concert Orchestra.

Composer Will Marion Cook writes *The Southerners*, the first interracial Broadway musical.

J. Rosamond Johnson and Bob Cole compose two Broadway shows, *Humpty Dumpty* and *In Newport*.

Will Rainey, leader of the Rabbit Foot Minstrels, marries Gertrude Pridgett, who later on becomes "Ma" Rainey, the "Mother of the Blues."

The World's Fair (with a National Ragtime Contest) is held in St. Louis, Missouri.

Daytona Normal and Industrial School (later to become Bethune-Cookman College) is founded by Mary McLeod Bethune in Florida.

Eighty-three African Americans are lynched.

Theodore Roosevelt is elected president of the United States.

 **1905**

Agba:

Jazz singer Ivie Anderson is born in Gilroy, California.

Jazz trombonist Jack Teagarden is born in Vernon, Texas.

Jazz pianist Earl Fatha Hines is born in Duquesne, Pennsylvania.

Jazz cornetist/bandleader Ernest "Red" Nichols is born in Ogden, Utah.

Blues singer Bertha "Chippie" Hill is born in Charleston, South Carolina.

Kuumba:

Concert singer Emma Azalia Smith Hackley has a debut recital in Philadelphia.

Composer Samuel Coleridge-Taylor publishes a collection of spirituals, *Twenty-Four Negro Melodies*, with an introduction written by Booker T. Washington, noting that: *Wherever companies of Negroes were working together, in the cotton fields and tobacco factories, on the levees and steamboats, on sugar plantations, and chiefly in the fervor of religious gatherings, these melodies sprang into life.*

Ernest Hogan composes and performs in *Rufus Rastus*.

Rev. Charles Albert Tindley composes *Stand By Me* and *We'll Understand It Better By & By*.

Ernest Hogan establishes a group of male and female singers, dancers and musicians, The Memphis Students. James Weldon Johnson calls the group a "playing-singing-dancing orchestra". The ensemble performs in New York and tours Paris, Berlin and London.

W. C. Handy organizes the Pythian Band, in Memphis, Tennessee. The group specializes in performing African American folk music.

James Reese Europe organizes the New Amsterdam Musical Association, the first black musicians' union in the country.

The Philadelphia Concert Orchestra, conducted by E. Gilbert Anderson, is established.

Sixty-two African Americans are lynched.

The Niagara Falls Movement begins, led by W.E.B. DuBois and William Monroe Trotter. It is organized in opposition to the conciliatory philosophy of Booker T. Washington, and calls for confrontation to end racial discrimination in the U.S.

Robert S. Abbott begins publication of the Chicago *Defender.*

The first U.S. movie theater opens in Pittsburgh, Pennsylvania.

The one-reeler film, *The Wooing and Wedding of a Coon*, is made with an all-black cast.

White actors are featured in blackface in the silent motion picture, *Everybody Works But Father.*

 **1906**

Agba:

Blues singer Victoria Spivey is born in Houston, Texas.

Singer/entertainer Josephine Baker is born in St. Louis, Missouri.

Jazz saxophonist John (Johnny) Cornelius Hodges is born in Cambridge, Massachusetts.

Jazz clarinetist Leon Albany (Barney) Bigard is born in New Orleans, Louisiana.

Concert pianist/accompanist William Duncan Allen is born in Portland, Oregon.

Kuumba:

Composer Samuel Coleridge-Taylor writes *Symphonic Variations on an African Air* (using the spiritual "I'm Troubled in Mind").

Robert Cole and J. Rosamond Johnson compose the first African American operetta, *The Shoo-Fly Regiment*, with libretto by James Weldon Johnson, conducted by James Reese Europe.

Robert Mott opens Chicago's Pekin Theater—a house for vaudeville/musical theater performance.

Charles Sullivan establishes and serves as manager of the Victorian Concert Orchestra in Boston, Massachusetts.

Bert Williams and Will Marion Cook compose the Broadway musical, *Abyssinia*, starring the comedy team of Bert Williams, George Walker and Ada Overton Walker.

Voice and music are broadcast on radio for the first time.

The black actors' union is organized by Williams and Walker—The Negro's Society.

The Azusa Street Revival, led by Rev. Philip Seymour, begins in Los Angeles, giving special impetus to the Pentecostal movement, and introducing the practice of "speaking in tongues".

Sixty-five African Americans are lynched.

Racial uprisings occur in Brownsville, Texas and Atlanta, Georgia.

Sculptor Meta Vaux Warrick Fuller exhibits *Portraits from Mirror* at the Pennsylvania Academy of the Fine Arts.

Alpha Phi Alpha Fraternity is founded at Cornell University—the first black male social fraternity.

Iku:

Soprano Flora Batson dies.

 **1907**

Agba:

Jazz saxophonist/composer/band leader Benny Carter is born in New York City.

Jazz bandleader/singer Cabell (Cab) Calloway is born in Rochester, New York.

Gospel singer Roberta Martin is born in Helena, Arkansas.

Composer Howard Swanson is born in Atlanta, Georgia.

Jazz band leader William (Chick) Webb is born in Baltimore, Maryland.

Boogie-woogie pianist Albert C. Ammons is born in Chicago, Illinois.

Popular music singer/dancer Clayton (Peg Leg) Bates is born in Fountain Inn, South Carolina.

Ethnomusicologist John Lovell, Jr. is born in Asheville, North Carolina.

Kuumba:

Jazz trumpeter Buddy Bolden is committed to a mental institution.

Scott Joplin moves to New York, continuing to compose and teach.

Sixty African Americans are lynched.

 **1908**

Agba:

Blues singer Fulton Allen "Blind Boy" Fuller is born in Wadesboro, North Carolina.

Blues singer Joshua Daniel "Josh" White is born in Greenville, Mississippi.

Jazz trumpeter Charles Melvin "Cootie" Williams is born in Mobile, Alabama.

Jazz trumpeter Oran Thaddeus (Hot Lips) Page is born in Dallas, Texas.

Jazz/R&B vocalist/saxophonist/bandleader Louis Jordan is born in Brinkley, Arkansas.

Kuumba:

The Howard Theatre opens in Washington, D.C., a 1200-seat vaudeville theatre that is managed by blacks.

Harry Pace and W. C. Handy found The Pace and Handy Music Publishing Company in Memphis, Tennessee.

Scott Joplin publishes the *School of Ragtime Exercises for Piano* to help students learn to play ragtime.

The Original Creole Band is founded by clarinetist George Bacquet in Louisiana the first jazz orchestra to feature a string bass.

Will Marion Cook composes the Broadway musical, *Bandanna Land* (starring Bert Williams, George Walker and Ada Overton Walker).

Robert Cole and J. Rosamond Johnson compose *The Red Moon*, produced in New York with an all-black cast. The plot is crafted as a celebration of African American and Native American culture.

James Weldon Johnson publishes the poem "O Black and Unknown Bards" in *Century Magazine*, in celebration of the spiritual and its creators.

Racial disturbances occur in Springfield, Illinois.

Ninety-seven African Americans are lynched.

William Howard Taft is elected president of the United States.

Alpha Kappa Alpha Sorority is founded at Howard University—the first black women's sorority.

Jack Johnson defeats Tommy Burns to earn the heavyweight boxing championship.

Iku:

Concert pianist Thomas Greene "Blind Tom" Bethune dies.

 **1909**

Agba:

Jazz vibraphonist Lionel Hampton is born in Louisville, Kentucky.

Jazz saxophonist Lester "Prez" Young is born in Woodville, Mississippi.

Jazz saxophonist Benjamin (Ben) Webster is born in Kansas City, Missouri.

White jazz artist Benny Goodman is born in Chicago, Illinois.

Jazz drummer William Cozy Cole is born in East Orange, New Jersey.

Kuumba:

Anselmo Barrasso establishes the Theatre Owners Booking Association (TOBA), a group of vaudeville theatres in the south, east and midwest that featured black entertainment The circuit came to be known as "Tough on Black Asses." It includes The Regal (Baltimore), The Howard (Washington, D.C.), The 81 (Atlanta), The Booker T (St. Louis) and The Monogram (Chicago). The circuit gradually expands to a network of fifty theatres.

Scott Joplin's *Solace-A Mexican Serenade* is published.

Bert Williams and J. Rosamond Johnson compose *Lode of Koal*, directed by James Reese Europe.

The Fisk Jubilee Quartet begins to tour the country (1909-1927) and record for Victor and Columbia, performing folk music and spirituals.

Howard University students rebel against being asked to sing spirituals.

Ada Overton Walker and the Abyssinian Girls begins to tour as a vaudeville act.

White composer Charles Ives composes *An Elegy For Our Forefathers* (originally entitled "An Elegy For Stephen Foster"). It is an orchestral work that uses the "Old Black Joe" theme.

Eighty-two African Americans are lynched.

The National Association for the Advancement of Colored People (NAACP) is founded.

Alpha Phi Alpha Fraternity, Inc. is established at Cornell University.

Harlem is advertised to blacks as the "Promised Land," thereafter becoming the center of black artistic and cultural life.

Booker T. Washington publishes *Story of the Negro*, a major contribution to the scholarship of Black History.

Matthew Henson explores the North Pole.

Sigmund Lubin begins to produce the "Sambo" series of all-black comedies.

Congress passes the first copyright laws giving copyright owners exclusive rights for the performance and the reproduction of their work.

Visual artist Henry Ossawa Tanner has his first one-man exhibition of religious painting in the American Art Galleries in New York.

New York City's daily black newspaper, *Amsterdam News,* begins publication.

Iku:

Composer/showman Ernest Hogan dies.

 **1910**

Agba:

Jazz guitarist/composer Jean Baptiste Django Reinhardt is born in Liverchies, Belgium.

Blues singer Howlin' Wolf (Chester Arthur Burnett) is born in Aberdeen, Mississippi.

Jazz pianist Mary Lou Williams is born in Atlanta, Georgia.

Jazz pianist Arthur (Art) Tatum is born in Toledo, Ohio.

Jazz drummer Sidney Catlett is born in Evansville, Indiana.

Blues singer/electric guitarist Aaron T-Bone Walker is born in Linden, Texas.

Opera singer/choral director Dorothy Maynor is born in Norfolk, Virginia.

Jazz bassist Milton (Milt) John Hinton is born in Vicksburg, Mississippi.

Kuumba:

Composer Shelton Brooks writes *Some of These Days,* a song that becomes the trade mark of Sophie Tucker.

Concert singer Emma Azalia Smith Hackley starts national tours lecturing about and performing black folk music.

French composer Claude Debussy writes *Golliwogs CakeWalk*, a piano composition that is part of the *Children's Corner*.

The Black Patti Troubadours perform in the Broadway musical, *A Trip to Africa.*

Bert Williams becomes the first African American performer featured in the Ziegfield Follies, performing his signature song, *Nobody,* and performing with the Follies until 1919.

French composer Claude Debussy composes *Minstrels* for his book of Preludes.

Black musical theatre flourishes in Harlem.

Monroe (Pink) Morton opens the 800-seat Morton Theatre in Athens Georgia. It is one of the largest theatres in the country to be owned by an African American.

Conductor James Reese Europe builds the Clef Club, a combined musicians' union and club date office, and organizes the Clef Club Orchestra.

Seventy-six African Americans are lynched.

The National Urban League is established, originally as The National League on Urban Conditions Among Negroes.

The NAACP publishes the first issue of *Crisis* magazine.

North Carolina Central University is founded in Durham.

The Boy Scouts of America is established.

The Great Migration begins the largest internal migration of African

American blacks, moving from the South to the North, a period that extends until 1940.

Heavyweight boxer Jack Johnson beats the "Great White Hope" Jim Jeffries, causing whites to riot.

William Foster forms the Will Foster Moving Picture Company, becoming the first African American to produce films using a black cast and marketing to a black audience.

 **1911**

Agba:

Jazz trumpeter David Roy Eldridge is born in Pittsburgh, Pennsylvania.

Gospel singer Mahalia Jackson is born in New Orleans, Louisiana.

Blues singer/harmonica player Sonny Terry (Saunders Terrell) is born in Durham, North Carolina.

Blues singer/songwriter "Ivory" Joe Hunter is born in Kirbyville, Texas.

Blues/R&B singer Big Joe Turner is born in Kansas City Missouri.

Composer Mark Fax is born in Baltimore, Maryland.

Kuumba:

The Black Patti Troubadours are featured in the Broadway musical, *In The Jungles.*

Tenor Roland Hayes tours with the Fisk Jubilee Singers.

Edward (Kid) Ory organizes his first jazz band in New Orleans, Louisiana.

William Wilkins opens the Wilkins School of Music in Los Angeles, California.

Ragtime composer Scott Joplin publishes his folk opera, *Treemonisha - Opera in Three Acts.*

White composer Irving Berlin writes *Alexander's Ragtime Band.*

J. Rosamond Johnson composes the Broadway musical, *Hello Paris*, and becomes the first black to conduct a white orchestra for a New York show.

Madam C. J. Walker Enterprises grosses more than one hundred thousand dollars annually.

Sixty-seven African Americans are lynched.

Kappa Alpha Psi Fraternity is founded at Indiana University.

Arthur Alfonso Schomburg and John Edward Bruce establish the Negro Society for Historical Research.

Iku:

Minstrel James Bland dies of pneumonia.

Broadway composer Bob Cole dies.

Minstrel/musical theater star George Walker dies.

 **1912**

Agba:

Blues singer Robert Johnson is born in Hazelhurst, Mississippi.

Blues artist Sam "Lightnin" Hopkins is born in Centerville, Texas.

Pop singer Herbert Mills (of the Mills Brothers) is born in Piqua, Ohio.

Jazz arranger Gil Evans is born in Toronto, Canada.

Jazz pianist/composer/arranger Theodore (Teddy) Wilson is born in Austin, Texas.

Kuumba:

J. Rosamond Johnson becomes musical director of London's Oscar Hammerstein Opera House.

Minstrel Billy Kersands takes his songs and his "buck and wing" soft-shoe dancing on a tour of Australia.

Concert singer Emma Azalia Smith Hackley establishes the Vocal Normal Institute in Chicago.

The Black Patti Troubadours are featured in the Broadway musical, *Captain Jaspar.*

James Reese Europe conducts the Clef Club Symphony Orchestra in concert at Carnegie Hall (145 players, including 47 mandolins, 27 harp-guitars, 11 banjos, 8 violins 13 cellos 1 saxophone, 1 tuba, 2 clarinets, 2 baritones, 8 trombones, 7 cornets, 1 timpani, 5 trap drums, 2 double basses, and 10 pianos), thereafter developing a list of 187 black musicians from all parts of the globe he could call for work. The concert is a benefit for the Music School Settlement for the Colored People of New York City.

W. C. Handy settles in Memphis, Tennessee and publishes *Memphis Blues*, the first published blues composition (published without lyrics).

Blues singer Bessie Smith begins her professional career, joining a minstrel show as a singer and tap dancer.

Blues singer Blind Lemon Jefferson begins performing on the streets of Dallas, Galveston and Houston, Texas.

Composer R. Nathaniel Dett writes the *Magnolia* piano suite.

White classical composer Henry F. Gilbert writes *Negro Rhapsody,* blending folk traditions with European classical tradition.

James Weldon Johnson publishes the novel *Autobiography of an Ex-Colored Man.*

White actors are featured in blackface in the silent motion picture, *A Close Call.*

New Mexico and Arizona join the Union, bringing the number of states to 48.

Tennessee State University is founded in Nashville.

Jarvis Christian College is founded in Hawkins, Texas.

The Girl Scouts of America is founded.

Sixty-three African Americans are lynched.

The Titanic sinks resulting in 1,503 deaths.

Woodrow Wilson is elected president of the United States, and oversees an administration that passes substantial legislation establishing apartheid in the country. Among other things, the legislation prevents blacks from holding commissions in the armed forces, segregates the federal work force, and segregates all eating and restroom facilities in federal facilities.

Iku:

Classical composer Samuel Coleridge-Taylor dies.

 **1913**

Agba:

Composer Margaret Bonds is born in Chicago, Illinois.

Jazz alto saxophonist Earl Bostic is born in Tulsa, Oklahoma.

Jazz singer Helen Humes is born in Louisville, Kentucky.

Pop singer Harry Mills (of the Mills Brothers) is born in Piqua, Ohio.

Kuumba:

James Reese Europe resigns from the Clef Club and establishes a new group, the Tempo Club.

Robert Nathaniel Dett composes the piano suite, *In The Bottoms*, and begins an appointment to Hampton Institute where he develops the Hampton Institute Choir.

Thirteen-year-old Louis Armstrong is arrested for shooting a revolver on New Year's Eve, and sent to the Waifs' Home, where he is given a horn by the man in charge of music. He shortly thereafter becomes the leader of the Home's band.

Will Marion Cook composes the Broadway musical, *The Traitor.*

William Vodery becomes a regular arranger for the Ziegeld Follies, working for them until 1932.

Billboard Magazine begins to publish the list of the most popular vaudeville songs.

Fifty-two African Americans are lynched.

Delta Sigma Theta Sorority is founded at Howard University.

Omega Psi Phi Fraternity is founded at Howard University.

Iku:

Harriet Tubman, "the Moses of her people," dies.

 **1914**

Agba:

Jazz drummer Kenneth (Kenny) Clarke is born in Pittsburgh, Pennsylvania.

Gospel artist Roebuck Staples is born in Winona, Mississippi.

Jazz singer Billy Eckstine is born in Pittsburgh, Pennsylvania.

Jazz trumpeter/bandleader Erskine Hawkins is born in Birmingham, Alabama

Avant-garde jazz band arranger Sun Ra is born in Birmingham, Alabama.

Jazz critic Leonard G. Feather is born in London, England.

Classical composer Noah Ryder is born in Nashville, Tennessee.

Conductor Leonard DePaur is born in Summit, New Jersey.

Kuumba:

Clarence Cameron White becomes the conductor of Boston's Victorian Concert Orchestra.

Jazz pianist James P. Johnson composes his first piano blues, *Mama and Papa Blues.*

J. Rosamond Johnson becomes the director of the Music School Settlement for the Colored People of New York City.

The All-Colored Composers' Concert is produced at Orchestra Hall in Chicago by tenor/impressario William Hackney, including performances by R. Nathaniel Dett, Anita Patti Brown and Ernest Amos.

Bert Williams becomes the first black to star in a movie, *Darktown Jubilee.*

Blues singer Gertrude "Ma" Rainey tours with Tollivers Circus and Musical Extravaganza.

Robert Nathaniel Dett composes the first choral-anthem spiritual, *Listen to The Lambs.*

Pianist Hazel Harrison completes a concert tour of the U.S., often performing works by black composers.

James Reese Europe's orchestra is signed by Victor Talking Machine Company. Europe begins an association with the white ballroom dance team of Vernon and Irene Castle, composing music for them, e.g. *Castle House Rag*, establishing the foundation for jazz dance and creating the music for two new popular dances: the fox-trot and the turkey-trot.

W.C. Handy's classic St. *Louis Blues* is published, and popularized by white vaudeville star Sophie Tucker.

The Black Patti Troubadours are featured in the Broadway musical, *Lucky Sam from Alabam.*

Jazz composer and band director Duke Ellington composes his first piece, *Soda Fountain Rag,* and he goes on to compose 1,012 copyrighted songs (243 of them written in collaboration with others).

The American Society of Composers, Authors and Publishers (ASCAP) is founded to establish and administer the process of royalties distribution for the live performance of copyrighted music in theatres, dance halls and restaurants.

The Great migration of blacks to urban centers such as Chicago, Detroit and New York continues and increases.

Fifty-five African Americans are lynched.

Minstrel/Actor Sam Lucas becomes the first black to play the title role in the film version of *Uncle Toms Cabin*.

Sculptor Meta Warrick Fuller produces a bronze work, *Water Boy*, inspired by the folk song.

The black film producer Oscar Micheaux makes *The Wages of Sin and The Broken Violin*.

Phi Beta Sigma Fraternity is founded at Howard University.

Henry Ford introduces the assembly line for the speedier production of the Model-T.

World War I breaks out.

Iku:

Musical theater star Ada Overton Walker dies.

 **1915**

Agba:

Blues singer Joshua Daniel "Josh" White is born in Greenville, South Carolina.

Conductor Dean Charles Dixon is born in New York City.

Composer Thomas Kerr, Jr., is born in Baltimore, Maryland.

Blues singer/bassist/composer Willie James Dixon is born in Vicksburg, Mississippi.

Jazz singer Billie Holiday (Eleanora Fagan) is born in Philadelphia, Pennsylvania.

Jazz singer William (Billy) Daniels is born in Jacksonville, Florida.

Pop singer Donald Mills (of the Mills Brothers) is born in Piqua, Ohio.

Composer/arranger Billy Strayhorn is born in Dayton, Ohio.

Jazz trumpeter Harry (Sweets) Edison is born in Columbus, Ohio.

Gospel guitarist/singer Roebuck "Pop" Staples is born in Winona, Mississippi.

Blues singer/guitarist "Muddy Waters" (McKinley Morganfield) is born in Rolling Fork, Mississippi.

Blues singer/guitarist Walter Brown "Brownie" McGhee is born in Knoxville, Tennessee.

Pop singer Albert "Al" Hibbler is born in Little Rock, Arkansas.

Archivist/folklorist Alan Lomax is born in Austin, Texas.

Gospel singer "Sister" Rosetta Tharpe is born in Cotton Plant, Arkansas.

Kuumba:

The General Phonograph Corporation issues discs on the Okeh record label.

Composer Shelton Brooks writes *Darktown Strutters Ball.*

Ragtime composer Scott Joplin produces the opera *Treemonisha.*

Will Marion Cook, composes the Broadway musical, *Darkeydom.*

Will Marion Cook, James Reese Europe and William Vodery compose the musical *Way Down South.*

Thomas A. Dorsey becomes a party pianist in Atlanta, Georgia.

Eubie Blake teams with Noble Sissle (a singer from Indianapolis), composing and performing as the Dixie Duo off and on for the next forty years.

The National Baptist Convention splits over a dispute about the ownership of the National Baptist Publishing Board, and hence, the National Baptist Convention, U.S.A., Inc. is created.

D. W. Griffiths racist feature film, *The Birth of A Nation*, the white southerners view of the story of the Civil War and Reconstruction, is released, causing boycotts by the NAACP.

Sixty-nine African Americans are lynched.

Carter G. Woodson founds the Association for the Study of Negro Life and History.

The United States invades Haiti.

W. E. B. DuBois publishes *The Negro*, a major contribution to the scholarship of Black History.

The YMCA and the YWCA implement "whites-only" policies.

Iku:

Minstrel William Billy Kersands dies.

 **1916**

Agba:

Jazz pianist/gospel performer and publisher Kenneth Morris is born.

Jazz trumpeter William Alonzo (Cat) Anderson is born in Greenville, South Carolina.

Jazz guitarist Charles (Charlie) Christian is born in Bonham, Texas.

Jazz pianist/organist/composer/arranger William Ballard (Bill) Doggett is born in Philadelphia, Pennsylvania.

Jazz bassist George Red Callender is born in Richmond, Virginia.

Kuumba:

The Aeolian Company begins the Vocalion record label.

Harry T. Burleigh arranges *Deep River* for solo voice performance - the model for future composers.

The National Baptist Publishing Board publishes *The National Jubilee Melodies* songbook, a collection of old plantation songs. It includes this description of the spiritual "Nobody Knows the Trouble I See": *A poor old negro slave who had been a model Christian but who had a most cruel master, sat and sung this refrain one day after he had been given a most merciless whipping.* (See *Black Hymnody* by Jon Michael Spencer, p.85).

The Original Dixieland Jazz Band, a group of five white musicians, makes its first public appearance in New Orleans.

Stride pianist James P. Johnson begins cutting piano rolls.

Preacher/composer Charles Tindley establishes the Paradise Publishing Company and publishes *New Songs of Paradise*, a collection of hymns for sunday schools. He also becomes the music director for the Baptist Training Union Congress.

The Apollo Theatre opens in Harlem.

The weekly newspaper, the *Chicago Defender*, begins a campaign to encourage blacks to purchase Victrolas and to demand records by "the Race's great artists."

Fifty-four African Americans are lynched.

Woodrow Wilson is reelected president of the United States.

Photographer James Van der Zee opens his own studio.

Iku:

Minstrel Sam Lucas dies.

 **1917**

Agba:

Jazz trumpeter/composer/bandleader John Birks Dizzy Gillespie is born in Cheraw, South Carolina.

Singer Nat King Cole (Nathaniel Adams Coles) is born in Montgomery, Alabama.

Blues artist John Lee Hooker is born in Clarksdale, Mississippi.

Classical composer Ulysses Kay is born in Tucson, Arizona.

Jazz/blues singer/saxophonist Eddie (Cleanhead) Vinson is born in Houston, Texas.

Classical composer Roque Cordero is born in Panama.

Jazz pianist/composer Thelonious Sphere Monk is born in Rocky Mount, North Carolina.

Jazz pianist/composer Tadley (Tad) Ewing Dameron is born in Cleveland, Ohio.

Singer/actress Lena Horne is born in Brooklyn, New York.

Blues/jazz violinist (Papa) Johnny Creach is born in Beaver Falls, Pennsylvania.

Kuumba:

Tenor Roland Hayes tours with the Hayes Trio, and makes a debut performance at Symphony Hall in Boston, Massachusetts.

Black Army regiments participate in World War I, each of which has a band: the 349th Infantry band, conducted by Norman Scott, the 350th Infantry Band, conducted by J. Tim Brymm, the 351st Infantry Band, conducted by Dorsey Rhodes, the 367th Infantry Band, conducted by Egbert Thompson, the 368th Infantry Band, conducted by Jack Thomas, the 369th Infantry Band, conducted by James Reese Europe, and the 370th Infantry Band, conducted by George Duff.

Harry T. Burleigh is awarded the Spingarn Medal for excellence in the field of creative music.

Music critic Nora Holt becomes the classical music critic for the *Chicago Defender*.

French composer Erik Satie includes a ragtime inspired movement, "Ragtime du Paquebot" in his ballet *Parade*.

Ma Rainey, the Mother of the Blues, establishes a touring company (female chorus line and string band) to back up her performances— Madam Gertrude Rainey and the Georgia Smart Set.

The first jazz recording is made by the Original Dixieland Jazz Band, selling one million copies.

Shelton Brooks composes *Darktown Strutters' Ball,* a piece that is recorded by The Original Dixieland Jazz Band.

At the behest of the United States Navy, Storyville closes, causing musicians to seek work first on the Mississippi River and thereafter in Chicago.

Ragtime wanes in popularity (taken over by jazz and stride piano).

Race riots break out in Houston, Texas and East St. Louis, Missouri.

Thirty-eight African Americans are lynched.

Marcus Garvey establishes a branch of the United Negro Improvement Association (UNIA) in Harlem.

James Weldon Johnson publishes *Fifty Years and Other Poems,* inaugurating the Harlem Renaissance.

Oscar Micheaux produces his first silent film, *The Homesteader,* starring Evelyn Preer.

The U.S. enters World War I. The war stimulates mass industrialization and begins what some call "the Machine Age."

Iku:

Ragtime composer Scott Joplin dies.

 **1918**

Agba:

Singer/entertainer Pearl Bailey is born in Newport News, Virginia.

Jazz singer Ella Fitzgerald is born in Newport News, Virginia.

Jazz singer Joe Williams is born in Cordele, Georgia.

Jazz bassist James (Jimmy) Blanton is born in Chattanooga, Tennessee.

Jazz trumpeter Gerald Wilson is born in Shelby, Mississippi.

Choral Conductor Kenneth Browne Billups is born in St. Louis, Missouri.

Blues singer/guitarist Elmore James is born in Richland, Mississippi.

Concert singer Carol Lovette Brice is born in Sedalia, North Carolina.

Kuumba:

Composer Clarence Cameron White writes *Bandanna Sketches*, an arrangement of four spirituals for violin and piano.

Harry T. Burleigh publishes a collection of spirituals that he arranged–*The Spirituals of Harry T. Burleigh*–with his suggestions for performance style contained in the introduction:

> *Success in singing these Folk Songs is primarily dependent upon deep spiritual feeling. The voice is not nearly so important as the spirit; and then rhythm, for the Negro's soul is linked with rhythm, and it is an essential characteristic of most all the Folk Songs.*

> *It is a serious misconception of their meaning and value to treat them as minstrel songs, or to try to make them funny by a too literal attempt to imitate the manner of the Negro in singing them, by swaying the body, clapping the hands, or striving to make the peculiar inflections of voice that are natural with the colored people. Their worth is weakened unless they are done impressively, for through all these songs there breathes a hope, a faith in the ultimate justice and brotherhood of man. The cadences of sorrow invariably turn to joy, and the message is ever manifest that eventually deliverance from all that hinders and*

oppresses the soul will come, and man—every man—will be free.
(Republished in 1984 by Belwin Mills Publishing Corp.)

Will Marion Cook organizes the Southern Syncopated Orchestra (also
known as The New York Syncopated Orchestra) and establishes the
foundation for symphonic jazz.

Trumpeter Louis Armstrong joins Kid Ory's band.

The Pace and Handy Music Publishing Company relocates to New York
City.

James Reese Europe and his 369th Infantry Band tour the United States
after the end of World War I, calling themselves "65 Musician Veterans
of the Champagne and Argonne."

Songwriters Henry Creamer and Turner Layton compose *After You've
Gone.*

Blues singer Leadbelly (Huddie Leadbetter) is jailed in the Texas State
Penitentiary for murder. He becomes known for his skillful guitar playing and his performance of prison work songs.

French composer Francis Poulenc composes *Rhapsodie negre.*

Emmett J. Scott produces the film *The Birth of a Race* in response to
The Birth of a Nation.

Producer Hal Roach begins to make the *Our Gang* series of comedies,
with Farina portrayed as a pickaninny.

Race riots break out in Chester and Philadelphia, Pennsylvania.

Sixty-four African Americans are lynched.

Marcus Garvey founds a weekly newspaper, *Negro World.*

World War I ends.

 **1919**

Agba:

Jazz drummer Arthur (Art) Blakey is born in Pittsburgh, Pennsylvania.

Jazz trumpeter/conductor Mercer Ellington is born in Washington, D.C.

Symphony Conductor Everett Lee is born in Wheeling, West Virginia

White jazz pianist George Shearing is born in London, England.

Jazz guitarist Charlie Christian is born in Dallas, Texas.

Jazz flutist Hubert Laws is born in Houston, Texas.

Kuumba:

The National Association of Negro Musicians is founded in Chicago. Charter members include Nora Holt, Henry L. Grant, Carl Diton, Alice Carter Simmons, Clarence Cameron White, Deacon Johnson and Robert Nathaniel Dett.

Fletcher Henderson arrives in New York City and is hired as piano player and arranger for the dance orchestra at Roseland Dance Hall.

Lucie Eddie Campbell Williams becomes the first major woman composer of gospel music, when her piece *Something Within* is introduced at the National Baptist Convention.

Will Marion Cook's Southern Syncopated Orchestra tours Europe.

Contralto Marian Anderson performs at the national meeting of the National Baptist Convention in Atlantic City.

Dance halls begin to emerge, first on the West Coast and then across the country, providing support for jazz musicians through 1929.

The Radio Corporation of America (RCA) is established.

White actors are featured in blackface in the silent motion picture, *Dark and Cloudy.*

83 African Americans are lynched.

Racial disturbances break out in 25 cities, and the summer comes to be known as Red Summer because of the number of riots.

The first Pan-African Congress meets in Paris, under the leadership of W.E.B. DuBois.

The Volstead Act is passed by the U.S. Congress, establishing the era of Prohibition (outlawing the sale, manufacture and transport of alcoholic beverages), and causing the rise of organized crime and the development of flourishing private clubs and speakeasies that cater to white sightseers and that use jazz to entice customers.

Iku:

James Reese Europe dies in Boston, Massachusetts, killed by a former member of his band.

1920

Agba:

R&B singer/pianist Percy Mayfield is born in Minden, Louisiana.

Blues singer Nehemiah (Skip) James is born near Bentonia, Mississippi.

Jazz trumpeter Clark Terry is born in St. Louis, Missouri.

Jazz drummer Sheldon (Shelly) Manne is born in New York City.

Jazz pianist/composer John Lewis is born in LaGrange, Illinois.

White jazz pianist/composer David Warren (Dave) Brubeck is born in Concord, California.

Jazz pianist/composer Marian Margaret Turner McPartland is born in Windsor, England.

Cabaret entertainer/Jazz pianist/composer Hazel Scott is born in Port-of-Spain, Trinidad.

Jazz singer Carmen MacRae is born in New York City.

Jazz saxophonist Charles Christopher (Charlie "Bird") Parker, Jr. is born in Kansas City, Kansas.

Baritone Wiliam Caesar Warfield is born in West Helena, Arkansas.

Kuumba:

Robert Nathaniel Dett is awarded the Bowdoin Prize by Harvard University for an essay entitled "The Emancipation of Negro Music."

The official year for the beginning of the "Jazz Age."

Concert singer Emma Azalia Smith Hackley performs and teaches black folk music in Japan.

Tenor Roland Hayes has a debut performance in London, England at Aeolian Hall.

The Classic blues period begins—the era of "race records". The first recording of black blues singers (Mamie Smith - *That Thing Called Love*) is made. She also records *Crazy Blues* (written by Perry Bradford), the first real blues record ever made, a hit that sold more than 800,000 copies:

> *I can't sleep at night, I can't eat a bite 'Cause the man I love, he don't treat me right. Now I got the crazy blues, since my baby went away I got no time to lose, I must find him today. Now the doctor gonna do all he can But what you're gonna need is an undertaker man I ain't had nothing but bad news Now I got the crazy blues.*

Bert Williams appears with Eddie Cantor in the show *Broadway Brevities*.

Pauline James Lee establishes the Chicago University of Music for the African American community of Chicago, Illinois.

Zeta Phi Beta Sorority is founded at Howard University.

Sixty-one African Americans are lynched.

Warren G. Harding is elected president of the United States.

Commercial radio broadcasts begin.

4

1921 - 1945
THE MUSIC OF THE RENAISSANCE

The music of this period reflects the tremendous creativity generated within the Black Renaissance, a time when the great African American writers, philosophers, visual artists, dancers and musicians seek to celebrate their artistic freedom and express pride in the race. While New York's Harlem is the center of activity, African American cultural expression emerges in urban centers all over the country, with Chicago, Kansas City and Los Angeles reflecting special vitality.

The period begins with the production of the Broadway musical *Shuffle Along*, a work that features a substantial number of the outstanding musicians of this period. The kick-off year also includes the publication of the major gospel music collection, *Gospel Pearls*, and the formal establishment of the concept of "Race Records," code language for the music (blues, jazz and gospel) marketed to African Americans.

The span of time encompasses spectacular achievements in the various genres of African American music, much of which is captured on the vinyl of the developing recording industry. It is also transmitted across the country through live broadcasts of the developing world of radio. And the music is incorporated into numerous films of the time. The evolution of jazz during this time period is particularly fascinating, as it develops from New Orleans Traditional into Chicago Hot Jazz into Swing and finally into Bop. Numerous racial barriers are challenged-particularly by jazz musicians and by performers of music in the European classical tradition.

The period concludes with the year that historians have designated as the formal end of Swing.

TRENDS
1921 - 1945

1920s

ɮ This is the period of the Harlem Renaissance (1917-1935), and its celebration of black culture as seen in the music, literature, dance, visual arts and philosophy of leading black artists and intellectuals.

ɮ The era of Classic Blues, featuring music that is usually performed by female contraltos accompanied by a small jazz combo.

ɮ The era of Country Blues recordings (a genre that develops before Classic Blues but is not documented on recordings until after the Classic Blues boom).

ɮ The decade that is sometimes characterized as the Jazz Age or the Chicago Era of the Roaring Twenties. It is filled with the hot jazz of Chicago's small ensembles (usually featuring trumpet, clarinet, saxophone, drums and piano), the scat singing of Louis Armstrong, the flourishing of jazz performance in Los Angeles at the Club Alabam, and the emergence of larger jazz bands in New York and Kansas City.

ɮ African American entrepreneurs establish recording companies.

ɮ A number of young whites (often described as artistic rebels, some of whom emerge from a juvenile delinquency background) begin performing the hot jazz style.

ɮ Whites begin the development of symphonic jazz.

ɮ The recording industry develops utilizing jazz and blues as its major product.

ɮ The era of rent parties (sometimes called chittlin' struts or blue Monday affairs)—parties with stride piano/blues entertainment being held to raise rent money.

ɮ Professional choirs emerge that are dedicated to the preservation of African American folk music.

◊ Jazz musicians and blacks in vaudeville shows and in Broadway shows tour the United States, Canada, Germany, Australia and Great Britain.

◊ Homes across the United States begin to acquire radios, the technology that helps change the concept of "audience." The large influx of radios is the main factor in the demise of vaudeville.

◊ The era of Prohibition.

1930s

◊ The Harlem Renaissance continues, and comparable cultural activity emerges in Chicago (identified by scholars as the Chicago Renaissance).

◊ Gospel music and the blues are combined by Baptist church musician Thomas Dorsey in the popular "Dorsey songs" (using the verse/chorus format). Additionally, a "jubilee" gospel style evolves, performed by male gospel groups (usually quartets) in a style that combines jazzy syncopation with a repertoire that included the more rhythmic spirituals.

◊ A number of quartets devote themselves to the performance of popular secular repertoire, including the Mills Brothers, the Four Southern Singers, the Four Blue Birds, the Five Jones Boys, the Golden Gate Quartet, and the Ink Spots.

◊ Classic Blues and Country Blues eras come to an end as the commercial support evaporates because of the Depression. The performers withdrew to the jook joints of the black community, "pleasure houses" where people went to dance, gamble and drink. With the end of Prohibition, the jook joints evolve into legal black-owned night clubs/cabarets.

◊ The era of Swing jazz, wherein the use of big bands requires the actual writing down (arranging) of jazz in a manner that incorporates improvised solos. The bands play a musical style that places emphasis on the steady accented beat in order to encourage dancing. The era is highlighted by the work of black big bands led by Jimmy Lunceford, Count Basie and Duke Ellington, centered in

New York City and Kansas City. These ensembles are distinguished by their outstanding soloists, placing emphasis upon improvisation and the use of individualized tone quality.

◊ Fletcher Henderson, an African American band leader, becomes the arranger for the Benny Goodman band. Mr. Goodman then markets himself as "The King of Swing," another example of the cultural appropriation practices that permeate the history of African American music. A number of white bands gain popularity, including those led by Charlie Barnet, Jimmy and Tommy Dorsey, Woody Herman, Glenn Miller and Artie Shaw. While not known for performing the truly innovative jazz that is associated with black bands, the white bands obtain superior financial success through performance on radio and by having the opportunity to perform in the white hotels and restaurants.

◊ Popular music (including Swing) provides the primary content for radio programming, with jazz being transmitted nationally via nightly broadcasts from ballrooms and nightclubs. At the same time, the growing popularity of radio has negative impact upon the sale of sheet music, phonograph records and pianos.

◊ A substantial number of black jazz musicians leave the United States and settle in Europe in response to the impact that segregation and discrimination has upon the development of their art.

◊ Boogie-woogie becomes a popular blues-based piano style. It is distinguished by its use of the "walking bass" ostinato left hand that is built on the harmonic structure of the blues. This supports an improvised, ornamented right-hand melody.

◊ African American composers of orchestral music begin to emerge, often infusing the music of African American folk/jazz/blues culture into their compositions.

◊ Hollywood produces a plethora of films that glorify the days of slavery, including *Anthony Adverse, The Little Colonel, Dixiana, Mississippi, The Littlest Rebel, So Red the Rose, Slave Ship, Stanley and Livingstone,* and *Gone with the Wind.* In many cases music is used to present the image of the happy slave.

◊ The United States Works Projects Administration (WPA) provides jobs for many artists in the U.S. during the time of the Depression, and undertakes a comprehensive oral history project, collecting oral interviews of hundreds of former slaves.

1940s

◊ The jukebox begins to flourish—with over 255,000 in operation.

◊ The blues tradition continues, developing into an urban blues style, featuring male solo singers like T-Bone Walker and B. B. King, performing with the increasingly popular electric guitar. It also evolves into Rhythm and Blues, a style that is sometimes called "Blues with a big beat" because it combines a small vocal ensemble accompanied by a strong rhythm group performing unifying repetitious rhythms. This evolution occurs at the same time as the development of radio stations that are targeted for the Black audience, since white disk jockeys will not play records that come with the "Black sound."

◊ Minton's Playhouse, a Harlem night club, becomes the after-hours site for jam sessions by musicians who were unhappy with the Swing style, resulting in the creation of Bebop (also known as re-bop or bop) and the era of Modern Jazz (with its new small-group instrumentation, innovative harmonic, rhythmic and melodic practices, and virtuoso technique). Jazz changes from dancing music to listening music, as performed by the leading proponents of the style-Miles Davis, Billy Eckstine, Charlie Parker, Max Roach, Dizzy Gillespie, Thelonius Monk, Kenny Clarke, Woody Herman, and others.

◊ Solo jazz singers, particularly known for their ability to improvise, begin to gain in popularity, including such people as Billy Eckstine, Sarah Vaughn, Ella Fitzgerald, Billie Holiday, Carmen McRae, Dinah Washington and Nat King Cole.

◊ Gospel music ensembles travel the Gospel Highway, performing on a circuit that includes churches and revival meetings. Gospel music radio shows begin in this decade.

♭ African American composers of the classical genre have works performed by the country's major musical organizations and many of these composers create works in the more contemporary Neo-classical style.

ACHIEVEMENT DATELINE
1921 - 1945

 **1921**

Agba:

Blues singer/guitarist Lowell Fulsom is born near Tulsa, Oklahoma.

Jazz composer/reed player William Marcell "Buddy" Collete is born in Los Angeles, California.

Jazz percussionist Foreststorn "Chico" Hamilton is born in Los Angeles, California.

Trumpeter Eddie "Lockjaw" Davis is born in New York City.

Jazz reed player Yusef Lateef is born in Chattanooga, Tennessee.

Jazz singer Jon Carl Hendricks is born in Newark, Ohio.

Jazz guitarist Mitchell Herb Ellis is born near Farmersville, Texas.

Baritone Robert McFerrin is born in Marianna, Arkansas.

Jazz pianist/composer/educator/broadcaster William "Billy" Taylor is born in Greenville, North Carolina.

Jazz pianist Erroll Louis Garner is born in Pittsburgh, Pennsylvania.

Kuumba:

Eubie Blake and Noble Sissle compose and produce the critically acclaimed historical Broadway musical *Shuffle Along*. It runs on Broadway for two years and then tours the country for two years. The show features Florence Mills, Caterina Jarboro, Paul Robeson and Josephine Baker in the cast. The book for the show is written by Aubrey Lyles and Flournoy Miller. The orchestra, led by Eubie Blake, includes composer William Grant Still on oboe, and Hall Johnson on viola. The show is also choreographed with jazz dancing. Overall, it is a tremendous success, attracting large white audiences to the show and to Harlem to find comparable talent. It contributes directly to the national popularity of black music and dance.

The National Baptist Publishing Board publishes *Gospel Pearls*, a historic collection of 165 'Pearls' of song. It contains hymns, spirituals and gospel songs compiled by a music committee that includes John Work, Jr., Frederick Work and Lucie E. Campbell among others. It establishes the main repertoire of the black church.

Harry Pace establishes the first black recording company, Pace Phonograph Corporation/Black Swan Phonograph Company. Fletcher Henderson is the recording manager and William Grant Still serves as arranger. Sociologist W.E.B. DuBois serves as a member of the board of directors.

Classic Blues singer Ethel Waters records *Down Home Blues/Oh, Daddy*, the first Black Swan label hit. She also tours the country, performing with the Black Swan Troubadours.

Country musician Charley Patton works as a musician on various Mississippi cotton plantations.

By this time the blues has developed into a regularized twelve-bar, three-line, multiple stanza structure, performed over a tonic, sub-dominant, dominant, tonic chord progression. In each three-line verse, the second line is usually a repeat of the first line, in both melody and lyrics. The third line is known as the kicker. The resulting form is AAB. The verses are most often performed by a singer using a melody that includes "blue notes" - meaning flatted thirds and sevenths. The singer is accompanied by a guitar in the case of Country Blues or by a small jazz combo in the case of Classic Blues.

The term 'Race Records' becomes the name for records intended for the black market. It is established as an advertising phrase for Okeh Records, which starts its 8000 series of race records. All major U.S. cities open race record shops.

The Music Publishers' Protective Association is organized by Tin Pan Alley publishers to monitor the lyrics of songs so that "indecent material" would not be published. This kind of organizational-corporate-legal control of product parallels the development of African American music.

Coleman Hawkins joins Mamie Smith's Jazz Hounds.

Kid Ory's Sunshine Orchestra becomes the first black jazz band to record in Los Angeles.

Joe King Oliver's band performs in San Francisco at the Pergola Dancing Pavilion on Market street.

Stride pianist James P. Johnson records *Carolina Shout*, the first recorded jazz piano solo.

Classical composer R. Nathaniel Dett completes *The Chariot Jubilee*, an oratorio premiered by the Cleveland Orchestra at the Syracuse New York Music Festival.

The Eastman School of Music is founded in Rochester, New York, with Howard Hanson as director. It maintains an open policy, providing instruction for black music students.

Tenor Roland Hayes gives a command performance for King George V in London, England.

Sixty-four African Americans are lynched.

Visual artist Meta Vaux Warrick Fuller creates *Ethiopia Awakening*, a sculptural rendering of black Americans. It is produced for New York's "Making of America" Festival, and becomes a symbol of the Harlem Renaissance.

 **1922**

Agba:

Classical composer George Walker is born in Washington, D.C.

Jazz bassist Oscar Pettiford is born in Okmulgee, Oklahoma.

Jazz bassist/bandleader Charles Mingus is born in Nogales, Arizona.

Jazz saxophonist Jean Baptiste (Illinois) Jacquet is born in Broussard, Louisiana.

Conga/bongo player Ramon (Mongo) Santamaria is born in Havana, Cuba.

Kuumba

King Oliver's Creole Jazz Band thrives in Chicago, Illinois, and hires Louis Armstrong.

Lil Hardin becomes the pianist for King Oliver's Creole Jazz Band - the first woman to play piano in a jazz band.

Jazz trumpeter Bix Beiderbecke begins to record with The Wolverines.

Thomas "Fats" Waller begins accompanying blues singers on recordings.

Paramount Records starts its 12000 series of race records.

Black-owned record company, Sunshine label, records blues songs by Roberta Duddley and Ruth Lee, and jazz records by Kid Ory (including *Ory's Creole Trombone*). The owner of the company is bandleader Reb Spikes.

Singer Ethel Waters stars in the musical *Oh Joy.*

Singer Florence Mills stars in the musical *Plantation Revue* with William Vodery as music director.

Popular song composer Armand Piron writes *I Wish I Could Shimmy Like My Sister Kate.*

The Mills Brothers quartet begins to perform in Ohio. Over a span of forty-plus years they become the most successful American male singing group.

Rev. Charles Albert Tindley organizes the Tindley Gospel Singers, a group that specialize in performing Tindley's music.

Composer George Gershwin writes the opera *Blue Monday Blues,* incorporating African American musical practice with a classical music form. William Vodery is the orchestrator of this work.

University professor Thomas Talley publishes the first major collection of African American secular songs, *Negro Folk Rhymes, Wise and Otherwise*, including a large grouping of "Rhyme Dance Songs."

James Weldon Johnson publishes *The Book of American Negro Poetry*.

Claude McKay publishes *Harlem Shadows*.

Carter G. Woodson publishes *The Negro In Our History*, a major contribution to the scholarship of Black History.

Fifty-seven African Americans are lynched.

Iku:

Concert singer Emma Azalia Smith Hackley dies.

Ragtime pianist/composer Tom Turpin dies.

Entertainer Bert Williams dies.

 **1923**

Agba:

Jazz vibraphonist Milt Jackson is born in Detroit, Michigan.

Jazz saxophonist Dexter Gordon is born in Los Angeles, California.

Jazz trumpeter/composer Thaddeus "Thad" Joseph Jones is born in Pontiac, Michigan.

Jazz pianist/composer Erroll Louis Garner is born in Pittsburgh, Pennsylvania.

Jazz pianist/composer/arranger/educator Melvin (Mel) Powell is born in New York City.

Jazz bassist Percy Heath is born in Wilmington, North Carolina.

Jazz drummer Joseph Rudolph Philly Joe Jones is born in Philadelphia, Pennsylvania.

Jazz pianist William M. (Red) Garland is born in Dallas, Texas.

Blues singer Jimmy Witherspoon is born in Gurdon, Arkansas.

Blues singer Albert King is born in Indianola, Mississippi.

Gospel composer/publisher and choir director Doris Akers is born in Brookfield, Missouri.

Percussionist Tito Puente is born in New York City.

Kuumba

The recording industry flourishes, with records selling at 75 cents per copy.

Ida Cox makes her first blues recording, *Any Woman's Blues.* As is typical of the blues, the lyrics are therapeutic for both the singer and the listener.

Blues singer Mamie Smith has a hit with the record *You've Got to See Mama Every Night (Or You Won't See Mama at All)*, accompanied by tenor saxophonist Coleman Hawkins.

"Ma" Rainey, the "Mother of the Blues," begins her recording career at Paramount Records, releasing such songs as *Bo Weevil Blues, Moonshine Blues,* and *Southern Blue.* She records ninety songs over a five-year period.

Columbia Records starts its 14000 series of race records. The series emerges as a major race records label, featuring recordings by Bessie Smith and Clara Smith.

Bessie Smith begins her recording career for Columbia Records, releasing such songs as *Down Hearted Blues/Gulf Coast Blues* (selling over a million copies), *Aggravatin' Papa, and Beale Street Mamma.* Her recording sales account for 20% of all the income from race records.

Clarence Williams becomes artist and repertoire director for Okeh Records.

The Cotton Club opens in Harlem at 142nd and Lenox Avenue, presenting glamorous black women in stage revues, and a sophisticated show orchestra (initially performing Chicago-style jazz) to an all-white audience. Eventually over two-hundred ballrooms open in New York.

Connie's Inn opens at 131st and Seventh Avenue, becoming an important whites-only Harlem club known for its bands and shows.

Fletcher Henderson organizes a band, the Black Swan Troubadours, who play at New York's Club Alabam.

Bandleader Armand J. Piron and His Novelty Orchestra perform at the Roseland Ballroom in New York. The ballroom serves an exclusively white clientele.

Duke Ellington opens with a band at Washington, D.C.'s Lafayette Theater, a group that ultimately becomes known as the Washingtonians.

Joseph (King) Oliver and his Creole Jazz Band make the first series of recordings by an African American jazz group. This includes *Dippermouth Blues* with Louis Armstrong on second cornet.

Jazz pianist/composer Lil Hardin Armstrong writes arrangements for Columbia Records—an early example of the accomplishment of women in the very male-dominated field of jazz.

The Bennie Moten Band begins to record for Okeh Records. The group becomes one of the major bands in Kansas City, performing in a style that imitates New Orleans traditional jazz.

Jazz pianist/composer James P. Johnson composes the Black Broadway show *Running Wild* a production that presents a new popular dance, the Charleston.

Spanish artist Pablo Picasso paints *Three Musicians*, a group of jazz musicians.

The Darius Milhaud 'ballet negre' *La Creation du Monde* is performed (a work inspired by African art and jazz).

Actor/athlete/singer/intellectual activist Paul Robeson graduates from Columbia University Law School.

French composer Maurice Ravel writes a blues as the second movement of his *Sonata for Piano and Violin.*

The Society for the Preservation of Spirituals is established by a group of whites in Charleston, South Carolina.

The Juilliard Graduate School is founded in New York City.

Tenor Roland Hayes achieves acclaim with a groundbreaking performance with the Boston Symphony Orchestra.

William Grant Still begins to study composition with the French avant-garde composer Edgard Varese.

The Curtis Institute of Music is founded in Philadelphia, Pennsylvania.

Marian Anderson wins the Philadelphia Harmonic Society voice contest.

Violinist Harrison Ferrell establishes the Ferrell Symphony Orchestra.

Black cowboy Bill Picket, "the world's colored champion," is featured in the film *The Bull-Dogger.*

Jean Toomer publishes the novel *Cane.*

Visual artist Henry Ossawa Tanner is made an honorary chevalier of the Order of the Legion of Honor, France's highest honor.

Thirty-three African Americans are lynched.

The migration of Blacks from the South to the North continues.

Russian inventor Vladimir Zworykin (working for Westinghouse) develops the iconoscope tube, a system that makes television possible.

 **1924**

Agba

Classical composer Julia Amanda Perry is born in Lexington, Kentucky.

Classical pianist Frances Walker is born in Washington, D.C.

Jazz drummer/bandleader Louis "Louie" Paul Balassoni Bellson is born in Rock Falls, Illinois.

Jazz saxophonist Paul Breitenfeld Desmond is born in San Francisco, California.

Cabaret entertainer/jazz pianist Dorothy Donnegan is born in Chicago, Illinois.

Jazz saxophonist Edward "Sonny" Stitt is born in Boston, Massachusetts.

Jazz pianist Earl "Bud" Powell is born in New York City.

Jazz trombonist James Louis "J. J." Johnson is born in Indianapolis, Indiana.

Jazz singer Sarah Vaughan is born in Newark, New Jersey.

Singer Dinah Washington (Ruth Lee Jones) is born in Tuscaloosa, Alabama.

Blues singer Mabel "Big Maybelle" Louise Smith is born in Jackson, Tennessee.

Blues guitarist Clarence "Gatemouth" Brown is born Vinton, Louisiana.

Gospel artist Clara Ward is born in Philadelphia, Pennsylvania.

Kuumba

The Mills Brothers receive a radio contract to broadcast on WLW in Cincinnati, Ohio.

Earl Hines forms a small jazz ensemble.

The Fletcher Henderson Orchestra opens at the Roseland Ballroom, performing there until 1928. Saxophonist Coleman Hawkins, trumpeter Louis Armstrong and arranger Don Redman join the band. *Sugar Foot Stomp* and *What'cha Call 'Em Blues* are examples of their arrangements.

The Pace Phonograph Company/Black Swan label, is sold to Paramount Records.

Paul Whiteman performs a concert at New York's Aeolian Hall, featur-

ing the premiere performance of George Gershwin's *Rhapsody in Blue.*
The work is an example of symphonic jazz, blending jazz with a 19th
century romanticism style.

Paul Robeson stars in the Eugene O'Neill production of *All God's
Chillun Got Wings.* The production causes significant controversy and
Ku Klux Klan death threats as a result of a scene where a black man
kisses a white woman. He also makes his film debut in Oscar
Micheaux's *Body and Soul.*

The Charleston, a dance that is derived from the juba, becomes the
dance craze of the country.

Blues singer Bessie Smith begins a twenty-week T.O.B.A. circuit tour.
Her performance in Chicago is reviewed in the *Defender: Bessie Smith,
the famous singer and Columbia record star, is the "piece de resistance" on an
excellent show at the Grand this week. Bessie, whose reputation is world wide,
had them howling long before her first number was half finished.* She continues to tour the country, earning more than $2,000 per week.

"Ma" Rainey records *Jelly Bean Blues, Counting the Blues* and *See-See
Rider* with cornetist Louis Armstrong on Paramount Records. The
accompanying ensemble is typical for Classic Blues singers: banjo,
clarinet or soprano saxophone, cornet, drums, piano, and trombone.

Robert Nathaniel Dett is elected president of the National Association
of Negro Musicians.

Gospel composer/preacher Charles Albert Tindley opens the Tindley
Temple United Methodist Church in Philadelphia, Pennsylvania.

Broadway musical star Florence Mills appears in *Dixie to Broadway,* a
show that features her trademark song "I'm Just A Little Blackbird
Lookin' For A Bluebird." Subsequently she tours London and Paris
with a "Blackbirds" revue.

Eubie Blake and Noble Sissle compose the Broadway show *Chocolate
Dandies,* starring Ivan Harold Browning and Josephine Baker.

Duke Ellington composes his first show, *Chocolate Kiddies,* a musical
that runs for two years in England and Germany starring Adelaide Hall.

Trumpeter Bix Beiderbecke makes his first recordings with the Wolverine Orchestra for Gennett Records.

Ku Klux Klan membership builds to 4.5 million people.

Sixteen African Americans are lynched.

Calvin Coolidge is elected president of the United States.

Baseball's "First Colored World Series" is held in Kansas City, Missouri.

Iku:

Concert singer Sidney Woodard dies.

 **1925**

Agba:

Classical composer Hale Smith is born in Cleveland, Ohio.

Gospel/Blues Singer Linda Hopkins is born in New Orleans, Louisiana.

Jazz pianist Oscar Peterson is born in Montreal, Canada.

Jazz saxophonist Eugene "Gene" Ammons is born in Chicago, Illinois.

Soprano Adele Addison is born in New York City.

Opera singer Mattiwilda Dobbs is born in Atlanta, Georgia.

Blues artist Riley (Blues Boy - B. B.) King is born in Indianola, Mississippi.

Jazz vibraphonist Callen "Cal" Radcliffe Tjader is born in St. Louis, Missouri.

Entertainer Sammy Davis, Jr. is born in New York City.

Jazz drummer Max Roach is born in New Land, North Carolina.

Jazz guitarist John Leslie "Wes" Montgomery is born in Indianapolis, Indiana.

Kuumba

Entertainer Josephine Baker opens as a dancer at Theatre des Champs-Elysees in Paris in the American production *La Revue Negre*, creating a sensation with a bare-breasted interpretation of "Danse Sauvage."

Ed Small's Paradise Club opens in Harlem.

Jazz bandleader Erskine Tate conducts a pit orchestra at Chicago's Vendome Theatre. The ensemble accompanies silent films and plays jazz between shows.

Trumpeter Louis Armstrong returns to Chicago to play with Erskine Tate. Additionally, he organizes a band, The Hot Five, to record for Okeh Records. The group includes Johnny Dodds on clarinet, Lillian Hardin Armstrong on piano, Johnny St. Cyr on banjo and Kid Ory on trombone.

Bessie Smith collaborates with Louis Armstrong on several records, including *St. Louis Blues.* The recording is described as the definitive recording of this W. C. Handy classic. Their work contributes to the merging of blues into jazz. The voice is imitated by the instrument as it is accompanied, using the inflections and emotions of the blues.

Various race record labels begin issuing sermons by black Baptist preachers.

Black-owned record company, Meritt Records, is established in Kansas City by Winston Holmes. The business operates for only three years.

Pop/blues singer Ethel Waters records the hits *Dinah* and *Sweet Georgia Brown* for Columbia Records.

Leadbelly (Huddie Leadbetter) is given a reprieve from prison.

Singer Lillian Evanti makes her debut with the Paris Opera.

Marian Anderson wins a singing contest that leads to her appearance with the New York Philharmonic at Lewisohn Stadium.

William Grant Still composes the three-movement work, *Levee Land* especially for Florence Mills.

Composer Florence Price wins the Wanamaker Award for her concert overture *Symphonic Love Poem.*

Bass-baritone Paul Robeson gives a debut concert of all spirituals at Greenwich Village Theatre in New York City. He also stars in the Broadway show *Emperor Jones.*

Conductor/arranger Hall Johnson establishes the first internationally acclaimed professional black choir - The Hall Johnson Negro Choir, with the primary mission of preserving and performing spirituals.

Composer/arranger William Levi Dawson publishes an arrangement of the spiritual *King Jesus Is A-Listening,* and a Trio in A for piano, violin and cello.

James Weldon Johnson and Rosamond Johnson edit and arrange two volumes of spirituals, publishing book one, *The Book of American Negro Spirituals* in 1925 and book two, *The Second Book of Negro Spirituals* in 1926.

Concert singer Roland Hayes gives a command performance for Queen Mother Maria Christina of Spain.

Bell Laboratories perfects the technique of electrical recording. The technology advances past the "horn" to the microphone.

The vitaphone is used in theatres for the first time, to synchronize recorded music with film action. This development contributes to the elimination of live music in movie houses.

Xavier University is founded in New Orleans, Louisiana.

Poet Countee Cullen publishes a volume of poetry, *Color.*

DuBose Heyward publishes *Porgy.*

The 35-millimeter camera and flash photography enter the commercial world.

Literary/art critic Alain Locke publishes *The New Negro* delineating the cultural accomplishments of the Harlem Renaissance, with illustrations by visual artist Aaron Douglas.

Carl Van Vechten writes the best-selling novel on life in Harlem, *Nigger Heaven*.

A. Philip Randolph founds the all-black International Brotherhood of Sleeping Car Porters, the first major African American trade union.

Iku:

Composer John Wesley Work II dies.

 **1926**

Agba:

Jazz saxophonist/composer John Coltrane is born in Hamlet, North Carolina.

Jazz saxophonist Lou Donaldson is born in Badin, North Carolina.

Jazz pianist/vocalist Robert Waltrip (Bobby) Short is born in Danville, Illinois.

Singer/folk-poet Oscar Brown, Jr., is born in Chicago, Illinois.

Gospel singer/composer Alex Bradford is born in Bessemer, Alabama.

Blues/R&B singer Willie Mae "Big Mamma" Thornton is born in Montgomery, Alabama.

Jazz pianist Randy Weston is born in Jamaica.

Jazz trumpeter Miles Dewey Davis is born in Alton, Illinois.

Jazz bassist Raymond (Ray) Matthews Brown is born in Pittsburgh, Pennsylvania.

Blues singer Charles Edward "Chuck" Berry is born in St. Louis, Missouri.

Jazz trombonist Melba Liston is born in Kansas City, Missouri.

Jazz artist Jimmy Heath is born in Philadelphia, Pennsylvania.

Classical composer Edward Bland is born in Chicago, Illinois.

R&B singer Eddie "Guitar Slim" Jones is born in Greenwood, Mississippi.

Folk singer Leon Bibb is born in Louisville, Kentucky.

Kuumba:

Blues singer Blind Lemon Jefferson makes his first recordings in Chicago for Paramount Records, *Booster Blues,* and *Dry Southern Blues.* He becomes their major artist after recording *Long Lonesome Blues,* achieving national popularity for the country blues form and establishing Chicago as a major center for the production of country blues recordings.

Blues pioneer Blind Blake begins his recording career at Paramount Records.

The recording industry reaches $128 million in sales.

Blues singer Peg Leg Howell begins to record for Columbia Records (receiving $15 per side).

Vocalion Records starts its 1000 series of race records.

Blues artist Big Bill Broonzy records his first 78 record, *House Rent Stomp.*

Columbia Records purchases all of the Okeh label's holdings.

Jelly Roll Morton, with the Red Hot Peppers, makes his most famous recordings.

Trumpeter Louis Armstrong records *Jazz Lips* with his Hot Five group.

Melody Maker debuts in England as a newspaper devoted to music, with specialization in jazz.

Composer/arranger William Levi Dawson publishes an arrangement of the spiritual *I Couldn't Hear Nobody Pray.*

The Hall Johnson Negro Choir gives its first public performance.

Composer/Conductor Eva Jessye publishes *My Spirituals*, a collection of sixteen songs that she heard in her native Kansas.

The Juilliard Graduate School and the Institute of Musical Art merge in New York City.

Broadway show *Blackbirds of 1926* opens with Florence Mills as star.

Trumpeter Louis Armstrong introduces scat singing (replacing words with nonsense syllables) on the Okeh recording *The Heebie Jeebies.*

F. E. Miller and Aubrey Lyles stage the all-black production of *Runnin' Wild.*

The Savoy Ballroom opens on Lenox Avenue in New York City, with a ballroom that soon has two bandstands in order to present two bands playing alternating sets. One of the continuing main attractions is The Royal Flush Orchestra, led by jazz clarinetist Stanley (Fess) Williams.

Harmonica player DeFord Bailey joins the Grand Ole Opry and becomes the first black star of country music, performing songs such as *Shoe Shine Boy Blues, John Henry, Alcoholic Blues,* and *Muscle Shoals Blues.*

NBC Radio links 19 stations to become the first nationwide radio network.

The number of radio stations in the country reaches 694, with a significant amount of the programming time devoted to jazz or "syncopation." The popularity of jazz leads to much complaint and condemnation from clergymen, women's clubs and "musically correct" people, and to the emergence of such organizations as the "Keep-the-Air-Clean-On-Sunday-Society."

The Harmon Foundation begins annual African American art exhibitions.

Poet Langston Hughes publishes *The Weary Blues.*

Twenty-three African Americans are lynched.

Carter G. Woodson and the Association for the Study of Negro Life and History create the one-week celebration, Negro History Week (in February), to raise consciousness of blacks about their culture and history and to draw the attention of others to the contributions of blacks.

Stepin Fetchit and Carolynne Snowden are featured in the first on-screen black movie romance, *In Old Kentucky.*

Iku:

Symphony conductor Edward Gilbert Anderson dies.

 **1927**

Agba:

Jazz drummer Connie Kay is born.

Jazz saxophonist/composer Gerald "Gerry" Joseph Mulligan is born in New York City.

Gospel singer Bessie Griffin is born in New Orleans, Louisiana.

Gospel singer Marion Williams is born in Miami, Florida.

Folk singer/actor Harry Belafonte is born in New York City.

Classical pianist Natalie Leota Henderson Hinderas is born in Oberlin, Ohio.

Opera singer Leontyne Price is born in Laurel, Mississippi.

Classical composer/ethnomusicologist Gertrude Rivers Robinson is born in Washington, D.C.

Ethnomusicologist Bette Cox is born in Twin Falls, Idaho.

Blues singer/harmonica player Herman "Little Junior" Parker is born in Clarksdale, Mississippi.

Jazz drummer Elvin Jones is born in Pontiac, Michigan.

English jazz singer Clementina "Cleo" Dinah Campbell Laine is born in Southall - Middlesex.

Blues/jazz singer Mose Allison is born in Tippo, Mississippi.

Kuumba:

Jules Bledsoe performs in the premiere of the Jerome Kern/Oscar Hammerstein Broadway musical *Showboat*. This is a landmark production, one that incorporates characters that are more three-dimensional and music that is more integrated into the libretto. Additionally, it has a plot that deals with non-typical subjects such as unhappy marriages, miscegenation and the hard life of black stevedores (as expressed through "Ol' Man River"). A well-known 1951 film adaptation of the musical stars William Warfield.

Clarence Williams composes the musical *Bottomland*.

Singer/actress Ethel Waters makes her Broadway debut in the show *Africana*.

Fletcher Henderson establishes the Big Band sound (3 trumpets, 2 trombones, 3 saxophones, 1 piano, 1 doublebass, and percussion)—the instrumentation of the Swing Band. He continues playing at the Roseland Ballroom where he comes to be called the "Colored King of Jazz." Radio station WHN regularly broadcasts his performances.

Duke Ellington and the Washingtonians are expanded and renamed Duke Ellington and His Orchestra, featuring the artistry of such noted musicians as Cootie Williams, Harry Carney, Johnny Hodges, Joe "Tricky Sam" Nanton and Barney Bigard. They play at Ciro's and at the Club Richman in New York, and they begin recording. They also start a residency and live CBS network radio broadcasts at the Cotton Club which continues until 1931. The period is known as his "jungle" period because of his performance in the lavish "Jungle Nights in Harlem" stage shows at the club.

The Lindy Hop becomes the popular dance at the Savoy Ballroom in Harlem (the home of Happy Feet), inspired by aviator Charles Lindbergh's solo flight.

The National Association of Music Merchants launches an effort to stop hotels, dance halls and night clubs from presenting music that stimulates "indecent dancing."

Count Basie settles in Kansas City, Missouri.

The Memphis Jug Band makes its recording debut.

Jazz artist Benny Goodman establishes his own band.

White jazz artists Bix Beiderbecke and Frankie Trumbauer join the Paul Whiteman "symphonic" ensemble.

Ernst Krenek composes a jazz-inspired opera, *Jonny Spielt Auf.*

Victor Records starts its series of race records.

Record companies are releasing up to five hundred race records a year.

"Ma" Rainey records *"Ma" Rainey's Black Bottom* on Paramount Records.

The language of the blues continues to use symbolic, code vocabulary. This is very apparent in this year's Bertha Chippie Hill recording of *Sport Model Mama:*

> *I'm a sports model mama out on the rack for sale,*
> *I'm a sports model mama out on the rack for sale,*
> *It's a mighty poor dog won't wag its own tail.*
>
> *I'm just a plain little sport, have punctures every day,*
> *I'm just a plain little sport, have punctures every day,*
> *You may want a limousine but they puncture the same way.*
>
> *When the men comes to buy me you'll always hear them say,*
> *When the men comes to buy me you'll always hear them say,*
> *'Give me a sports model mama because they know the way.*

The Black Patti opens as a black-owned recording company operated by J. H. Mayo Williams.

Columbia Broadcasting System begins with sixteen radio stations.

The Radio Act is passed by Congress to license stations, including a section that states that *no person within the jurisdiction of the United States shall utter any obscene, indecent or profane language by means of radio communication.*

Sound is added to motion picture bringing about the advent of the "talkies," the demise of the theater pit orchestra and the death of vaudeville.

Mary Cardwell Dawson establishes the Cardwell School of Music in Pittsburgh, Pennsylvania.

Opera singer Lillian Evanti makes her debut in Nice, France.

The Rodman Wanamaker Musical Composition Prizes are established for African American composers.

The National Baptist Publishing Board releases *Spirituals Triumphant Old and New,* a compilation of arrangements for choir, by Edward Boatner. He is the Chorister of the National Baptist Convention.

Composer Clarence Cameron White publishes a collection of spirituals, *Forty Negro Spirituals.*

Composer/conductor R. Nathaniel Dett publishes a collection of arrangements of spirituals, *Religious Folk-Songs of the Negro.*

Jazz artist James P. Johnson composes *Yamekraw,* an orchestral rhapsody orchestrated by William Grant Still.

Al Jolson, appearing in blackface, stars in *The Jazz Singer*, the first film with a sound track.

Uncle Tom's Cabin is released as a film.

Porgy is produced as a play in New York, starring Rose McClendon and Frank Wilson.

Visual artist Aaron Douglas paints *Crucifixion,* published as an illustration for James Weldon Johnson's *God's Trombones.*

The 15th Amendment to the U.S. Constitution is passed: *The right of citizens of the United States to vote shall not be denied or abridged by the United States or by any State on account of race, color, or previous condition of servitude.*

Sixteen African Americans are lynched.

Marcus Garvey is deported and settles in London.

Iku:

Musical theatre singer Florence Mills dies of a routine appendectomy.

 **1928**

Agba:

Jazz trumpeter Maynard Ferguson is born in Montreal, Canada.

Jazz organist James Oscar "Jimmy" Smith is born in Norristown, Pennsylvania.

Blues guitarist Aaron T-Bone Walker is born in Linden, Texas.

R&B singer/composer/guitarist Ellas McDaniel "Bo" Diddley is born in McComb, Mississippi.

R&B singer Tony Williams (of The Platters) is born in Elizabeth, New Jersey.

Classical composer Arthur Cunningham is born in Piedmont, New York.

Jazz pianist/composer/arranger Horace Ward Martin Tavares Silver is born in Norwalk, Connecticut.

Jazz alto saxophonist Julian "Cannonball" Adderley is born in Tampa, Florida.

Jazz saxophonist Harold DeVance Land is born in Houston, Texas.

Classical composer Thomas Jefferson Anderson is born in Coatesville, Pennsylvania.

Jazz trumpeter Art Farmer is born in Council Bluffs, Iowa.

Soul singer James Brown is born in Pulaski, Tennessee.

R&B singer Ruth Brown is born in Portsmouth, Virginia.

Jazz composer/saxophonist/clarinetist Eric Allan Dolphy is born in Los Angeles, California.

Choral conductor/composer Lena Johnson McLin is born in Atlanta, Georgia.

Singer Eartha Kitt is born in Columbia, South Carolina.

Jazz pianist/composer Hampton Hawes is born in Los Angeles, California.

Classical composer Betty Jackson King is born in Chicago, Illinois.

Kuumba:

Many of Chicago's hot jazz musicians have moved to New York, the center of the music industry. This is the place to build a reputation and to secure personal appearance bookings, radio jobs and recording dates.

The Cotton Club allows blacks to begin attending the club with seating in the back.

Jazz artists Louis Armstrong and Earl (Fatha) Hines record together.

The Sonny Clay "Plantation" Band tours Australia.

Paul Robeson and Alberta Hunter star in the Jerome Kern/Oscar Hammerstein production *Show Boat.*

Record company talent scouts search the South to discover authentic country bluesmen.

Country blues singer/farmer "Mississippi" John Hurt records twenty songs for Okeh Records, including *Stagolee.* He receives twenty dollars per side, with no royalties, and then retires to his farm.

Country blues singer/composer Blind Lemon Jefferson writes and records *See That My Grave Is Kept Clean: There's one kind favor I'll ask of you; There's one kind favor I'll ask of you; Lord, there's one kind favor I'll ask of you: See that my grave is kept clean.*

Bessie Smith, the Empress of the Blues, makes it to Broadway to perform at Connie's Inn.

Boogie-woogie pianist Pinetop Smith releases his first recordings.

Over 500 race record titles are released in this year.

The gospel chorus is formed by Magnolia Butler in Chicago at the Metropolitan Community Church.

Gospel singer Sister Arizona Dranes records *You Shall Wear a Golden Crown.*

Mahalia Jackson moves to Chicago, Illinois, and begins singing with the choir of the Greater Salem Baptist Church.

Gospel composer Thomas A. Dorsey writes his first gospel piece, *If You See My Savior, Tell Him That You Saw Me.*

Harry Lawrence Freeman's opera, *Voodoo* is produced on Broadway at Palm Garden with an all-black cast.

The Hampton Institute establishes the School of Music, and names Robert Nathaniel Dett Director.

French composer Maurice Ravel visits Chicago, Illinois and is introduced to jazz and the blues.

Composer Florence Price wins the G. Schirmer Prize for her piano piece *At the Cotton Gin.*

Country music singer/harmonica player Deford Bailey appears at the Grand Ole Opry, becoming the first African American to perform at this venue.

The Golden Age of radio begins with the coast-to-coast broadcast of the New York Symphony, and the daily national broadcast of the blackface *Amos 'n' Andy* series, (continuing until 1943) .

Herbert Hoover is elected president of the United States.

Writer Claude McKay Publishes *Home To Harlem.*

 **1929**

Agba:

R&B singer LaVern Baker (Delores Williams) is born in Chicago, Illinois.

Motown owner Berry Gordy, Jr. is born in Detroit, Michigan.

Jazz pianist Toshiko Akiyoshi is born in Dairen, China.

R&B singer/pianist Antoine "Fats" Domino is born in New Orleans.

Composer Eugene Wilson Hancock is born in St. Louis, Missouri.

Jazz pianist/composer Cecil Percival Taylor is born in New York City.

Jazz guitarist Joseph "Joe" Anthony Pass is born in New Brunswick, New Jersey.

Jazz drummer Melvin "Mel" Lewis is born in Buffalo, New York.

Jazz composer/pianist/flutist William John (Bill) Evans is born in Plainfield, New Jersey.

R&B singer Johnny Ace (John Marshall Alexander, Jr.) is born in Memphis, Tennessee.

Singer Roy Hamilton is born in Leesburg, Georgia.

Jazz/blues singer Arthur Prysock is born in Spartanburg, North Carolina.

R&B singer David Lynch (of The Platters) is born.

Composer Noel Da Costa is born in Lagos, Nigeria.

Kuumba:

Country blues artist Charley Patton begins his recording career with Paramount.

The Victor Talking Machine Company merges with RCA (Radio Corporation of America), an example of the centralization of the entertainment business.

The Duke Ellington Orchestra is featured in Ziegfeld's *Show Girl*, performing music by George Gershwin, including *An American in Paris*. He and his orchestra become the first to receive official billing in a movie, *Black and Tan Fantasy*. This is partially a reflection of the development of the concept of a movie soundtrack.

The Chick Webb orchestra is featured performing *Sweet Sue* in the film *After Seben*.

Jazz trumpeter Louis Armstrong comes to New York to star in the show *Hot Chocolates*, composed by Fats Waller and Andy Razaf. The musical includes the song *Ain't Misbehavin'*.

Count Basie joins the Bennie Moten Orchestra in Kansas City, Missouri, helping to create a more modern sound for the group.

The Gospel male quartet, the Dixie Hummingbirds, is organized in Greenville, South Carolina. Members include James Davis, Barney Gipson, Barney Parks and J. P. Matterson.

The New Pleasant Green Gospel Singers are organized. Ultimately the group comes to be known as The Soul Stirrers in 1935.

Country blues singer John Adam "Sleepy John" Estes makes his first recordings. He builds a career of recording and touring, centering his activities in Memphis and Chicago.

Bessie Smith, "the Empress of the Blues," appears in the short, 17-minute film, *St. Louis Blues,* with James P. Johnson as music director and pianist, and members of the Fletcher Henderson orchestra. J. Rosamunde Johnson is conductor of the Hall Johnson chorus. W. C. Handy is the co-producer of the film. She records *Nobody Knows You When You're Down and Out* for Columbia Records, a song that becomes the national anthem of the Depression. She also appears on Broadway in the very short-lived black musical *Pansy.*

Eva Jessye becomes the choral director for the all-black film, *Hallelujah.* The production features the performance of several spirituals. Blues singer Victoria Spivey appears in the film, directed by King Vidor.

Robert Nathaniel Dett travels to Fontainebleau to study with Nadia Boulanger.

Marian Anderson wins the Julius Rosenwald Scholarship to support her studies in Europe.

W. Llewellyn Wilson establishes the Baltimore City Colored Orchestra.

The Howard Theatre closes (not to reopen until 1931).

The tap-dancing duo Fayard and Harold Nicholas make their debut in Philadelphia, Pennsylvania. Their style is precursor to the breakdances of the 1980s.

The year of the Al Capone Valentine's Day Massacre, an event that causes many jazz musicians to reconsider the general practice of playing in clubs owned by gangsters.

The U. S. stockmarket crashes as the Great Depression begins.

Grambling State University is established in Louisiana.

Seven African Americans are lynched.

Visual artist Archibald Motley, Jr. produces a celebration of Black music, *Blues,* depicting African and West Indian expatriates in a Parisian cafe.

Iku:

Boogie-woogie pianist Clarence (Pine Top) Smith dies.

 **1930**

Agba:

Gospel music conductor Thurston Gilbert Frazier is born in Houston, Texas.

Concert singer Betty Lou Allen is born in Campbell, Ohio.

Jazz trumpeter Clifford Brown is born in Wilmington, Delaware.

Jazz pianist Ahmad Jamal (Fritz Jones) is born in Pittsburgh, Pennsylvania.

Jazz trumpeter Richard "Blue" Mitchell is born in Miami, Florida.

Jazz flutist Herbert "Herbie" Jay Mann is born in Brooklyn, New York.

Jazz saxophonist Ornette Coleman is born in Fort Worth, Texas.

Blues singer/songwriter Robert Calvin "Bobby Blue" Bland is born in Rosemark, Tennessee.

R&B singer/pianist/composer Ray Charles Robinson (Ray Charles) is born in Albany, Georgia.

Blues singer/pianist/harmonica player Otis Spann is born in Jackson, Mississippi.

Singer Abbey Lincoln is born in Chicago, Illinois.

Jazz singer Betty Carter (Lillie Mae Jones/Betty Bebop) is born in Flint, Michigan.

Jazz singer Morgana King is born in Pleasantville, New York.

Gospel singer Albertina Walker is born.

Folk singer Odetta (Holmes Felious Gordon) is born in Birmingham, Alabama.

Jazz saxophonist Sonny Rollins is born in New York City.

Kuumba:

The T.O.B.A. (Theater Owners Booking Association) closes, reflecting the impact of the Depression.

U.S. record production falls 65%, reflecting the impact of the Depression.

The official history of gospel music begins with the public endorsement of the music by the National Baptist Convention.

Gospel singer Theodore Frye begins to perform and promote the songs of Thomas A. Dorsey.

Country blues singer Son House records *Preachin' the Blues* for Paramount Records.

Blues artist Leadbelly (Huddie Leadbetter) is jailed a second time, this time in the Texas State Penitentiary for intent to murder. Once again he becomes a chain gang leader known for his performance of prison songs.

Robert Nathaniel Dett and the Hampton Institute Choir complete a European concert tour.

Pianist Hazel Harrison makes her New York debut at Town Hall.

Raymond Lowden Smith establishes the E. Gilbert Anderson Memorial Symphony (subsequently renamed the Philadelphia Concert Orchestra).

William Grant Still composes the ballet, *Sahdji*, and the first in his trilogy of symphonies, *Africa*.

Concert artist/actor Paul Robeson appears in the starring role of the London production of *Othello* and in the Kenneth McPherson film, *Borderline*.

The Eva Jessye Choir is established, an ensemble that performs the music of black culture, keeping the heritage of the spiritual alive.

Josephine Baker debuts with star billing as a singer/dancer at the Casino de Paris.

Eubie Blake and Andy Razaf write the Broadway musical *Blackbirds of 1930*.

Jazz vibraphonist Lionel Hampton makes his first recording as a solo vibraphonist with Louis Armstrong.

Louis Armstrong appears at Frank Sebastian's Cotton Club in Los Angeles, billed as the "King of the Trumpet."

The Duke Ellington Orchestra accompanies French entertainer Maurice Chevalier at New York's Fulton Theatre.

The Fletcher Henderson Orchestra plays at Connie's Inn.

Ethel Waters stars in *Check and Double Check*, and Duke Ellington appears in the same film.

Fats Waller receives a contract to broadcast on WLW in Cincinnati, Ohio.

Jazz pianist/composer James P. Johnson composes the song *If I Could Be With You.*

The show *Green Pastures* opens in New York at Broadway's Mansfield Theater, with the Hall Johnson Choir performing 24 Johnson arrangements of spirituals.

White composer Daniel Gregory Mason composes *String Quartet in G Minor on Negro Themes.*

Sculptor Sargent Johnson creates *Copper Mask.*

Twenty African Americans are lynched.

The Black Muslims organization is founded in Detroit and New York by W. D. Ford.

Iku:

Blind Lemon Jefferson dies.

 **1931**

Agba:

Singer/actress Della Reese (Deloreese Patricia Early) is born in Detroit, Michigan.

Opera singer Shirley Verrett is born in New Orleans, Louisiana.

Classical pianist Philippa Duke Schuyler is born in New York City.

Composer/educator David Baker is born in Indianapolis, Indiana.

Gospel singer/conductor/composer James Cleveland is born in Chicago, Illinois.

Soul singer Benjamin Franklin Peay "Brook" Benton is born in Camden, South Carolina.

R&B singer/guitarist/producer Ike Turner is born in Clarksdale, Mississippi.

R&B singer Jimmy McCracklin is born in St. Louis, Missouri.

Pop singer/organist Earl Grant is born in Oklahoma City.

Jazz pianist Phineas Newborn, Jr., is born in Whiteville, Tennessee.

Jazz guitarist Kenneth Earl "Kenny" Burrell is born in Detroit, Michigan.

Jazz pianist/composer Raphael (Ray) Bryant is born in Philadelphia, Pennsylvania.

Jazz cornetist/trumpeter Nathaniel "Nat" Adderley is born in Tampa, Florida.

Kuumba:

Cab Calloway's band becomes the Cotton Club band, becoming known as the "hi-de-ho" band (named for the lyrics of Calloway's big hit *"Minnie the Moocher).*

Blanche Calloway becomes the leader of an all-male band, Blanche Calloway and the 12 Clouds of Joy.

Count Basie joins the Bennie Moten Band in Kansas City, Missouri.

Singer Ivy Anderson joins the Duke Ellington Orchestra, staying with them until 1941.

Duke Ellington composes *Mood Indigo.* Additionally, he composes the jazz tone-poem *Creole Rhapsody,* using a more sophisticated, symphonic approach to orchestration and a more extended form. He also performs at the gala that celebrates the reopening of Washington, D.C.'s Howard Theatre.

Trumpeter Louis Armstrong tours the South, earning up to $1,000 per week.

Fats Waller opens with the Otto Hardwicke band at The Hot Feet Club in New York.

Jazz pianist Mary Lou Williams becomes the chief arranger for the Clouds of Joy Band, a Kansas City group led by Andy Kirk.

The influence of jazz and the blues is reflected in the *Piano Concerto in D* of French composer Maurice Ravel.

Columbia Records drops Bessie Smith from its roster of artists after she records her last four sides, *Blue Blues, In the House Blues, Long Old Road* and *Shipwreck Blues.*

The Mills Brothers record their first hit, *Tiger Rag.*

The pop singing group The Ink Spots is organized as the Swingin' Gate Brothers.

R. Nathaniel Dett conducts the Hampton Institute Choir in a performance at Carnegie Hall.

The first major gospel chorus is organized in Chicago, with Thomas A. Dorsey and Theodore Frye as co-founders.

Composer/conductor William Dawson becomes the conductor of the choir at Tuskegee Institute.

Composer William Grant Still's *Afro-American Symphony*, a classical symphony that blends European musical practice with the blues musical practice, is performed by the Rochester Philharmonic. It is the first symphony by an African American composer to be performed by a major orchestra.

Conductor/composer Eva Jessye composes a folk oratorio, *The Life of Christ in Negro Spirituals.*

Ethel Waters stars in *Rufus Jones for President,* and Sammy Davis, Jr. makes his debut in this film.

Twelve African Americans are lynched.

Choreographer Katherine Dunham establishes the Negro Dance Group in Chicago.

Iku:

Jazz trumpeter Buddy Bolden dies in New Orleans, Louisiana.

Bix Beiderbecke dies in New York of alcohol-induced pneumonia. He is immortalized in the novel, *Young Man With a Horn.*

 **1932**

Agba:

Blues guitarist/singer Albert Collins is born in Leona, Texas.

Composer Coleridge-Taylor Perkinson is born in New York City.

Jazz trombonist Locksley Wellington "Slide" Hampton is born in Jeannette, Pennsylvania.

Jazz pianist Josef (Joe) Zawinul is born in Vienna, Austria.

Jazz trumpeter Donald Toussaint L'Ouverture Byrd is born in Detroit, Michigan.

Classical composer Leslie Adams is born in Cleveland, Ohio.

R&B artist "Little Richard" (Wayne Penniman) is born in Macon, Georgia.

R&B singer/songwriter Jesse Belvin is born in San Antonio, Texas.

R&B/Soul singer Ocie Lee (O. C.) Smith is born in Mansfield, Louisiana.

Gospel/soul singer Cissy Houston is born in Newark, New Jersey.

Singer Miriam Makeba is born in Johannesburg, South Africa.

Conductor Henry Lewis is born in Los Angeles, California.

Jazz vocalist Ethel Llewellyn Ennis is born in Baltimore, Maryland.

Kuumba:

Thomas A. Dorsey composes *Precious Lord, Take My Hand,* following the death of his wife and his newborn child. It is premiered by singer Theodore Frye. Dorsey also is appointed choral conductor of Chicago's Pilgrim Baptist Church, and establishes a gospel chorus, with Roberta Martin as pianist. He also establishes the first gospel publishing company, Dorsey House. He goes on to write over 400 gospel songs— "Dorsey Songs."

Gospel artist Mahalia Jackson begins her career by touring with the Johnson Gospel Singers.

The Cleveland Opera Company produces *Tom-Toms*, an opera for a cast of 500 by Shirley Graham DuBois.

Conductor Dean Dixon organizes the Dean Dixon Symphony Orchestra and the Dean Dixon Choral Society in Harlem.

Clarence Cameron White composes the opera, *Ouanga*, with libretto by John F. Matheus—the story of Jean-Jacques Dessalines.

Florence Price wins the Wanamaker Prize for her *Symphony in E minor*.

Lyric soprano Lillian Evans Evanti makes her New York Town Hall debut.

The Tuskegee Institute Choir, conducted by William L. Dawson, appears at Radio City Music Hall in New York City. Dawson also composes *Negro Folk Symphony,* a work that blends folk culture with European traditional practices.

Robert Nathaniel Dett composes the oratorio *The Ordering of Moses*.

Singer Etta Moten Barnett performs at the White House for president Franklin Roosevelt.

Columbia Records releases blues singer Bessie Smith's last record, *Shipwreck Blues.* Her career is ruined by the Depression.

The Mills Brothers record *Rockin' Chair,* a record that includes the first example of a talking-bass part. In the same year their hits include *Sweet Sue* and *It Don't Mean a Thing (If It Ain't Got That Swing)*, the latter composed by Duke Ellington.

Louis Armstrong tours London and Paris where he picks up the nickname "Satchelmouth." He is featured in the film *Rhapsody in Black and Blue,* a movie that places him in "Jazzmania," meaning jazz heaven.

Cab Calloway appears in the Paramount film *The Big Broadcast,* performing his hit song *Minnie the Moocher.* His make-up is blackened in order to underscore his racial identity. The Mills Brothers are also featured in the movie.

Blues singer Leadbelly records for the Library of Congress' Archive of Folksongs.

ASCAP establishes the policy requiring radio to pay fees on a percentage of total income. They sign their first contract with the National Association of Broadcasters (NAB) for the sum of $4.5 million per year.

Actress Hattie McDaniel makes her movie debut in *The Golden West.*

Up to 14 million people in the U.S. are unemployed because of the depression.

Six African Americans are lynched.

Franklin D. Roosevelt is elected president of the U.S and the New Deal begins.

 **1933**

Agba:

Jazz band conductor/arranger Quincy Delightt Jones is born in Chicago, Illinois.

Jazz pianist Cecil Taylor is born in New York City.

R&B singer Clyde McPhatter is born in Durham, North Carolina.

R&B singer Lloyd Price is born in New Orleans, Louisiana.

Jazz/Blues singer Nina Simone (Eunice Kathleen Waymon) is born in Tryon, North Carolina

Jazz saxophonist Wayne Shorter is born in Newark, New Jersey.

Kuumba:

The Duke Ellington Orchestra tours Europe. While there he is featured on a BBC radio program. *Fortune* magazine reports the band is earning $250,000 per year.

Louis Armstrong leads the way in extending the range of the trumpet, with reports that "one night in Paris, he played seventy successive high C's in one song."

Jazz pianist Earl Hines records *Cavernism, Darkness* and *Madhouse* for the Brunswick label.

White bandleader Benny Goodman begins including African Americans in his recording sessions.

Billie Holiday is discovered by newspaper columnist John Hammond singing at Monette's Supper Club in Harlem. Immediately thereafter her recording career begins. She and other blues artists sing about infidelity, dancing, hard luck, and other aspects of life in the black community.

Harold Arlen and Ted Koehler composed *Stormy Weather* for Ethel Waters to perform at the Cotton Club.

The Archive of Folksongs of the Library of Congress starts to add recordings of spirituals to its collection. Additionally, John Alan Lomax begins extensive field recording of Southern country blues for inclusion in the Archive.

Prohibition is repealed, signaling the reemergence of legal nightclubs and saloons.

Coin-operated juke boxes are manufactured by Wurlitzer. Initially they are leased for use in places such as jook joints.

The National Convention of Gospel Choirs and Choruses is chartered by Thomas A. Dorsey and Sallie Martin.

Gospel artists Roberta Martin and Theodore Frye establish the Martin-Frye Quartet.

Clarence Cameron White becomes the conductor of the Hampton Institute Choir.

Classical pianist Margaret Bonds becomes the first black to appear with the Chicago Symphony Orchestra.

Soprano Caterina Jarboro performs with the Chicago Civic Opera, becoming the first African American singer to appear with a major opera company.

Symphony in E Minor by Florence Price, is performed by the Chicago Symphony Orchestra at the Chicago World's Fair.

The film version of Eugene O'Neill's *The Emperor Jones* is released, starring Paul Robeson.

The black Broadway show by Hall Johnson, *Run, Little Chillun*, premieres.

The Les Hite band is featured in the film *Sing, Sinner, Sing.*

Ethel Waters and Sammy Davis, Jr., appear in the film *Rufus Jones For President.*

The dancing Nicholas Brothers team star in *Barbershop Blues.*

Sculptor Richmond Barthe produces *African Dancer*, a work that is purchased by the Whitney Museum.

White actor Eddie Cantor appears in the film *Roman Scandals* in blackface.

Twenty-four African Americans are lynched.

Author E. Franklin Frazier writes that "only 19% of black children of high school age were in high schools."

Iku:

Gospel Composer Rev. Charles Albert Tindley dies.

Singer Sissieretta Joyner-Jones, "The Black Patti," dies.

Cornetist Freddie Keppard dies.

 **1934**

Agba:

Tenor George Shirley is born in Indianapolis, Indiana.

R&B singer Jackie Wilson is born in Detroit, Michigan.

Blues guitarist Milton "Little Milton" Campbell is born in Inverness, Mississippi.

Jazz saxophonist Stanley Turrentine is born in Pittsburgh, Pennsylvania.

Jazz pianist/composer/arranger/conductor Horace Elva Tapscott is born in Houston, Texas.

Latin jazz percussionist William "Willie" Correa Bobo is born in New York City.

Jazz trumpeter Donald "Don" Johnson Ellis is born in Los Angeles, California.

Jazz vocalist Shirley Horn is born in Washington, D.C.

Jazz pianist Ellis Marsalis is born.

Kuumba:

The Apollo Theatre opens in New York City, becoming the prime venue for African American entertainers. It establishes an amateur night on Wednesdays, that is subsequently won by such leading entertainers as Ella Fitzgerald, Pearl Bailey, Ruth Brown, Sam Cooke, King Curtis, Marvin Gaye, Lena Horne and Sarah Vaughan.

Lena Horne makes her debut in the chorus at Harlem's Cotton Club with the Jimmie Lunceford band.

The Chick Webb Orchestra, the unofficial house band at the Savoy, records *Stomping At The Savoy*.

White jazz clarinetist Benny Goodman forms his first big band. The ensemble begins to gain a national audience by performing on the NBC *Let's Dance* radio program.

Leon Herriford leads a band at the Cotton Club in Los Angeles, featuring Lionel Hampton on vibraphone. Eventually Lionel Hampton becomes the leader of the group.

Coleman Hawkins moves to Europe, remaining there for several years. He performs with ensembles in London, Paris, Geneva, Copenhagen, Zurich, and Amsterdam. He records for Parlophone Records.

Singer/pianist/composer Fats Waller begins recording for RCA Victor.

Black film producer Oscar Micheaux makes *Harlem After Midnight,* featuring the Leon Gross swing band.

Decca Records starts its 7000 series of race records.

Blues singer Big Blue Broonzy records *Take Your Hands Off Her* and *The Sun Gonna Shine in My Back Door Some Day* for the Bluebird label. Throughout his career he records two hundred sixty blues songs.

Singer Lillian Evanti performs at the White House for President and Mrs. Roosevelt.

Composer William Levi Dawson's *Symphony No. 1, Negro Folk Symphony* receives its world premiere with the Philadelphia Orchestra, conducted by Leopold Stokowski.

Classical conductor/composer Eva Jessye composes the folk oratorio *Paradise Lost and Regained.*

Russian composer Dimitri Shostakovitch composes *Suite for Jazz Orchestra,* an example of the influence of African American music on music of the European classical tradition.

Asadata Dafora produces the first black ballet-opera, *Kykuntor* (meaning The Witch Woman), in New York.

Composer/pianist Florence Price performs her own Piano Concerto with the Chicago Women's Symphony.

Composer William Grant Still wins a Guggenheim Fellowship.

Anthropologist Zora Neale Hurston publishes an essay, *Spirituals and Neo-Spirituals*, decrying the current performance practices, calling for more authentic performances, stating the following position: *There never has been a presentation of genuine Negro spirituals to any audience anywhere. What is being sung by the concert artists and glee clubs is the work of Negro composers or adapters based on the spirituals. Glee clubs and concert singers put on their tuxedos, bow prettily to the audience, get the pitch and burst into magnificent song—but not Negro song....Let no one imagine that they are the songs of the people, as sung by them.*

The Hampton Institute Quartet (a group of male singers) is organized by Noah Ryder. It becomes a professional ensemble known as the Deep River Boys.

Eva Jessye becomes the choral director for the Virgil Thomson opera, *Four Saints In Three Acts*, a work performed on Broadway with an all black cast.

Billboard Magazine begins to publish the list of the most-played songs on network radio.

Down Beat magazine begins publication.

Visual artist Aaron Douglas produces a series of panels entitled *Aspects of Negro Life*, for the Countee Cullen Branch of the New York Public Library. They depict the history of blacks in America.

Fifteen African Americans are lynched.

The Universal pictures film, *Imitation of Life* is released, featuring two black women performers, Louise Beavers and Fredi Washington, as a mammy figure and a mulatto daughter.

Sculptor Augusta Fells Savage becomes the first black member of the National Association of Women Painters and Sculptors.

Actor Stepin Fetchit appears in the films *Stand Up and Cheer* and *The World Moves On.*

Iku:

Delta blues singer Charley Patton dies.

 **1935**

Agba:

Singer Johnny Royce Mathis is born in San Francisco, California.

Singer Louis "Lou" Allen Rawls is born in Chicago, Illinois.

Singer/actress Diahann Carroll (Carol Diahann Johnson) is born in New York City.

Jazz pianist Ramsey Emanuel Lewis is born in Chicago, Illinois.

Jazz pianist Leslie Coleman "Les" McCann is born in Lexington, Kentucky.

Blues singer "Little" Esther Phillips is born in Galveston, Texas.

Gospel/R&B singer Sam Cooke is born in Chicago, Illinois.

Classical composer William S. Fischer is born in Shelby, Mississippi.

Jazz percussionist Albert William "Tootie" Heath is born in Philadelphia, Pennsylvania.

Ethnomusicologist/educator Horace Clarence Boyer is born in Winter Park, Florida.

Kuumba:

The official start date for the Swing era - the music that helps the U.S. recover from the Depression.

The Benny Goodman band continues performing on NBC radio, and he becomes known as "The King of Swing."

Swing bands begin using singers to perform ballads and the blues with the ensembles. The singers come to be known as Blues Shouters, and include performers such as Big Joe turner and Eddie Cleanhead Vinson.

Ella Fitzgerald appears with the Tiny Bradshaw Band at the Harlem Opera House, in her first professional appearance. She then becomes the star of the Chick Webb Orchestra, performing at the Savoy Ballroom in Harlem. She makes her first records, *Love and Kisses* and *I'll Chase the Blues Away* and eventually becomes "The First Lady of Jazz."

Billie Holiday gets her break with a successful engagement at Harlem's Apollo Theater.

Blues singer "Ma" Rainey retires.

Blues singer/composer Huddie Ledbetter (Leadbelly) receives a pardon from prison, and goes on to work with John Lomax who records his songs for the archives of the Library of Congress. He bills himself as the "King of the Twelve-String Guitar."

Benny Carter travels to Paris and London, playing an important role in the development of jazz in Europe.

Count Basie forms his own band, the Barons of Rhythm, and performs at Kansas City's Reno Club. Saxophonist Lester Young joins the band.

Jazz pianist Jelly Roll Morton moves to Washington, D.C. and opens a small club, the Jungle Club.

The Swingin' Gate Brothers, now renamed The Ink Spots, make their first recording for RCA, *Swingin' On The Strings.*

The New Pleasant Green Gospel Singers become known as The Soul Stirrers. They help create the modern gospel music quartet style.

The Charioteers, a gospel group formed at Wilberforce University, begins recording for the Decca label. An early record was *Little David Play On Your Harp.*

Roberta Martin establishes the Roberta Martin singers.

William Grant Still composes the three-act opera, *Blue Steel,* and the tone-poem, *Kaintuck.* His symphony, *Afro-American Symphony*, is given a New York premiere by the New York Philharmonic.

George Gershwin's *Porgy & Bess, ("An American Folk Opera"),* is performed, with Eva Jessye as the choral director, Todd Duncan in the role of Porgy, Ann Brown as Bess and John Bubbles in the role of Sportin' Life. Numerous revivals of this popular work will be performed throughout the twentieth century.

Marian Anderson makes her New York Town Hall debut. She goes on to perform all over the world, hailed as the greatest contralto of the twentieth century.

The U.S. begins the Federal Arts Projects of the WPA (Works Progress Administration), providing jobs from 1935-1939 for artists in the areas of music, writing, theatre and visual arts.

Jazz pianist Fats Waller appears in the Alice Faye film *King of Burlesque.*

Shirley Temple, Bill "Bojangles" Robinson, and Stepin Fetchit appear in *The Littlest Rebel,* the Civil War film noted for the song and dance numbers that present the happy slave image.

Chicago continues to flourish as a center of The Renaissance (1935-1950).

Race riots occur in Harlem.

New York's Museum of Modern Art presents the first large exhibition of traditional African art, *African Negro Art*.

Joe Louis wins his first big boxing match.

Elijah Muhammad becomes the leader of the Black Muslims.

Eighteen African Americans are lynched.

The National Council of Negro Women is founded by Mary McLeod Bethune.

Visual artist Aaron Douglas completes *Portrait of William L. Dawson*.

Visual artist Lois Mailou Jones creates the watercolor *Negro Boy*.

W. E. B. DuBois publishes *Black Reconstruction*, a major contribution to the scholarship of Black history.

Iku:

Pop singer/guitarist John Mills dies.

Piedmont Blues singer Arthur Phelps (Blind Blake) dies.

Bandleader Bennie Moten dies of complications from a tonsillectomy.

 **1936**

Agba:

Symphony conductor Paul Douglas Freeman is born in Richmond, Virginia.

Opera singer Martina Arroyo is born in New York City.

Blues guitarist George "Buddy" Guy is born in Lettsworth, Louisiana.

Jazz cornetist Don Cherry is born in Oklahoma City, Oklahoma.

Jazz drummer Billy Higgins is born in Los Angeles, California.

Jazz saxophonist Albert Ayler is born in Cleveland, Ohio.

Jazz saxophonist Roland Rahsaan Kirk is born in Columbus, Ohio.

Jazz bassist Scott LaFaro is born in Newark, New Jersey.

R&B/Big Band/Gospel Music arranger/producer H. B. Barnum is born in Houston, Texas.

Soul singer Solomon Burke is born in Philadelphia, Pennsylvania.

Symphony conductor James DePriest is born in Philadelphia, Pennsylvania.

Kuumba:

The Gibson instrument company begins the electric guitar revolution, producing the ES-150 guitar with matching EH-150 amp. This instrument imitates the double bass, keeping the beat in the ensembles that accompany blues singers.

Blues singer Alberta Hunter appears in the film *Radio Parade.*

Country blues singer Robert Johnson makes his first recordings, including *Dead Shrimp Blues:*

> *I got dead shrimps, baby, someone is fishing in my pond. I got dead shrimps, baby, someone's fishing in my pond. I've tried my best bait, baby, and I can't do that no more;*

> If I Had Possession Over Judgement Day: *If I had possession over Judgement day. If I had possession over judgement day. Lord, then the little woman I'm lovin' wouldn't have no right to pray;* and

> Kind Hearted Woman: *I got a kind-hearted woman, do anything in the world for me. I got a kind-hearted woman, do anything in this world for me. But these evil hearted women, man, they will not let me be.*

The first biographies and academic studies of jazz begin to emerge, including *Swing That Music,* an autobiography by Louis Armstrong, and *Hot Jazz,* an English translation of a study by French author Hugues Panassie.

Count Basie and his Barons of Rhythm, enlarged and renamed the Count Basie Orchestra, obtains a recording contract. They perform at the Roseland Dance Hall in New York. The group is distinguished by its strong rhythm section and outstanding soloists.

Tenor saxophonist Benny Carter becomes a staff arranger for the BBC orchestra in London, England.

The Cotton Club closes in Harlem and relocates in downtown New York.

The Village Vanguard jazz club opens in New York.

Benny Goodman's trio is integrated by pianist Teddy Wilson.

Noble Sissle leads the first black orchestra, the Noble Sissle Society Orchestra, to perform at the Ritz-Carlton Hotel in Boston. He features Lena Horne as the band's singer.

The Duke Ellington and Cab Calloway Bands alternate at the relocated Cotton Club (moved to Downtown New York at 48th and Broadway). Duke Ellington and Juan Tizol compose *Caravan*, an early example of Afro-Cuban jazz.

Cab Calloway is featured with Al Jolson in the film *The Singing Kid.*

Singer Billie Holiday records her first hit *I Cried For You.*

Josephine Baker appears in New York with the Ziegfeld Follies.

The Ink Spots record *T'ain't Nobody's Business If I Do* for the Decca label.

Jazz pianist/composer Lil Hardin Armstrong becomes the house pianist for Decca Records.

Actor/bass-baritone/political activist Paul Robeson travels to the U.S.S.R. to meet with the Soviet film director Sergei Eisenstein to discuss making a film on the life of Haitian leader Toussaint L'Ouverture. He also stars in the Hammer-British Lion production of *Song of Freedom.*

Universal releases a film remake of *Showboat,* featuring Paul Robeson (distinguished for his performance of *Old Man River*).

The Broadway musical *The Green Pastures* is released as a film, with the Hall Johnson Choir performing. Additionally The Hall Johnson choir appears in three films: *Dimples, Banjo on My Knee,* and *Rainbow on the River.*

William Grant Still writes orchestrations for the film *Pennies From Heaven,* a Bing Crosby movie that includes performances by Louis Armstrong and Lionel Hampton. Still also conducts the Los Angeles Philharmonic at the Hollywood Bowl, becoming the first black to conduct a major American orchestra.

Composer R. Nathaniel Dett publishes a collection of arrangements, *The Dett Collection of Negro Spirituals.*

Conductor Leonard DePaur becomes the musical director of the Negro Unit of New York's Federal Theatre Project.

The Delta Rhythm Boys, a popular music group formed at Langston University and subsequently developed by Dr. Frederick Hall at Dillard University, makes its professional debut in Buenos Aires. They spend seven months touring South America and performing on Argentina Radio Splendid.

Alan Lomax records the gospel group The Soul Stirrers for the Library of Congress.

Gospel composer/arranger Kenneth Morris becomes an arranger for the Lillian M. Bowles Music House.

Shirley Graham DuBois becomes director of the Black division of the Chicago Federal Theatre Project.

Track star Jesse Owens wins four gold medals at the Berlin Summer Olympics.

Eight African Americans are lynched.

Franklin D. Roosevelt is elected to a second term.

Visual artist Palmer Hayden produces the painting *Mid-Summer Night in Harlem.*

Iku:

Pianist/musicologist Maud Cuney Hare dies.

 **1937**

Agba:

Composer Olly Wilson is born in St. Louis, Missouri.

Opera singer Grace Bumbry is born in St. Louis, Missouri.

Jazz artist Alice McLeod Coltrane is born in Detroit, Michigan.

Jazz bassist Charlie Haden is born in Shenandoah, Iowa.

Jazz bassist Ronald Levin "Ron" Carter is born in Ferndale, Michigan.

Jazz vocalist Nancy Wilson is born in Chillicothe, Ohio.

Pop singer Shirley Bassey is born in Cardiff, Wales.

Ethnomusicologist Samuel Floyd, Jr., is born in Tallahassee, Florida.

R&B singer O'Kelly Isley (of The Isley Brothers) is born in Cincinatti, Ohio.

R&B singer/keyboardist John "Little Willie John" Davenport is born in Camden, Arkansas.

R&B singer Arthur Lanon Neville is born in New Orleans, Louisiana.

Jazz saxophonist Archie Shepp is born in Fort Lauderdale, Florida.

Jazz bassist Malachi Favors (of the Art Ensemble of Chicago) is born in Chicago, Illinois.

Kuumba:

Actor/bass-baritone/political activist Paul Robeson co-founds with W.E.B. DuBois the Council of African Affairs, to aid national liberation struggles. In this same year, he appears in the film *Song of Freedom*, depicting a successful black singer who, after discovering his aristo-cratic African origins, returns to take over the leadership of the country.

Blues singer Alberta Hunter becomes the first African American to have a radio program on NBC. The program airs until 1939.

The Wings Over Jordan Choir begins a radio show on a local Cleveland station WGAR that ultimately becomes a national CBS broadcast, continuing until 1949.

Mahalia Jackson makes her first record for Decca, *God Gonna Separate the Wheat From the Tares.*

The Golden Gate Jubilee Quartet is formed by a group of students from Booker T. Washington High School in Norfolk, Virginia, using a name that describes the gates to heaven. They record the popular *Golden Gate Gospel Train* and *Gabriel Blows His Horn* for the Bluebird label.

The Mills Brothers record *Pennies From Heaven* for the Decca label.

Singer Josephine Baker becomes a French citizen to avoid racial discrimination.

Jazz artist Count Basie composes *One O'Clock Jump* and singer Billie Holiday signs on with his band for one year. Together they open at Harlem's Apollo theatre.

Ella Fitzgerald wins the *Down Beat* magazine poll as Best Female Vocalist of the year.

Singer Ivie Anderson is featured in the Marx Brothers film *A Day At The Races.* She performs *All God's Chillun Got Rhythm.*

The Chick Webb Orchestra faces the Benny Goodman Band in a battle of the bands at The Savoy.

Jazz pianist Nat King Cole forms The King Cole Trio in Los Angeles and the group plays at a number of Central Avenue clubs.

Trumpeter Louis Armstrong is featured in the Mae West film *Every Day's A Holiday.*

White composer Igor Stravinsky composes *Prelude pour ensemble de jazz*, reflecting the influence of jazz upon music of the European classical tradition.

Composer Howard Swanson wins a Rosenwald Fellowship to study in France with Nadia Boulanger.

The Cincinnati Symphony gives the premiere performance of Robert Nathaniel Dett's *The Ordering of Moses*.

William Grant Still composes the third in his trilogy of symphonies, *Symphony In G Minor*, subtitled, *Song of a New Race*. He publishes a collection of arrangements of spirituals, *Twelve Negro Spirituals*, and writes orchestration for the film *Lost Horizon*.

White classical composer Morton Gould writes *Spirituals for Orchestra* which blends folk traditions with European classical traditions.

Comedian Eddie (Rochester) Anderson begins to appear on the Jack Benny radio show.

Joe Louis defeats Jim Braddock to become heavy-weight boxing champion of the world.

Painter Lois Mailou Jones creates *Les Fetiches*.

The Negro Art Association is founded in Los Angeles by sculptor Beulah Woodard.

Iku:

Blues artist Bessie Smith bleeds to death after a car accident in Mississippi.

Visual artist Henry Ossawa Tanner dies.

 **1938**

Agba:

Gospel singer Shirley Caesar is born in Durham, North Carolina.

Jazz trumpeter/bandleader Freddie Dewayne Hubbard is born in Indianapolis, Indiana.

Jazz pianist Alfred McCoy Tyner is born in Philadelphia, Pennsylvania.

Jazz saxophonist/bandleader/composer Charles Lloyd is born in Memphis, Tennessee.

Bass-baritone/opera singer Simon Lamont Estes is born in Centerville, Iowa.

Tenor William Brown is born in Jackson, Mississippi.

Country singer Charley Pride is born in Sledge, Mississippi.

R&B/Soul bassist James Jamerson is born in South Carolina.

R&B singer Ben E. King (Benjamin Earl Nelson) is born in Henderson, North Carolina.

Soul singer Levi Stubbs (of The Four Tops) is born in Detroit, Michigan.

Soul singer Lawrence Payton (of The Four Tops) is born in Detroit, Michigan.

Soul singer Abdul Fakir (of The Four Tops) is born in Detroit, Michigan.

Blues singer Etta James is born in Los Angeles, California.

Gospel singer Jessy Dixon is born in San Antonio, Texas.

Kuumba:

The multiple-act jazz concert becomes an important performance venue. Record producer/talent scout John Hammond organizes a show at Carnegie Hall dedicated to Bessie Smith, *From Spirituals to Swing.* It features performances of spirituals, gospel, blues and jazz.

The Count Basie Orchestra performs at New York's Savoy Ballrooom. The orchestra faces the Chick Webb Orchestra in a battle of the bands.

Fats Waller is playing at New York's Yacht Club. He also tours Europe, a trip that inspires the six-movement composition of *London Suite.*

Violinist Eddie South leads a jazz orchestra in Amsterdam, featuring singer Mabel Mercer.

Trumpeter Roy Eldridge leads a big band at New York's Arcadia Ballroom.

Trumpeter Louis Armstrong is featured in the Bing Crosby film *Doctor Rhythm.*

Singer Billie Holiday begins a nine-month engagement at the Cafe Society nightclub in New York's Greenwich Village.

Ella Fitzgerald and the Chick Webb band record a swing version of the nursery rhyme, *A-Tisket A-Tasket.*

The International Sweethearts of Rhythm, a black female swing band drawn from the marching/concert bands of Piney Woods Country Life School in Mississippi, becomes the primary fund-raising vehicle for the school.

The first major jazz magazine is published, *H.R.S. Rag (Hot Record Society Rag),* edited by Russell Sanjek and Heywood Hale Broun.

Jazz band director Benny Goodman commissions Hungarian composer Bela Bartok to write *Contrasts.* He also becomes the first white band-leader to include African Americans in his ensemble—Lionel Hampton and Teddy Wilson.

George "Trombone Happy" Johnson leads a big band at the Vogue Ball-room in Los Angeles (9th and Grand Avenue).

Library of Congress folklorist/archivist John Alan Lomax completes a series of interviews and recordings of jazz pianist Jelly Roll Morton, thereby beginning a small Morton revival. Morton is interviewed by *DownBeat* Magazine, attacking W. C. Handy, the commercially acclaimed "Father of the Blues": *Mr. Handy cannot prove that he has created any music. He has possibly taken advantage of some unprotected material that sometimes floats around. I would like to know how a person could be an originator of anything without being able to do at least some of what they created.* He culminates his attack by claiming to be the inventor of jazz.

The Federal Music Project rhythm band provides musical experience for black children in New York City.

With the support of the Federal Theater Project, Jester Hairston directs a production of the musical *Run Little Children* in San Francisco.

Gospel singer Sister Rosetta Tharpe performs gospel music at the Cotton Club in Harlem.

The Gospel quartet, The Swan Silvertones, is organized, originally using the name The Four Harmony Kings.

Musicologist/pianist Eileen Southern makes her debut performing a concerto with the Chicago Musical College symphony orchestra.

White conductor Ignatz Waghalter organizes the Negro Symphony Orchestra in Harlem.

Composer W. C. Handy publishes a collection of arrangements of spirituals, *Book of Negro Spirituals.*

Marian Anderson performs 92 recitals in 70 cities over a five-month period, becoming one of the most popular and highest paid performers on the concert circuit.

Jack and Jill of America, Inc. is established in Philadelphia, Pennsylvania.

New York's Museum of Modern Art presents a solo exhibition of the work of self-taught sculptor William Edmondson.

The CBS radio network grows to one-hundred and ten stations.

Television is demonstrated by RCA at the New York World's Fair.

Six African Americans are lynched.

Hitler invades Austria.

Iku:

Ragtime pianist/composer James Scott dies.

Jazz cornetist/bandleader Joe King Oliver dies.

Blues singer Robert Johnson dies.

 **1939**

Agba:

R&B singer Tina Turner (Anna Mae Bullock) is born in Brownsville, Tennessee.

R&B singer Marvin Pentz Gaye is born in Washington, D.C.

Soul singer Eddie Kendricks (of The Temptations) is born in Union Springs, Alabama.

Soul singer Rudolph Isley (of the Isley Brothers) is born in Cincinatti, Ohio.

Soul singer Paul Williams (of The Temptations) is born in Birmingham, Alabama.

R&B singer Harold James Melvin (of The Bluenotes) is born in Philadelphia, Pennsylvania.

R&B singer Jerry Butler is born in Sunflower, Mississippi.

Soul/pop singer Roberta Flack is born in Black Mountain, North Carolina.

Jazz pianist Joseph "Joe" Sample (of The Crusaders) is born in Houston, Texas.

Jazz trombonist Wayne Henderson (of The Crusaders) is born in Houston, Texas.

Jazz trumpeter Hugh Masekela is born in Johannesburg, South Africa.

Classical pianist Althea Waites is born in New Orleans, Louisiana.

Classical violinist Sanford Allen is born in New York City.

Kuumba:

Because of segregation policies, Marian Anderson is refused permission by the DAR to sing in Washington, D.C.'s Constitution Hall. She had been invited to sing for the inauguration of president Franklin Roosevelt. In response to the actions of the DAR, Eleanor Roosevelt resigns from the organization. The concert is then moved to the Lincoln Memorial where she performs before 75,000 on Easter Sunday. Millions hear the concert on national radio.

With Paul Robeson as soloist, the cantata *Ballad For Americans*, a patriotic song of brotherhood, is performed on the CBS "Voice of America" radio program.

William Grant Still is commissioned to compose music for the New York World's Fair.

Soprano Dorothy Leigh Maynor makes her New York debut.

Dizzy Gillespie joins the Cab Calloway band.

Charlie Parker joins the Jay McShann Orchestra as first saxophonist.

Charlie Christian begins to champion the use of the electric guitar in jazz.

Trumpeter Roy Eldridge leads a band at The Arcadia in New York.

The Duke Ellington Orchestra tours Europe. He composes *Concerto for Cootie,* a piece that reflects the Ellington practice of spotlighting the unique talents of his individual band members. He also forms his own music publishing company, thereby taking financial control of his compositions.

Count Basie, Ella Fitzgerald and Earl (Fatha) Hines all lead bands at the Roseland Ballroom.

Count Basie records the classic *Lester Leaps In,* an example of Lester Young's cool saxophone.

Singer Lena Horne stars in the revue *Blackbirds of 1939* with the Hall Johnson Choir.

The Hot Mikado, a jazz version of Gilbert and Sullivan's operetta, *The Mikado*, opens on Broadway, starring Bill "Bojangles" Robinson with the Delta Rhythm Boys.

Blue Note Record Company is founded.

Billie Holiday composes and records *Strange Fruit*, a song that uses the poetry of Lewis Allen to describe the lynchings of the South. She also integrates the all-white Artie Shaw band, becoming their singer.

The pop singing group The Ink Spots record the hit *If I Didn't Care*, a song noted for its wonderful tenor solo line. The record sells over one million copies. In this same year they record *My Prayer,* a song that later becomes a hit for two other groups - the Golden Gate Quartet and The Platters.

Coleman Hawkins returns to the U.S. and records the classic *Body and Soul.* He leads a big band at Kelly's Stables, one of the many clubs on New York's 52nd Street.

Jimmy Yancey records several boogie-woogie pieces for The Solo Art label.

Gospel music is increasingly performed outside of the church setting, most notably on radio, e.g. "The Gold Hour" on the Los Angeles station KGFJ, sponsored by the Gold Furniture Company.

Gospel singer Roberta Martin opens a publishing firm, the Roberta Martin Studio of Music.

Gospel group The Five Blind Boys of Alabama is organized at the Talladega Institute for the Deaf and Blind, becoming a professional ensemble in 1945.

Gospel group The Five Blind Boys of Mississippi is organized in the Piney Woods School near Jackson, Mississippi, becoming a professional ensemble in 1944.

Mahalia Jackson goes on the road with Thomas Dorsey, touring the gospel highway.

Gospel composer Thomas A. Dorsey composes *When I've Done the Best I Can.*

The first FM radio station goes on the air.

Sculptor Augusta Savage creates *Lift Every Voice and Sing*, a sculptural celebration of black contributions to music, exhibited at the New York World's Fair.

Two African Americans are lynched.

Iku:

Jazz conductor Chick Webb dies of tuberculosis. The Chick Webb Orchestra is renamed Ella Fitzgerald and Her Orchestra and tours the U.S. for the next two years.

Blues singer "Ma" Rainey dies in Columbus, Georgia of a heart attack.

 **1940**

Agba:

Classical composer Wendell Logan is born in Thomson, Georgia.

Classical composer/educator/singer Dorothy Rudd Moore is born in New Castle, Delaware.

Ethnomusicologist William Komla Amoaku is born in Ghana.

Classical composer Talib Rasul Hakim (Stephen Alexander Chambers) is born in Asheville, North Carolina.

Symphony conductor James Frazier is born in Detroit, Michigan.

Blues singer/guitarist Taj Mahal is born in New York City.

R&B singer Anthony Gourdine (of Little Anthony and the Imperials) is born in New York City.

R&B singer Addie Micki Harris (of The Shirelles) is born in Passaic, New Jersey.

Pop/soul singer Billy Davis (of The Fifth Dimension) is born in St. Louis, Missouri.

Pop/soul singer LaMont McLemore (of The Fifth Dimension) is born in St. Louis, Missouri.

Soul singer/songwriter William "Smokey" Robinson is born in Detroit, Michigan.

R&B singer Eugene "Gene" Dixon Chandler is born in Chicago, Illinois.

Singer Marie Dionne Warwick is born in East Orange, New Jersey.

Jazz pianist/composer/bandleader Herbert Hancock is born in Chicago, Illinois.

Jazz/rock/blues bass guitarist Charles Walter Rainey III is born in Cleveland, Ohio.

Jazz singer/composer Al Jarreau is born in Milwaukee, Wisconsin.

Kuumba:

Virginia adopts the James Bland song, *Carry Me Back to Ole Virginny*, as its official State song.

New York's Cotton Club closes.

The performing-rights organization, Broadcast Music, Inc. (BMI) is organized by the National Association of Broadcasters to compete with ASCAP (signing on many composers of popular and folk music).

Jazz pianist Billy Strayhorn joins the Duke Ellington band.

Jazz saxophonist Charlie Parker makes his first recordings.

Vibraphonist Lionel Hampton leaves Benny Goodman to establish his own orchestra.

W. C. Handy and William Grant Still are honored at the ASCAP Festival of American Music in San Francisco.

William Grant Still composes the two-act opera, *A Bayou Legend*, and the cantata *And They Lynched Him on a Tree*.

Composer William Levi Dawson composes *A Negro Work Song for Orchestra*.

Baritone Theodore Charles Stone makes his debut at New York's Town Hall.

Composer Asadata Dafora composes a dance opera, *Zunguru*.

Blues singer Ida Cox records *Last Mile Blues*.

Singer Dinah Washington (Ruth Jones) joins the Sallie Martin Colored Ladies Quartet, an all-woman gospel group.

The gospel ensemble The Golden Gate Quartet, records a popular secular hit, *My Prayer.* The song hits the charts again in 1956 with an arrangement by The Platters.

The Deep River Boys, a popular music group that develops at the Hampton Institute, begins to record for Bluebird records. Their first hit is *Nothing But You.*

Billboard Magazine begins to publish the "Best-Selling Retail Records" list.

Todd Duncan, Ethel Waters and Katherine Dunham star in the Broadway production of *Cabin in the Sky.*

Dancer Katherine Dunham debuts in New York.

Benjamin O. Davis, Sr. is appointed Brigadier General in the U.S. Army.

Author Richard Wright's *Native Son* is published and becomes a bestseller.

Visual artist Sargent Claude Johnson produces the lithograph *Singing Saints.*

Hattie McDaniel becomes the first African American to win an Academy Award for her performance as the stereotypical mammy character in *Gone With The Wind.*

Franklin D. Roosevelt is elected to a third term as president of the United States.

Four African Americans are lynched.

Author E. Franklin Frazier writes that "only 35% of black children of high school age are in high schools".

Entertainer Josephine Baker joins the resistance movement after the German invasion of France. Ultimately she wins both the Medal of Resistance and the Legion of Honor for her service.

 **1941**

Agba:

Stage composer Micki Grant is born in Chicago, Illinois.

R&B singer Otis Redding is born in Dawson, Georgia.

Soul singer David Ruffin (of The Temptations) is born in Meridian, Mississippi.

Soul singer Otis Williams (of The Temptations) is born in Texarkana, Texas.

Pop/soul singer Ron Townson (of The Fifth Dimension) is born in St. Louis, Missouri.

R&B/soul singer William Guest (of Gladys Knight and the Pips) is born in Atlanta, Georgia.

R&B singer Clarence Collins (of Little Anthony and the Imperials) is born in New York City.

R&B singer Ernest Wright (of Little Anthony and the Imperials) is born in New York City.

R&B singer Beverly Lee (of The Shirelles) is born in Passaic, New Jersey.

R&B singer Doris Kenner (of The Shirelles) is born in Passaic, New Jersey.

R&B singer Shirley Owens (of The Shirelles) is born in Passaic, New Jersey.

R&B singer Aaron Neville is born in New Orleans, Louisiana.

Soul singer Wilson Pickett is born in Prattville, Alabama.

Soul singer Percy Sledge is born in Leighton, Alabama.

R&B singer Chubby Checker (Ernest Evans) is born in Philadelphia, Pennsylvania.

R&B singer Martha Reeves is born in Detroit, Michigan.

R&B singer Ronald Isley (of The Isley Brothers) is born in Cincinatti, Ohio.

Folk singer Richie Haven is born in Brooklyn, New York.

Classical composer Adolphus C. Hailstork is born in Albany, New York.

Jazz /rock/fusion keyboardist Armando Anthony "Chick" Corea is born in Chelsea, Massachusetts.

Kuumba:

Mary Cardwell Dawson establishes the National Negro Opera Company in Pittsburgh, Pennsylvania with supporting guilds in Chicago, New York and Washington, D.C. The Company provides performance opportunities for African American singers who face career limitations because of continuing racial discrimination.

Dean Dixon leads the New York Philharmonic and the NBC Summer Symphony, making his debut appearance as a conductor of a major orchestra.

William Grant Still composes the cantata *Plain-Chant for America* and the opera *A Bayou Legend.*

Composer/Conductor Noah Francis Ryder becomes the director of the Hampton University Choir.

KFFA radio in Helena, Arkansas, begins broadcasting "King Biscuit Time," a fifteen-minute program of live country blues (the first of its kind).

Leadbelly and The Golden Gate Quartet record the hits *Midnight Special, Ham and Eggs, Pick a Bale of Cotton,* and *Alabama Bound.*

The Delta Rhythm Boys release the hit *Gimmie Some Skin/Chilly 'n Cold.*

Pearl Bailey begins USO concert tours.

Trumpeter Roy Eldridge becomes a featured soloist in Gene Krupa's orchestra, pioneering as the only black artist in a white band.

The black female swing band, the International Sweethearts of Rhythm becomes a professional ensemble.

Billy Strayhorn composes the Duke Ellington orchestra theme song, *Take the 'A' Train*. The piece is featured in the Ann Miller film *Reveille with Beverly* in 1943.

Jazz artists Buddy Collette and Chico Hamilton appear in the Fred Astaire/Rita Hayworth film *You'll Never Get Rich*.

W. C. Handy publishes his autobiography, *Father of the Blues*.

The Japanese attack Pearl Harbor, the U. S. enters World War II, and the big-band era begins to die with musicians joining the armed forces, and gasoline rationing making touring impossible. Curfews are also imposed during this time, affecting audiences. At the same time, the war stimulates a massive migration of African Americans from the South to new jobs in the urban centers (particularly to Chicago). Soon R&B becomes the musical expression for this new audience.

Visual artist Horace Pippin completes the folk painting, *Marian Anderson*, an image that celebrates black music and musicians.

Visual artist William H. Johnson is inspired by musical culture to paint the *Jitterbug* series. Note the description of scholar Richard J. Powell in *Homecoming: The Art and Life of William H. Johnson* (New York: Rizzoli, 1991) re *Jitterbug V: completing the dance cycle with the characteristic "throwing" of the partner in the air...the heads, bodies and appendages... along with a double belled trumpet, snare drum, and cymbals...evoke movement, creating an almost whirling gestural pattern against the solid background. As overtures to a palpable living cubism, the Jitterbugs...indicate that Johnson fully understood that hyper kinetic dances and fashion extremes of contemporary Black culture were appropriate inspirations for a modern African American art. (150)*

African-Americans migrate from the South to the North and West during the war years.

Alain Locke organizes the exhibition American Negro Art: 19th and 20th Centuries at New York's Downtown Gallery.

Choreographer Ruth Beckford founds the African-Haitian Dance Company.

Jacob Lawrence completes the 61-panel series, *The Migration of the Negro*, depicting the mass movement of Southern blacks to the North.

President Franklin Roosevelt issues an executive order, establishing the Fair Employment Practices Commission.

Four African Americans are lynched.

The U.S. Army establishes a school for black pilots in Tuskegee, Alabama.

The Congress of Racial Equality (CORE) is organized by James Farmer in Chicago, Illinois.

Artist Elizabeth Catlett is awarded first prize in sculpture at Chicago's American Negro Exposition.

Iku:

Jazz artist Jelly Roll Morton dies.

Blues singer "Blind Boy" Fuller dies.

 **1942**

Agba:

Jazz trumpeter Don Ayler is born in Cleveland, Ohio.

Jazz drummer/pianist/composer Jack DeJohnette is born in Chicago, Illinois.

R&B singer/composer Isaac Hayes is born in Covington, Tennessee.

R&B singer/composer Curtis Mayfield is born in Chicago, Illinois.

R&B singer/songwriter Nikolas Ashford (of Ashford & Simpson) is born in Fairfield, South Carolina.

Soul singer Melvin Franklin (of The Temptations) is born in Montgomery, Alabama.

Gospel singer/composer/pianist Andrae Edward Crouch, and his twin sister, singer Sandra Crouch are born in Los Angeles, California.

R&B singer Carla Thomas is born in Memphis, Tennessee.

R&B/soul singer Aretha Franklin is born in Memphis, Tennessee.

R&B/soul singer Major Lance is born in Chicago, Illinois.

R&B singer Eddie Levert (of The O'Jays) is born in Canton, Ohio

R&B singer Walter Williams (of The O'Jays) is born in Canton, Ohio.

R&B/soul singer Merald 'Bubba' Knight (of Gladys Knight and the Pips) is born in Atlanta, Georgia.

R&B bandleader Autry "Junior" Walker is born in Blytheville, Arkansas.

Guitarist/acid rock artist Johnny (Jimi) Hendrix is born in Seattle, Washington.

Kuumba:

Saxophonist Charlie Parker joins the Earl Hines Orchestra. He joins a number of other musicians who are experimenting with the new Bop sound.

Pop idol Billy Eckstine begins to build a singing career with his recording of *Skylark.*

Duke Ellington and Juan Tizol compose *Perdido*, an early example of Afro-Cuban jazz.

Singer Sarah Vaughan wins in the Apollo Theatre amateur night contest, and launches her career.

Singer Dinah Washington tours with the Lionel Hampton orchestra.

Capitol Records is established in Hollywood by Glenn Wallichs, Johnny Mercer and Buddy DeSylva. The company is the first to establish the practice of giving records to disc jockeys. Nat King Cole signs a contract with the company, and his many hits help build the company.

Billboard magazine creates a ratings chart for African American music, known as *The Harlem Hit Parade.*

A musicians' strike by the American Federation of Musicians creates a ban on recording which lasts until 1944.

The Mills Brothers record *Paper Doll,* a song that becomes a major hit in 1943. It sells more than six million copies. They also record *Lazy River* in this year. Over the span of their career they have at least seventy-one hit singles.

The Deep River Boys release the hit *By The Light Of The Silvery Moon.*

The Delta Rhythm Boys begin performing in Las Vegas.

William Grant Still composes the two-act opera, *A Southern Interlude.*

Howard Swanson composes the art song *The Negro Speaks of Rivers,* using a text by Langston Hughes. It is performed in recital by contralto Marian Anderson, who often includes the works of African American composers in her many recitals.

Composer Thomas Kerr, Jr. receives a Rosenwald Fellowship in composition.

The U.S. Department of the Interior dedicates a mural to commemorate Marian Anderson's 1939 Lincoln Memorial concert.

The computer is developed.

Franklin D. Roosevelt is elected to his fourth term as president of the United States.

Six African Americans are lynched.

John H. Johnson publishes his first magazine, *Negro Digest.*

Iku:

Jazz guitarist Charles "Charlie" Christian dies.

Jazz bassist James (Jimmy) Blanton dies.

Composer Frederick J. Work dies.

 **1943**

Agba:

Conductor Margaret Harris is born in Chicago, Illinois.

Singer/actress Eloise C. "Leslie" Uggams is born in Washington Heights, New York.

Pop/Soul singer Marilyn McCoo (of The Fifth Dimension) is born in Jersey City, New Jersey.

R&B singer Florence Ballard (of The Supremes) is born.

Gospel singer Edwin Hawkins is born in Oakland, California.

Jazz guitarist George Benson is born in Pittsburgh, Pennsylvania.

Jazz saxophonist Grover Washington, Jr., is born in Buffalo, New York.

Jazz vibraphonist Gary Burton is born in Anderson, Indiana.

Kuumba:

Lena Horne stars in the Vincente Minnelli film *Cabin in the Sky,* joined by John Bubbles, Ethel Waters, Eddie "Rochester" Anderson, Louis Armstrong, the Duke Ellington Orchestra and the Katherine Dunham Dance Company. It is a film that comes to be called "Uncle Tom's Cabin in the Sky" because of the stereotypical presentation of blacks. Lena Horne also stars in *Stormy Weather* a film based on the lives of James Reese Europe, Adelaide Hall and Noble Sissle. The movie also stars Cab Calloway, the Nicholas Brothers, Katherine Dunham, Bill Robinson and Fats Waller. Known as "the most beautiful woman in the world," Lena Horne is profiled in feature articles in *Time, Life* and *Newsweek* magazines.

Billie Holiday is voted Best Female Vocalist in an *Esquire* magazine poll.

Jazz vocalist Ella Fitzgerald records *Cow Cow Boogie* with the Ink Spots.

Singer Dinah Washington joins the Lionel Hampton band.

Trumpeter Dizzy Gillespie joins the Earl Hines Orchestra.

Duke Ellington composes the jazz tone-poem *Black, Brown and Beige*, written for a Carnegie Hall concert with Mahalia Jackson as soloist. It is an outstanding example of the fusion of jazz with the European classical musical tradition.

The Count Basie Band is featured in the film *Stage Door Canteen.*

Russian composer Igor Stravinsky writes *Ebony Concerto*, a composition in the European classical tradition that reflects significant jazz influence.

Four radio stations in the country provide programming for African-Americans.

The jitterbug becomes the dance craze of the United States.

The Ink Spots record the hit *Don't Get Around Much Anymore,* a song that was later recorded by The Isley Brothers and by The Belmonts.

Savoy Records and DeLuxe Records begin releasing recordings for the black audience.

Sister Rosetta Tharpe becomes the first to sing gospel music at New York's Apollo Theater.

Gospel composer Thomas A. Dorsey composes *The Lord Will Make a Way Somehow*, an example of the verse-chorus format of gospel music.

The Golden Gate Quartet records the gospel hit *Run On/Comin' In On A Wing And A Prayer* for the Okeh label.

The Ward Singers gospel trio debuts at the meeting of the National Baptist Convention.

Gospel singer Roberta Martin composes the song *Try Jesus, He Satisfies.*

The Negro Units of the USO Camp Shows begin to tour the European theater.

William Grant Still composes the tone poem, *In Memoriam: The Colored Soldiers Who Died For Democracy.*

Oscar Hammerstein produces an all-black Broadway version of the Bizet opera *Carmen Jones*, starring Muriel Rahn and Muriel Smith.

Porgy and Bess opens on Broadway in a revival performance.

Sculptor Selma Hortense Burke designs the portrait of President Franklin D. Roosevelt that appears on the dime, becoming the first black sculptor to design a United States coin.

Three African Americans are lynched.

A series of race riots erupt across the country (Mobile, Alabama, Detroit, Michigan, Beaumont, Texas, and Harlem).

Visual artist Charles White produces a mural at Hampton Institute, *Contribution of the Negro to American Democracy,* depicting significant blacks in history.

The influence of jazz on the visual arts is reflected in works of Piet Mondrian—*Broadway Boogie Woogie and Victory Boogie Woogie.*

* Iku:*

Jazz pianist/composer Fats Waller dies.

Composer Robert Nathaniel Dett dies.

Music publisher/record producer Harry Pace dies.

Concert singer Julius (Jules) Bledsoe dies.

 **1944**

Agba:

R&B singer Patti LaBelle (Patricia Louise Holte) is born in Philadelphia, Pennsylvania.

Soul singer Florence LaRue (of The Fifth Dimension) is born in Pennsylvania.

Contralto Florence Quivar is born in Philadelphia, Pennsylvania.

Symphonic conductor Tania Leon is born in Cuba.

R&B singer/actress Diana (Diane Earle) Ross is born in Detroit, Michigan.

R&B singer Gladys Knight is born in Atlanta, Georgia.

Jazz/soul singer Freda Payne is born in Detroit, Michigan.

R&B singer Robert Dwayne "Bobbi" Womack is born in Cleveland, Ohio.

R&B singer Barry White is born in Galveston, Texas.

Rock singer Sylvester Stewart (Sly Stone) is born in Dallas, Texas.

Jazz guitarist George Benson is born in Pittsburgh, Pennsylvania.

R&B singer Booker Taliaferro Jones (of Booker T & The MGs) is born in Memphis, Tennessee.

Blues harmonica player Charlie Musselwhite III is born in Kosciusko, Missouri.

Ethnomusicologist/educator/conductor Hansonia L. Caldwell is born in Washington, D. C.

Kuumba:

White promoter Norman Granz begins the "Jazz at the Philharmonic" (JATP) concert in the Los Angeles Philharmonic Auditorium. The first concert features Illinois Jacquet, Barney Kessel and Jack McVea. The concert also becomes a tour that crosses the country twice a year, ten weeks per tour (1944-1957). The promoter is noted for contracts that prohibit discrimination in ticket sales and seating.

Esquire Magazine produces a jazz concert at the Metropolitan Opera House in New York.

Charlie Parker and Dizzy Gillespie join the popular Billy Eckstine band, and with that ensemble helped to generate the modern sound of jazz.

Jazz trumpeter Dizzy Gillespie composes one of his most well known hits *A Night in Tunisia.* He becomes the leading trumpeter of the bebop style.

Jazz artists Lester Young, Red Callender, Harry Edison, Sidney Catlett, Barney Kessel and Illinois Jacquet appear in the Gjon Mili film *Jammin' the Blues.*

Trumpeter Roy Eldridge becomes a featured soloist in Artie Shaw's band.

Thelonious Monk makes his recording debut with the Coleman Hawkins ensemble.

Jazz vocalist Carmen McRae becomes a featured singer with the Benny Carter band.

Jazz pianist Oscar Peterson begins his career in Canada.

Louis Jordan, the "Father of R&B," records *Is You Is Or Is You Ain't My Baby?*

The Nat King Cole Trio has a hit in *Straighten Up and Fly Right,* selling more than 500,000 copies.

The Mills Brothers record the hit *You Always Hurt The One You Love.*

Nora Holt becomes the music critic of New York's *Amsterdam News.*

Ulysses Kay composes *Of New Horizons*, an overture performed by the New York Philharmonic in Lewissohn Stadium.

Actor/bass-baritone/political activist Paul Robeson performs *Othello* on Broadway, setting an all-time record of 296 performances for a Shakespearean play.

Baritone Todd Duncan makes his debut at New York's Town Hall.

William Grant Still composes *Festive Overture.*

Visual artist Horace Pippin completes the painting, *Harmonizing*, a portrayal of four young black men singing on a street corner.

The United Negro College Fund (UNCF) is founded.

Iku:

Composer/conductor Will Marion Cook dies.

 **1945**

Agba:

Opera singer Jessye Norman is born in Augusta, Georgia.

Reggae singer Robert "Bob" Marley is born in St. Ann, Jamaica.

Jazz pianist Keith Jarrett is born in Allentown, Pennsylvania.

Orchestra conductor Isaiah Jackson is born in Richmond, Virginia.

Singer/composer/arranger Donny Hathaway is born in Chicago, Illinois.

Latin R&B/pop singer/songwriter/guitarist Jose Feliciano is born in Lares, Puerto Rico.

Singer Beatrice Moorman "Melba Moore" is born in New York City.

Classical singer/educator Gwendolyn Lytle is born in Jersey City, New Jersey.

Kuumba:

World War II ends - the era of Swing fades.

Louis Jordan records *Let the Good Times Roll*, a precursor of R&B.

King Records begins releasing records for the black audience.

Blues singer Huddie "Leadbelly" Ledbetter begins hosting his own radio show on the West Coast.

The Berklee College of Music (a school for jazz musicians) is founded in Boston by Lawrence Berk.

The black female swing band, the International Sweethearts of Rhythm, tours France and Germany for the USO.

Trumpeter Miles Davis joins the Benny Carter band.

Jazz vocalist Billie Holiday makes her debut at New York's Town Hall.

Jazz vocalist Ella Fitzgerald and The Delta Rhythm Boys record the hit *It's Only A Paper Moon/Cry You Out Of My Heart.*

Charlie Parker and Dizzy Gillespie release the first recordings that showcase the new Bop movement. This includes *Mean To Me* with vocalist Sarah Vaughn.

The New Jazz Foundation produces a series of modern jazz concerts at Town Hall in New York. Charlie Parker and Dizzy Gillespie are among those featured.

Woody Herman forms the first white band to have a bop orientation.

White banjoist Eddie Condon opens a club in New York that specializes in presenting the Dixieland style of jazz. New York becomes a center for the revival of Dixieland, as performed at various clubs including Condon's, the Central Plaza and Nick's.

Blues guitarist T-Bone Walker plays in the clubs on Central Avenue in Los Angeles.

Nora Holt is sponsored by Virgil Thomson to become the first black member of the Music Critics Circle of New York.

Baritone Todd Duncan makes his debut with the New York City Opera, in *Il Pagliacci.*

South Carolina Food and Tobacco Union workers adapt the song *I'll Overcome Someday* into *We Shall Overcome* and use it during their strike.

Dancer Katherine Dunham choreographs "Carib Song," a work inspired by her Haitian travels and study.

Richard Wright publishes *Black Boy.*

The United Nations Charter is approved.

Visual artist Elizabeth Catlett is awarded the Julius Rosenwald Foundation grant to produce a series on black women.

Richmond Barthe becomes the first black sculptor elected to the National Academy of Arts and Letters.

Johnson Publication Company publishes the first issue of *Ebony* magazine.

President Franklin Roosevelt dies and vice president Harry S. Truman becomes president.

Seven African Americans are lynched.

The NAACP increases the systematic attack on the legal basis for segregation.

5

1946 - 1959
THE MUSIC OF INTERNATIONAL
COMMUNICATION

Performers in the genres of African American music that have become fundamental to the music of the United States (Blues, Jazz, and Gospel Music), excel and continually create new forms. These performers and genres achieve international recognition. They become the driving force in creating product for the rapidly expanding recording market. Indeed, the music of African Americans becomes a major product for all aspects of the growing communications field (radio and television). Additionally, African Americans develop exceptional abilities within genres generally associated with white culture— European classical music and the Broadway stage.

The period begins with the formation of The Vibranaires, one of the earliest R&B doo-wop groups. The period ends with musical experimentation and economic enterprise. That is, in 1959 a number of jazz artists (Miles Davis, Ornette Coleman, Leonard Feather, Dave Brubeck, Charles Mingus and others) are performing and recording in a variety of new styles. And, Hitsville USA is established, the company that becomes Motown and creates the primary musical product for the next decade.

TRENDS
1946 - 1959

1940s

ℓ Rhythm and Blues replaces Swing as the popular music of the African American community. Urban black audiences provide the primary market for new style.

ℓ Jazz becomes more of a listening experience as the genre evolves into the collaborative art form known as bop. It is performed by instrumentalists and vocalists in small ensembles that eliminate the regularity of dance rhythm from their style. The larger swing bands either go out of business or find new audiences by changing their styles to either bop or the newer, hard-driving rhythms of rhythm and blues.

ℓ Some black composers of music in the Americanized European classical tradition increasingly write music that utilizes contemporary musical vocabulary in a manner that minimizes the presence of recognizably African American musical characteristics.

1950s

ℓ Black entertainers begin to make enormous sums of money performing in the nightclubs of New York, Las Vegas, Lake Tahoe and Los Angeles, including Nat King Cole, Sammy Davis, Jr., and Lena Horne.

ℓ Professional gospel groups emerge and tour the country. Soloists move out from the church, acquiring international fame by performing on television, in concert halls and at jazz festivals in this country and in Europe.

ℓ Chicago Blues enters its golden age, as performed by Chuck Berry, Eddie Boyd, Bo Diddley, Buddy Guy, Elmore James, Jimmy Rogers, Otish Rush, Little Walter, Muddy Waters, Sonny Boy Williamson, Howlin' Wolf, Arthur Spires Memphis Slim, Johnny Shines, Otis Spann, Snooky Pryor and John Lee Hooker. It is recorded on the Chess, J.O.B., Chance, United, Vee Jay, Parrot and Cobra labels.

◊ Teenagers begin to own their own radios, and they rapidly become the major market for popular music. Rhythm & Blues groups emerge from the street corners and high school stairwells of urban America and create the music for this new market. The R&B music category is nationalized by *Billboard* magazine, as code language for music designated for the black market.

◊ Initially the R&B groups perform doo-wop, created as an a cappella, single gender vocal ensemble style known for the use of simple lyrics that feature repetitive nonsense syllables. The ensemble often includes a lead singer, thus facilitating the continuation of African call and response structure.

◊ Through the period the R&B style expands, using more sophisticated technology and arrangements. For example, the small ensembles often use arrangements that have recognizable hooks, recognizable harmonic practices and distinctive voice parts (including the popular falsetto). The accompaniments are provided by strongly accented, often boogie-woogie piano, drums, guitar, and growling, howling saxophones. The rhythm is highlighted by the singers through hand-clapping and finger-snapping.

◊ At the beginning of the period, R&B groups are usually made up of male members and often take their names from birds, and cars. Toward the end of the decade, much of the music is performed by girl groups, many of which use the names of flowers and jewels.

◊ The R&B music is the dance music of the decade, accompanying dances such as the mashed potato, the jerk and the shout.

◊ R&B recording companies proliferate in Memphis, New York, Chicago, Cincinnati, Los Angeles and New Orleans, with mostly white A&R (artist and repertoire) people deciding the people and the music to be recorded and promoted. At the same time, a few African American entrepreneurs establish recording companies.

⟨ R&B begins to blend with Gospel music, incorporating its melismatic melodic practices. Gospel singers cross-over to record in the R&B genre.

⟨ R&B reaches the white teenage market through covered versions in a style known as Rock and Roll. It combines with country music to create rockabilly.

⟨ Bebop evolves into East and West Coast schools of Cool Jazz, as performed by Miles Davis, Dave Brubeck, Gerry Mulligan, Stan Getz, Thelonius Monk, and Lennie Tristano. Third Stream jazz becomes popular, as performed by the Modern Jazz Quartet—a concert jazz style that blends classical and jazz elements. And funk/hard bop develops as a back to the roots response to the styles that some feel have become too restrained and cool. Additionally Afro Cuban jazz gains in popularity.

⟨ Jazz evolves into a self-conscious art music that increasingly is performed in community and college concert venues around the world and at festivals rather than in nightclubs.

⟨ New York is described as the jazz capitol of the world.

⟨ Millions of Americans attend college with the support of the GI Bill. Numerous African American artists and musicians receive educational training.

⟨ The United States political leadership focuses upon a "red scare" of Communism. Jazz and African American classical musicians are sent by the State Department on goodwill tours to encourage emerging countries to align themselves with the West. Some jazz musicians assert that these tours should also be sent to the Southern states.

⟨ African Americans continue the use of street cries throughout the U.S. to generate public response needed to sell their wares.

⟨ Racial segregation is enforced as the law of the land. African Americans are not permitted to vote, to serve on juries, to enjoy mainstream public accommodations like restaurants, movie theaters, concert halls, hotels and swimming pools, to enroll in white public schools or to even use certain public toilets.

ACHIEVEMENT DATELINE
1946 - 1959

 **1946**

Agba:

Gospel/soul singer Al Green is born in Forest City, Arkansas.

Soul singer Brenda Holloway is born in Atascadero, California.

Soul singer/keyboardist Billy Preston is born in Houston, Texas.

Singer/dancer Ben Vereen is born in Miami, Florida.

R&B singer Valerie Simpson (of Ashford & Simpson) is born in New York.

Soul/Pop singer Ruth Pointer (of the Pointer Sisters) is born in Oakland, California.

R&B singer Maurice White (of Earth, Wind and Fire) is born in Memphis, Tennessee.

R&B/psychedelic rock bass guitarist Larry Graham is born in Beaumont, Texas.

Classical pianist Andre Watts is born in Nuremburg, Germany.

Classical pianist Cecil Lytle is born in Jersey City, New Jersey.

Jazz pianist George Duke is born in San Rafael, California.

Jazz percussionist Don Moye (of the Art Ensemble of Chicago) is born in Rochester, New York.

Kuumba:

The pioneering era of Rhythm and Blues begins. Erlington "Sonny" Til organizes a group that comes to be known as the first R&B singing group. With the name The Vibranairs, they begin harmonizing together on a corner on Baltimore's Pennsylvania Avenue. Ultimately the group changes its name to Sonny Til and the Orioles, and their performance style helps define the harmonic practices of R&B.

The Ink Spots record the popular hit *Prisoner of Love,* a song that is subsequently covered by James Brown and His Famous Flames.

Gospel singer Mahalia Jackson has a hit on Apollo Records, *I Will Move On Up a Little Higher* (composed by Rev. William Herbert Brewster). It sells over two million copies and launches her commercial career.

Singer/jazz artist Nat King Cole has a fifteen-minute radio show.

Jazz pianist Erroll Garner releases *Laura,* a record that sells over 500,000 copies.

Duke Ellington composes the jazz tone-poem *Deep South Suite.*

Jazz saxophonist Charlie Parker suffers a nervous breakdown and spends several months in California's Camarillo State Hospital. He later reminisces about the stay with the piece *Relaxin' at Camarillo.*

Jazz singer Sarah Vaughan wins the Female Vocalist of the Year award from *DownBeat* magazine.

Singer Billie Holiday and Louis Armstrong appear in the movie *New Orleans.*

Singer/entertainer Pearl Bailey makes her Broadway debut in the musical *St. Louis Woman.*

Jazz trumpeter Miles Davis join the Billy Eckstine band.

Dizzy Gillespie creates the Dizzy Gillespie Orchestra, and adds two Cuban musicians to the group, Mario Bauza and conga drummer Chano Poz, mixing bebop and Latin rhythms to create Afro-Cuban jazz. He later forms a remarkable bebop quintet, with Charlie Parker, Bud Powell, Max Roach and Ray Brown.

Ulysses Kay composes *A Short Overture,* winner of the 1947 George Gershwin award.

George Walker composes *Lyric for Strings (Lament for Strings)*, a work that utilizes serial technique and complex rhythms.

Actor/bass-baritone/political activist Paul Robeson warns President Truman that unless the U.S. Government begins to protect blacks from lynching, blacks would take the necessary steps of self-defense, thus articulating a philosophy that precedes the teachings of Malcolm X.

White composer Igor Stravinsky writes the *Ebony Concerto for Dance Orchestra* for Woody Herman, reflecting the influence of jazz on music of the European classical tradition.

Conductor Hall Johnson organizes the 300-voice Festival Negro Chorus of New York, and composes the Easter Cantata, *Son Of Man.*

The Links, Inc. is founded as a black women's public service volunteer organization.

Sculptor Richmond Barthe creates a bust of Booker T. Washington, for New York University's American Hall of Fame.

Walt Disney continues presenting the image of the docile, happy slave in *Song of the South.*

The influence of jazz on the visual arts is reflected in the work of Romare Bearden—*A Blue Note.*

Jackie Robinson plays baseball with the Kansas City Monarchs, one of the professional teams in the Negro Leagues.

Six African Americans are lynched.

The U.S. Supreme Court prohibits segregation in interstate bus travel (Morgan vs. Virginia).

Network television begins.

Iku:

Blues singer Mamie Smith dies.

 **1947**

Agba:

Singer Minnie Riperton is born in Chicago, Illinois

Soul singer Renaldo Benson (of The Four Tops) is born in Detroit, Michigan.

Keyboardist/trumpeter/composer David Darius Brubeck is born in San Francisco, California.

Kuumba:

Balladeer Nat King Cole has a #1 hit in *Nature Boy*, making him the first black male singer to successfully crossover into the white market.

Louis Jordan has a popular hit with his jump band, *Open The Door, Richard,* an early example of the strong rhythms found in R&B. His songs are recognized as having lyrics that have a special humor.

The Chess record label is established in Chicago, Illinois, and the Imperial record label is established in Los Angeles, California, both releasing records for the black audience.

The R&B group known as the Vibranairs sign with the It's Natural recording label after appearing on Arthur Godfrey's Talent Scouts. They release their first hit, *It's Too Soon To Know.*

The R&B group known as The Clovers start performing together at Armstrong High School in Washington, D.C.

Blues artist Aaron "T-Bone" Walker records *Call It Stormy Monday*, a modern version of country blues.

The Delta Rhythm Boys record the hit *Dry Bones* for RCA, and a version of the Duke Ellington song *Take The A Train.*

Jazz singer Ella Fitzgerald tours with the Dizzy Gillespie Orchestra, and begins developing her scatting abilities, as reflected in the bebop style recordings, *Oh Lady Be Good,* and *How High The Moon.* She develops an impressive reputation for her two-and-one-half octave vocal range and her sense of pitch and rhythm.

John Coltrane joins the Dizzy Gillespie band.

Charlie Parker reforms his quintet with Miles Davis on trumpet, Duke Jordan on piano, Tommy Potter on bass and Max Roach on drums. The group is known for a number of outstanding recordings, including *Embraceable You.* It reflects Charlie Parker's use of impressive improvisation and complicated chord progressions.

Billy Eckstine disbands his band and refocuses his career into solo/ballad singing.

Louis Armstrong stops performing with his large swing band. He forms a new septet, Louis Armstrong and the All Stars, with Barney Bigard on clarinet, Dick Cary on piano, Sid Catlett on drums, Arvell Shaw on bass, Jack Teagarden on trombone, and singer Velma Middleton singing.

John Alan Lomax records work songs and hollers at Parchman State Penitentiary.

Billie Holiday is arrested on a drug possession charge. She is sentenced to federal prison in West Virginia.

Gospel singer Marion Williams joins the Ward Singers.

The Golden Gate Quartet records the gospel hit *Shadrack.*

Comedian Jackie "Moms" Mabley appears in *Killer Diller*, her first film.

Poet/author Langston Hughes writes lyrics for the Kurt Weill Broadway show *Street Scene.*

CORE sends the first freedom riders into the south to test the Supreme Court's ban against segregation on interstate buses.

Martin Luther King, Jr. becomes an assistant preacher at his father's church, Ebenezer Baptist, in Atlanta, Georgia.

Jackie Robinson joins the Brooklyn Dodgers, playing second base and breaking the major league baseball color barrier.

All federal employees are subjected to loyalty investigations in response to the growing fear of Communism and the House Committee on Un-American Activities begins hearings to identify Communist sympathizers in the film industry. The committee's anticommunist witch hunt extends until 1952.

The First Negro Classic Ballet is established in Los Angeles, California by Joseph Rickard, and is the nation's first black classical ballet group (with organization archives now available at the Huntington Library).

The United States starts the Marshall Plan.

Round-the-world passenger service is inaugurated by Pan American Airways.

Iku:

Blues harmonica player Sonny Boy Williamson I dies.

New Orleans Traditional Jazz pianist/bandleader Fate Marable dies.

Swing bandleader James (Jimmy) Lunceford dies.

 **1948**

Agba:

R&B singer Jeffrey Linton Osborne is born in Providence, Rhode Island.

Opera singer Kathleen Battle is born in Portsmouth, Ohio.

Opera singer Carmen Balthrop is born in Washington, D.C.

Opera singer Clamma Churita Dale is born in Chester, Pennsylvania.

French horn player Robert Lee Watt is born in Neptune, New Jersey.

Singer/actress Nell Carter is born in Alabama.

Soul/Pop singer Anita Pointer (of The Pointer Sisters) is born in Oakland, California.

Disco singer LaDonna Andrea Gaines (Donna Summers) is born in Boston, Massachusetts.

Reggae singer James Chambers (Jimmy Cliff) is born in West Kingston, Jamaica.

Kuumba:

Paul Robeson and others participate in a major civil rights campaign—the first significant voter registration drive in the deep South since Reconstruction. In so doing, he changes the words of his signature song, *Ol' Man River* - changing the phrase:

> *Darkies all work on the Mississippi; Darkies all work while the white folks play* to *There's an old man called the Mississippi; That's the old man I don't like to be.*

> Also, the phrase *I gits weary and sick of tryin'; I'm tired of livin' and scared of dyin'* becomes *I keeps laffin instead of cryin'; I must keep fightin' until Im dyin'.*

Classical composer Ulysses Kay composes *Concerto for Orchestra* and the score for the film *The Quiet One.*

Dean Dixon makes his conducting debut with the New York Philharmonic Orchestra.

Classical composer Howard Swanson writes *Short Symphony.*

Soprano Adele Addison gives her debut concert at Boston's Jordan Hall.

The Southeast Symphony Association is founded in Los Angeles to serve the black community. The ensemble supports an annual season of concerts, and has outstanding black musicians as its conductor, including William Grant Still, Leroy Hurt, Leon Thompson, Henry Lewis, Luther L. Henderson, III, Yvette Devereaux and John Dennison.

A number of technological developments have impact upon the world of music. The long-playing 33rpm (LP) record is introduced and Dr. Peter Goldmark of Columbia Records invents high fidelity. The transistor is invented. Magnetic tape is marketed for the first time. This means that longer performances and live performances can be recorded. It also means that recordings can be edited and mistakes eliminated.

The Dizzy Gillespie band tours Europe.

The first jazz festival is established in Nice, France. It features Louis Armstrong.

The Fender Musical Instruments Company of California begins to produce a new electric guitar—the Telecaster, an instrument that resists feedback.

Blues singer/guitarist John Lee Hooker starts his career with *Boogie Chillen* and *Wednesday Evening Blues*.

B. B. King becomes a blues disc jockey at WDIA radio in Memphis, Tennessee. WDIA becomes the first radio station to feature all black-oriented programming.

The *Billboard* magazine race records chart includes *Run Joe* by Louis Jordan, *Tomorrow Night* by Lonnie Johnson, *Messin' Around* by Memphis Slim, *Pretty Mama Blues* by Ivory Joe Hunter, and *Send For Me If You Need Me* by The Ravens.

The Atlantic Soul record label is established in New York, by Herb Abramson and Turk Ahmet Ertegun. It becomes the primary producer/distributor for the R &B singers of the Big Apple.

The Roberta Martin Singers record the gospel music hit *Only A Look*.

The Ward Singers record the gospel music hit *Surely God Is Able*.

Mahalia Jackson and Theodore Fry organize the National Baptist Music Convention, an auxiliary to the National Baptist Convention.

The Staple Singers (Mavis, Cleotha, Yvonne, and their father, Pops) are organized as a group.

Eubie Blake's song, *I'm Just Wild About Harry* (from his 1921 musical *Shuffle Along)*, becomes the campaign theme song for Harry Truman's presidential election.

Pianist/cabaret singer Hazel Scott becomes first black performer to have a network television program.

A full season is offered on network television, featuring Milton Berle and Ed Sullivan.

Ralph J. Bunche is named acting United Nations mediator in Palestine.

Martin Luther King, Jr. becomes an ordained Baptist minister.

Jackie "Moms" Mabley is featured in the movie *Boarding House Blues.*

Oscar Micheaux releases the film *The Betrayal.*

Baseball star Leroy (Satchel Paige) is signed as a 42-year-old rookie by the Cleveland Indians.

Alice Coachman becomes the first African American woman to win the Olympic gold medal for the long jump.

Harry Truman is elected president of the United States. He issues Executive Order 9981 requiring equality of treatment and opportunity for all Americans in the armed forces, responding to the pressures of A. Philip Randolph and the League for Non-Violent Civil Disobedience Against Military Segregation.

Iku:

Archivist/folklorist John Lomax dies.

 **1949**

Agba:

R&B singer Lionel Richie is born in Tuskegee, Alabama.

R&B/Soul pianist/composer William Everett (Billy) Preston is born in Houston, Texas.

Classical composer Primous Fountain III is born in St. Petersburg, Florida.

Bluesologist/Jazz poet Gil Scott-Heron is born in Chicago, Illinois.

Kuumba:

William Grant Still, the Dean of African American composers, writes the three-act opera, *Troubled Island*, with libretto by Langston Hughes. He is the first black American to have an opera performed by a major opera company, the New York City Opera (with Robert McFerrin in a starring role). He also composes the song cycle *Songs of Separation,* setting the poetry of five black poets (Arna Bontemps, Philippe-Thoby Marcelin, Paul Laurence Dunbar, Countee Cullen, and Langston Hughes).

Clarence Cameron White's opera, *Ouanga,* is premiered by the Harry T. Burleigh Music Association in South Bend, Indiana.

California's College of the Pacific employs composer/conductor Jester Hairston to teach spirituals, and a generation of young people and their teachers are introduced to African American folk song.

Conductor Albert McNeil establishes the McNeil Singers, a Los Angeles-based group that specializes in performing spirituals.

Conductor Dean Dixon settles in Europe in order to find work.

The concert halls of the U.S. continue to be segregated, causing singer Marian Anderson to require vertical seating that assures the designation of seats for blacks throughout the hall.

Baritone Paul Robeson performs concerts in black churches across the United States because municipal auditoriums and concert halls refuse to book his concerts. Protestors follow his public appearances, voicing opposition to his affiliation with the Communist Party. Often their protests generate riots that stop the performances. This is evident at a scheduled Westchester County outdoor concert and at a Peekskill, New York event.

Singer Juanita Hall appears in the Broadway musical *South Pacific,* ultimately winning a Tony award for her performance.

The Mills Brothers release the pop hits *I Love You So Much It Hurts* and *I've Got My Love to Keep Me Warm.*

The Deep River Boys release the hit record *Don't Ask Me Why/Wrapped Up In A Dream.*

The Delta Rhythm Boys tour Europe, and begin recording Swedish and Finnish folk songs.

B. B. King has a hit, *Three O'Clock Blues,* with Ike Turner on the piano.

Sonny Til and The Orioles release the R&B hits *Tell Me So/Deacon Jones* and *Lonely Christmas/What Are You Doing New Year's Eve.*

Henry Roland (Roy) Byrd (Professor Longhair) records the hit song *Mardi Gras in New Orleans,* a song that becomes the unofficial anthem of the city. He is one of the creators of modern New Orleans blues.

Billboard drops the term "race records" and the Harlem Hit Parade list, substituting "rhythm & blues" as the category title until 1969.

The RCA Corporation produces the 45rpm record. This format eventually replaces the 78 record.

Miles Davis, Charlie Parker, Sidney Bechet and Clyde Hart all perform in the summer at the International Jazz Festival in Paris.

The jazz club Birdland opens on Broadway in New York, named after Charlie "Bird" Parker. Hot Lips Page, Charlie Parker, Lennie Tristano and Lester Young all played at the December 15th opening, a performance that is transmitted to Europe via The Voice of America. The club becomes the site for numerous live recordings.

Louis Armstrong is featured on the cover of *Time* Magazine.

Boogie-woogie pianist Albert Ammons performs at the inauguration of President Harry Truman.

WERD is established as the first black-owned radio station, in Atlanta, Georgia.

Jackie Robinson is voted the National League's Most Valuable Player.

Boxer Joe Louis retires from the ring.

Photographer Gordon Parks joins the staff of *Life* Magazine.

NATO (The North Atlantic Treaty Organization) is established.

Iku:

Singer/composer Harry T. Burleigh dies.

Boogie-woogie pianist Albert C. Ammons.

Dancer Bill "Bojangles" Robinson dies.

Jazz singer Ivie Anderson dies.

Jazz Cornetist Bunk Johnson dies.

Blues singer Leadbelly (Huddie Ledbetter) dies of Lou Gehrigs disease.

Agba:

Conductor Calvin Simmons is born in San Francisco, California.

Singer/composer "Little Stevie Wonder" - Stevland Morris, is born in Saginaw, Michigan.

Singer Natalie Cole is born in Los Angeles, California.

Singer/conductor Bobby McFerrin is born in New York City.

Soul singer Teddy Pendergrass is born in Philadelphia, Pennsylvania.

Soul singer Billy Ocean (Les Charles) is born in Trinidad.

Soul/Pop singer Bonnie Pointer (of The Pointer Sisters) is born in Oakland, California.

Disco/funk singer/bassist Robert 'Kool' Bell (of Kool and the Gang) is born in Youngstown, Ohio.

Kuumba:

The State Department cancels singer/actor/activist Paul Robesons passport, preventing him from traveling abroad for international concert tours, despite the fact that he is accused of no crime. He is blacklisted from public performances in the U.S., and his income falls from $104,000 annually to $2,000. Louis Farrakhan describes this situation in his essay, "I Am An Alarm Clock" (*The Black Scholar,* January/February 1979, page 12): *When Paul Robeson, our dear brother, who had the power of God in his voice, in his oratorical ability, in the brilliance of his mind*

*to see and want good for us—no pain blinded that man to his people's desires—
but because he would speak something that would stir the masses, the public
policy was to ostracize him, vilify him, malign him, and let us get our Negro
intellectuals to help us do it. I'm an alarm clock to you, brothers and sisters,
because history is going to repeat itself and what side of the fence are you going
to be on in 1979?*

Jazz pianist/composer Hazel Scott is accused of being a Communist
sympathizer and loses her television show.

Jazz vocalist Sarah Vaughn records *Nice Work If You Can Get It,* accompanied by Miles Davis. She is named the best vocalist by *Down Beat*
magazine.

Charlie Parker performs with a quintet at Birdland in New York. He also
performs and records with a group in Sweden.

Duke Ellington composes the symphonic jazz tone-poem *A Tone Parallel to Harlem,* a work that is commissioned by Arturo Tossanini for the
NBC Symphony Orchestra.

The Count Basie Orchestra breaks up.

Saxophonist Ornette Coleman joins the band of bluesman Pee Wee
Crayton.

The jazz clubs on Central Avenue in Los Angeles begin to close.

White composer Aaron Copland composes *Concerto for Clarinet* for
Benny Goodman, reflecting the influence of jazz upon classical music.

Howard Swanson's second symphony, *Short Symphony* is performed by
the New York Philharmonic and wins the New York Critic's Circle
Award for being the best work performed during the 1950-51 season.

William Grant Still composes the opera *Costaso.*

The ABC radio network begins a regular Sunday morning show, *Negro
College Choirs.*

Zelma George performs in the Broadway production of Gian Carlo
Menotti's *The Medium.*

Roland Hayes is appointed to the music faculty of Boston University.

221

Nat King Cole has a hit in the ballad *Mona Lisa* (an Oscar-winning song from Alan Ladd's film *Captain Carey, U.S.A.*).

Singer Lena Horne makes her debut on The Ed Sullivan Show - *Toast of the Town*.

Harry Belafonte signs a recording contract with RCA Victor.

Huddie "Leadbelly" Ledbetters lumberjack ballad, *Goodnight, Irene*, (composed in 1936) becomes the biggest song of the year. Recorded in a cover version by The Weavers, a white folk group, it sells over 2 million copies.

R&B artist/boogie-woogie pianist Antoine "Fats" Domino cuts his first record - *Fat Man* - for Imperial Records of Los Angeles, California.

Louis Jordan has an R&B hit with *Blue Light Boogie.*

Singer Ruth Brown has R&B hit with *Teardrops From My Eyes.*

Blues singer Jimmy Witherspoon has a hit with *Real Ugly Woman.*

R&B artist Little Esther (Phillips) makes her debut with Johnny Otis.

An annual Rhythm and blues jubilee is staged at the Shrine Auditorium in Los Angeles.

The Roberta Martin Singers record a gospel music hit, *The Old Ship Of Zion,* as arranged by Thomas A. Dorsey.

Sam Cooke joins the gospel group, The Soul Stirrers. The group records the hit, *By And By.*

Gospel artist Mahalia Jackson debuts at New York's Carnegie Hall, and becomes responsible for elevating gospel music from its folk music base into a "refined art" with a mass audience appeal. She also becomes the official soloist of the National Baptist Convention.

Ethel Waters stars in the Broadway show *Member of the Wedding.*

The ABC weekly television comedy about a black maid, "Beulah," debuts, featuring Ethel Waters in the first year, Hattie McDaniel in the next season, and Louise Beavers in the last season.

The film *The Jackie Robinson Story* is released, featuring Jackie Robinson and Ruby Dee.

Ruby Dee, Ossie Davis and Sidney Poitier appear in the film *No Way Out.*

Gwendolyn Brooks receives the Pulitzer Prize for the book *Annie Allen.*

Elma Lewis establishes the Elma Lewis School of Fine Arts (in Boston, Massachusetts), subsequently renamed the National Center of Afro-American Artists.

The first African American players integrate the National Basketball Association (Chuck Cooper, Nathaniel Sweetwater Clifton and Early Lloyd).

Ralph Bunche receives the Nobel Peace Prize for his service as United Nations Mediator in the Palestine dispute.

The U.S. enters the Korean War.

Iku:

Blues singer Bertha Chippie Hill dies.

Boogie-Woogie pianist Jimmy Yancey dies.

 **1951**

Agba:

Soul singer Robert Peabo Bryson is born in Greenville, South Carolina.

Singer Deniece Williams is born in Gary, Indiana.

Soul singer Jeffrey Osborne is born in Providence, Rhode Island.

Soul singer Luther Vandross is born in the Bronx, New York.

Jazz bassist Stanley Clarke is born in Philadelphia, Pennsylvania.

Soul/pop singer Sigmund Esco (Jackie) Jackson (of The Jackson Five) is born in Gary, Indiana.

Disco/funk saxophonist Ronald Bell (of Kool and the Gang) is born in Youngstown, Ohio.

Kuumba:

Gospel singer Shirley Caesar makes her first recording, *I'd Rather Have Jesus.*

The Soul Stirrers, with Sam Cooke as lead, record the gospel hit *Peace In The Valley,* a record that is later covered by Elvis Presley.

The Dominoes record the R&B song *Harbor Lights* and *Sixty Minute Man.*

Blues singer Howlin' Wolf has hits with *Moaning at Midnight* and *How Many More Years.*

Nat King Cole has a Pop hit with *Too Young.*

Chicago blues artist Big Bill Broonzy performs in England, becoming influential upon the development of English rock groups.

Ray Charles starts recording for the Atlantic label.

The Dave Brubeck Quartet is established.

Charlie Parker's cabaret card is revoked in New York because of his association with drug dealers, and is not restored until 1953.

Thelonious Monk is arrested on a narcotics charge - he loses his cabaret card, and is thereafter unable to work in New York City establishments that sell alcohol until 1957.

Jazz bassist Ray Brown joins the Oscar Peterson Trio.

Jazz guitarist Django Reinhardt records *Nuages.*

Rev. William Herbert Brewster composes *How I Got Over.*

Paul Robeson works with a committee that petitions the U.S. government to stop its policy of genocide against African Americans.

Conductor Hall Johnson and his Festival Negro Chorus of New York tours Europe on behalf of the U.S. Department of State. Included is a performance at the International Festival of Fine Arts in Berlin.

Janet Collins joins the Metropolitan Opera corps de ballet, becoming the first black prima ballerina to perform in a major American ballet company. She makes her debut in *Aida*.

The Jerome Kern/Oscar Hammerstein II, 1927 musical *Show Boat* is released as a film, with William Warfield performing the famous "Ol' Man River" song.

Harry Belafonte begins performing folk songs at the Village Vanguard.

Arna Bontemps writes the novel *Chariot in the Sky* based upon the story of the Fisk Jubilee Singers.

Amos 'n' Andy debuts as a television comedy series, with an all-black cast.

Richard Wright's *Native Son* is released as a film

Johnson Publication Company publishes its first issue of *Jet* magazine.

Ralph Bunche is appointed Undersecretary of the United Nations.

Videotape technology emerges.

CBS begins to telecast in color.

Iku:

Arranger/music director William Henry Bennet Vodery dies.

Jazz drummer Sidney Catlett dies.

 **1952**

Agba:

White jazz bassist Jaco Pastorius is born in Norristown, Pennsylvania.

Kuumba:

The Modern Jazz Quartet is established (with John Lewis on piano, Milt Jackson on vibraharp, Percy Heath on Bass, and Kenny Clarke, later replaced by Connie Kay) on drums. The ensemble becomes the premiere performer of the tightly arranged Third-stream jazz.

The Jazz Crusaders is organized in Houston, Texas, with Wilton Felder on bass and saxophone, Wayne Henderson on trombone, Nesbert (Stix) Hooper on percussion and Joe Sample on keyboard.

Count Basie forms a new orchestra.

Jazz pianist Mary Lou Williams records *Bebop Waltz.*

White composer John Cage writes *Imaginary Landscape No. 5,* a musical collage of forty-two jazz records.

Recordings become the major source of revenue in the music industry, surpassing sheet music. The radio becomes the primary vehicle through which hits are made.

Polish immigrants Phil and Len Chess establish the Chess and Checker recording labels, Chicago-based companies that are active in the recording of the blues.

The Mills Brothers record the hit *Glow Worm.*

Blues singer Elmore James records the hit *Dust My Broom.*

R&B singer Joe Turner records *Sweet Sixteen* for Atlantic Records.

R&B singer Johnny Ace has a debut recording *My Song.*

The Royals record the R&B hit *Every Beat of My Heart,* written by Johnny Otis, the white singer/composer/pianist who becomes known as the godfather of Rhythm and Blues.

R&B singer Lloyd Price records *Lawdy Miss Clawdy* for Specialty Records, with Fats Domino on piano.

R&B singers Shirley Goodman and Leonard Lee become the Sweethearts of the Blues and record a hit for Aladdin Records, *I'm Gone.*

R&B singer Ray Charles signs with Atlantic Records.

Gladys Knight and the Pips begin singing together in Atlanta, Georgia.

Disc jockey Alan Freed invents the phrase rock 'n' rool, a term with significant sexual overtones. The term becomes code language for R&B-influenced music performed by white singers.

White radio engineer/announcer Sam Phillips establishes the Sun Label in Memphis, the company that ultimately became the producer of the early Elvis Presley records (until 1955), and of the performers known for their Rockabilly style, Carl Perkins, Johnny Cash and Jerry Lee Lewis.

Gospel singer Albertina Walker organizes The Caravans.

Gospel singer Mahalia Jackson makes her first tour to Europe.

The Gospel quartet The Dixie Hummingbirds, record *I Know I've Been Changed/Trouble In My Way.*

Contralto Marian Anderson makes her television debut on "The Ed Sullivan Show."

Leontyne Price, William Warfield and Cab Calloway perform in a revival of *Porgy & Bess.*

Soprano Leontyne Price makes her debut in Paris, France, performing in Virgil Thomson's *Four Saints in Three Acts.*

Eartha Kitt stars in the Broadway musical *New Faces.*

Ralph Ellison publishes *The Invisible Man.*

Iku:

Band conductor/arranger Fletcher Henderson dies.

 **1953**

Agba:

Singer Yvette Marie Stevens (Chaka Khan) is born in Chicago, Illinois.

Soul/pop singer Toriano Adaryll (Tito) Jackson is born in Gary, Indiana.

Blues singer/guitarist Robert Cray is born at Fort Benning, Georgia.

Kuumba:

The number of radio stations in the country that provide programming for African American audiences expands to 260.

Blues artist B. B. King records *Every Day I Have the Blues.*

Blues artist Muddy Waters records *I'm Your Hoochie Coochie Man.*

The Gibson company begins to produce the new solid-body Les Paul electric guitar.

Vee Jay Records, a black-owned recording company, is founded by James Bracken, Vivian Carter Bracken and Calvin Carter.

Blues shouter Willie Mae "Big Mama" Thornton records the R&B No. 1 hit, *Hound Dog,* the song, written by lyricist Jerry Leiber and composer Mike Stoller, is later covered by Elvis Presley. Thornton is one of the rare women blues singers of the 1950s.

Singer Ruth Brown has R&B hit *(Mama) He Treats Your Daughter Mean,* a song that reflects the strong beat that is typical of R&B.

Sonny Til and The Orioles have a hit with *Crying in the Chapel,* an early example of an R&B song that becomes popular with white audiences. The song reflects the use of a high tenor lead with close backup harmonies, typical of the R&B call and response style.

The Drifters - an R&B group - begin to record with Clyde McPhatter as lead singer, releasing the blockbuster hit, *Money Honey.* The group's recording career extends until 1979, using as many as twelve different lead singers.

The Clovers record the R&B hit *Good Lovin'.* The group goes on to record twenty-one major R&B hits throughout the decade.

The Harptones, an R&B group, record *A Sunday Kind of Love.*

Music critic Nora Holt produces a classical-music radio program on WLIB in New York, *Nora Holt's Concert Showcase, WLIB.*

Baltimore's Lyric Theater refuses to book Marian Anderson because of their segregation policy.

Symphony conductor Dean Dixon serves as musical director of the Goeteborg Symphony in Sweden until 1960.

Mattiwilda Dobbs makes her operatic debut at La Scala in Milan, Italy.

Gospel composer Doris Akers composes *Lead Me, Guide Me.*

Albertina Walker forms an all-female gospel group, The Caravans. The group becomes one of the leading gospel ensembles of the decade.

Under the leadership of Marl Young and Buddy Collette, the black and white musicians unions merge in Los Angeles. The historic segregation of the two unions had an impact upon the type of work available for African American musicians. An "amalgamation" of the two unions (#767 and #47) was imperative.

Dizzy Gillespie begins to use his tilted trumpet after someone falls on the instrument and bends it upward.

Charlie Parker tours this country and Canada and performs primarily with pickup groups.

Trumpeter Clifford Brown records the hit *Cherokee.*

The ChaCha becomes a popular dance in Cuba, driven by the popular recording of *La Enganadora* (composed by Enrique Jorrin and performed by his Orquesta America). This dance style eventually becomes popular in the United States.

James Baldwin publishes *Go Tell It On the Mountain.*

Paul Williams becomes the first black architect fellow of the American Institute of Architects.

Louise Evans becomes the first black woman to be accepted into the designers' union, the United Scenic Artists Association.

Segregation in Washington, D.C. restaurants is struck down by the U.S. Supreme Court.

Roy Campanella receives the National Leagues Most Valuable Player. Only six out of the sixteen baseball teams have black players.

Iku:

Composer Florence Price dies.

 **1954**

Agba:

Soul/pop singer Jermaine Jackson (of The Jackson Five) is born in Gary, Indiana.

Soul/Pop singer June Pointer (of The Pointer Sisters) is born in Oakland, California.

Jazz pianist/composer Patrice Rushen is born in Los Angeles, California.

White jazz bassist Steve Rodby is born in Joliet, Illinois.

White jazz/New Age guitarist/composer Pat Metheny is born in Kansas City, Missouri.

Kuumba:

The Newport Jazz Festival is established in Rhode Island. This is the first American jazz festival.

Thelonious Monk writes the classic jazz ballad *Round Midnight.* He records *Bag's Groove* with the Miles Davis All-Stars.

Miles Davis and Sonny Rollins record *Nigeria, Oleo* and *Doxy.*

Jazz pianist Horace Silver composes *Doodlin'.*

Jazz bassist Charles Mingus records *Gregarian Chant.*

Jazz vocalist Ella Fitzgerald begins recording the music of America's songwriters for Verve Records, with her first album, *The Cole Porter Songbook.*

Jazz vocalist Sarah Vaughn has a hit with *Lullaby of Birdland,* accompanied by Clifford Brown.

Tumpeter Louis Armstrong releases *Louis Armstrong Plays W. C.*

Handy, a Columbia Records album that reflects the use of the newest tape editing capabilities.

The Modern Jazz Quartet record the well known *Django* as a memorial to Django Reinhardt.

The Clifford Brown/Max Roach Quintet is founded, with Max Roach, Fats Navarro and Dizzy Gillespie.

Charlie Parker tours as a guest soloist with the Stan Kenton band. This is the year his daughter dies and he attempts suicide, ending up in New York's Bellevue Hospital. He also separates from his wife and finally has to pawn his horn.

Jazz pianist/composer Dave Brubeck is featured in a cover article in *Time* magazine.

Jazz singer Carmen McRae records her first album.

Billie Holiday has a successful tour of Europe.

Blues singer/bass guitarist Willie Dixon becomes a house producer for Chess Records. He subsequently produces the work of numerous blues artists, including Chuck Berry, Buddy Guy, Otis Rush, Muddy Waters and Howlin' Wolf.

R&B singer Johnny Ace is named the most programmed R&B artist of 1954 by *Cashbox* magazine.

Blues artist Lowell Fulsom has an R&B hit on Checker Records, *Reconsider Baby*.

R&B singer Guitar Slim has a hit with *The Things That I Used To Do*, recorded for Specialty Records.

Blues singer Big Joe Turner records the original version of *Shake, Rattle & Roll*.

White rock and roll artists Bill Haley & His Comets cover Big Joe Turner's *Shake, Rattle And Roll*. Covering becomes a popular practice wherein whites perform songs from the R&B chart, often with enhanced production elements. The white versions reach the mass radio market, particularly since the white-run radio stations refuse to play the originals. Only the songwriters (or the song rights owners, who often are not the same people as the original composers) receive royalties from the white releases.

The Penguins record the R&B classic *Earth Angel.* It is covered in 1955 by The Crew-Cuts.

The Chords, an R&B doo-wop group, record *Sh-Boom*, the first R&B song to make it to the top of the Pop charts.

The Cadillacs record the R&B hit *Gloria.* The group becomes known for its use of choreography in its live performances. Their choreographer eventually becomes the choreographer for Motown.

The R&B group The Four Aims is formed in Detroit. They eventually become The Four Tops (in 1956), producing hits over the next forty years.

The R&B group The Spaniels record *Goodnight, Well It's Time To Go.*

R&B group The Midnighters have R&B hits with *Work With Me Annie* and *Annie Had a Baby.* This is part of the Annie craze.

The R&B group, The Drifters, record *Honey Love.*

R&B artist B. B. King records *Every Day I Have The Blues*.

Ray Charles releases *I Got A Woman*, an R&B song that is based on the gospel song *My Jesus Is All the World To Me.*

Gospel singer Mahalia Jackson has a successful local show on Chicagos CBS television station.

Gospel singer/composer James Cleveland joins The Caravans.

Diahann Carroll and Pearl Bailey star in the Broadway musical, *House Of Flowers.*

Carmen Jones is released as a film produced by Otto Preminger. It features Dorothy Dandridge (singing dubbed by Marilyn Horne), Harry Belafonte, Pearl Bailey, Diahann Carroll, Brock Peters, Joe Adams (singing dubbed by Marvin Hayes) and Carmen DeLavallade, and uses music from Georges Bizet's 1875 opera with lyrics from the Oscar Hammerstein II 1943 Broadway adaptation.

Composer Julia Amanda Perry completes the opera *The Cask of Amontillado,* staged by Columbia University.

Singer Mattiwilda Dobbs makes her debut with the San Francisco Opera.

Singer Leontyne Price gives her Town Hall debut recital.

Sylvia Olden Lee joins the coaching staff of the Metropolitan Opera, becoming the first black member of the Metropolitan's musical staff.

Classical pianist Natalie Leota Hinderas gives her Town Hall debut recital.

Harry Belafonte receives a Tony Award for his performance in *John Murray Anderson's Almanac.*

Visual artist Charles White completes the ink drawing *Piano Player,* an image that celebrates Black music and musicians.

Willie Mays becomes the National League's Most Valuable Player.

Martin Luther King, Jr. becomes pastor of the Dexter Avenue Baptist Church in Montgomery, Alabama.

Norma Sklarek becomes the first black woman registered architect.

The Brown vs. Board of Education of Topeka, Supreme court decision is made. It declares the racial segregation that emerged in public schools from the application of the separate but equal doctrine to be unconstitutional. Public school desegregation begins.

The United States outlaws the Communist Party, and McCarthyism flourishes in Congress.

Iku:

R&B singer Johnny Ace dies (playing Russian Roulette).

Jazz trumpeter Oran Thaddeus (Hot Lips) Page dies.

Composer Harry Lawrence Freeman dies.

Composer/lyricist J. Rosamond Johnson dies.

 **1955**

Agba:

Soul Singer Rick James (James Johnson) is born in Buffalo, New York.

Jazz saxophonist David Murray is born in Los Angeles, California.

Kuumba:

Marian Anderson makes her debut at the Metropolitan Opera House in Verdis *Un Ballo In Maschera*, becoming the first African American to sing on the stage of the Met.

Baritone Robert McFerrin debuts with the Metropolitan Opera, in *Verdi's Aida*, and he becomes the first African American to accept a permanent position with the Metropolitan Opera.

Soprano Leontyne Price makes her debut with the NBC-TV Opera Company in the coast-to-coast presentation of *Tosca*.

Composer Hale Smith creates the four-part song cycle *The Valley Wind.*

Berry Gordy opens a jazz record store in Detroit.

Rock and Roll explodes into national popularity, generating much opposition from the church, educators, parents and politicians.

The rock and roll cover syndrome continues, with Pat Boone covering the Fats Domino song *Ain't That a Shame,* and the Ivory Joe Hunter song *I Almost Lost My Mind.* The McGuire Sisters cover the Moonglows hit *Sincerely,* and Georgia Gibbs covers the Etta James hit *Roll With Me Henry* (changing it to *Dance With Me Henry*) and the LaVern Baker hit *Tweedle Dee.* Note that the 1909 copyright law does not apply to recorded material and does not cover arrangements.

While in a Detroit high school, Smokey Robinson forms a group known as The Matadors, soon to be renamed The Miracles.

Carver Bunkum, Carl Fisher, Dave Govan and Jimmy Johnson form The Vibrations while at Jefferson High School in Los Angeles.

Ray Charles incorporates gospel music style into his R&B recording style, changing *This Little Light of Mine* to *This Little Girl of Mine*, and recording *Hallelujah, I Love Her So.*

Rockabilly emerges as a style that combines rhythm and blues with country and western music

Rock Around the Clock by Bill Haley & His Comets is popular as a record and as a movie.

R&B/rock & roll pioneer Little Richard records *Tutti Frutti*. The song reflects his use of particularly fast tempos and his overall special dynamic style. It becomes popular with both blacks and whites.

R&B singer Chuck Berry records *Maybelline*, attracting a large, white teenage audience and winning the *Billboard* Triple Award. He eventually becomes very influential on white popular musicians, including The Beatles.

R&B singer Fats Domino records the Glenn Miller hit *Blueberry Hill*, and a million-seller, *Ain't That a Shame.*

R&B singer/guitarist Bo Diddley has a hit with *She's Mine, She's Fine.* He is considered to be a pioneer of rock and roll, and he becomes very influential on future British rock groups.

R&B singer Roy Hamilton records the hit *Unchained Melody.*

A group known as The Robins record the R&B hit *Smokey Joe's Cafe.* Part of this group become members of a new Los Angeles-based ensemble named The Coasters.

R&B group The Platters record *The Great Pretender* and *Only You*, hits in both the United States and England. Over the years *Only You* sells more than five million copies.

R&B singer Johnny Ace has a pop chart hit, after his death—*Pledging My Love.*

The Deep River Boys perform at the White House for president Dwight Eisenhower.

Trumpeter Miles Davis triumphs at the Newport Jazz Festival. Later in the year he forms The New Miles Davis Quintet (with John Coltrane, Red Garland, Paul Chambers, and Philly Joe Jones).

Jazz singers Ella Fitzgerald and Carmen McRae are named Best Female Vocalists by *Metronome* magazine.

Jazz bassist Charles Mingus records *Haitian Fight Song.*

Drummer Art Blakey and pianist Horace Silver establish The Jazz Messengers, a group that goes on to specialize in the crossover, blues-rooted Hard Bop performance style with a spotlight placed on the solo abilities of the individual players. Separately from this group, Art Blakey explores Latin American rhythm/percussion with the two-volume album set, *Orgy in Rhythm.*

Jazz pianist Ahmad Jamal records *Ahmad Jamal at the Pershing,* including a setting of the Broadway tune "Poinciana"—an album that remains on the top of the *Billboard* charts for 108 weeks.

Antonio Carlos Jobim composes the jazz-inspired/bossa-nova inspired work *Sinfonia de Rio de Janeiro.*

Vocalist Joe Williams has a hit with the Count Basie Orchestra - *Every Day I Have The Blues.*

Jazz singer Gaby Lee starts her singing career performing at the Moulin Rouge nightclub in Los Angeles. She eventually changes her name to Abbey Lincoln.

Pianist Lennie Tristano records *Requiem* as a tribute to Charlie Parker. It is an example of West Coast Cool jazz.

Harry Belafonte stars in the Broadway show *Three For Tonight.* He also stars with Dorothy Dandridge in the film *Bright Road.*

Dorothy Dandridge becomes the first black woman nominated for an Oscar Award as best actress for her performance in the film *Carmen Jones.*

Sidney Poitier is featured in the film *Blackboard Jungle.*

Visual artist Charles White completes *Jazz (Jimmy Rushing Sings The Blues),* in celebration of black music and musicians.

Segregation in interstate bus travel is banned by the Interstate Commerce Commission.

Roy Wilkins becomes executive secretary of the NAACP.

Dancer/choreographer Arthur Mitchell dances with the New York City Ballet company, becoming the first black to dance with a major company.

Dancer Carmen de Lavellade joins the dance company of New York's Metropolitan Opera Company.

Dr. Jonas E. Salk develops a vaccine to fight polio.

Rosa Parks refuses to give up her bus seat (December 5). With the leadership of Martin Luther King, Jr., the 381-day Montgomery Bus Boycott begins.

Fourteen-year-old Emmett Till is lynched in Mississippi.

Iku:

Stride pianist/composer James P. Johnson dies.

Saxophonist Charlie Parker dies of a heart attack.

 **1956**

Agba:

Classical composer Regina A. Harris Baiocchi is born in Chicago, Illinois.

Entertainer Yvonne LaToya Jackson is born in Gary, Indiana.

Jazz singer Dianne Reeves is born in Detroit, Michigan.

Jazz saxophonist George Howard is born in Philadelphia, Pennsylvania.

Kuumba:

Dick Clark becomes the host of the *Bandstand* television dance party, a show that introduces the technique of lip-synching for the performance of popular hit records.

R&B groups tour the country, performing on the grits and gravy circuit. They appear at a group of theatres that include the Apollo in New York, the Flame in Detroit, the Howard in Washington, D.C., the Regal in Chicago, the Royal in Baltimore and the Royal Peacock in Atlanta.

R&B group the Platters have a hit with *My Prayer,* and become the first black group to have a hit at the top of the pop charts.

R&B group The Five Satins record *In the Still of the Night,* a classic doo-wop song known for its "shoo-doo-shoo-be-doo" background. The song has come to symbolize the music of the 1950s.

Rock 'n' Roll artist Elvis Presley records *Heartbreak Hotel,* and has a megahit covering Big Mama Thornton's song, *Hound Dog.* He becomes the "King of Rock and Roll," after performing on the Ed Sullivan television show. During his career, he performs a number of works composed by black songwriter Otis Blackwell, including *Don't Be Cruel, All Shook Up* and *Return to Sender.*

The Del-Vikings release the pop/R&B hit *Come Go With Me,* the first hit by a racially mixed group.

R&B singer Ivory Joe Hunter records *Since I Met You Baby.*

The Dells release the R&B hit *Oh What a Nite,* distinguished by its use of call and response.

R&B singer Fats Domino records *I'm In Love Again* and *Blueberry Hill.*

R&B singers Shirley and Lee, the Sweethearts of the Blues, have a hit with *Let The Good Times Roll,* selling over a million copies

R&B group The Clovers record *Devil or Angel.*

R&B singer Clyde McPhatter records *Treasure of Love.*

R&B singer Chuck Berry records *Roll Over, Beethoven.*

R&B singer James Brown records his first hit, *Please, Please, Please!.* The song is built on one word and his electrifying screams. It becomes popular with both black and white audiences. He continues building a career that encompasses over one hundred and fourteen hits.

R&B artist William "Bill" Doggett records the popular *Honky Tonk.*

R&B singer Aretha Franklin begins to record for the Chess label.

R&B singer Tina Turner joins Ike and his Kings of Rhythm band in St. Louis, Missouri.

R&B singer Little Richard appears in the rock 'n' roll film *The Girl Can't Help It.* He also records *Long Tall Sally.*

R&B singers Frankie Lymon and the Teenagers have an R&B and Pop chart hit with *Why Do Fools Fall In Love.* The song is subsequently covered by white singers—Gale Storm and again by The Diamonds.

Ray Charles records *Drown in My Own Tears*, using gospel piano style as accompaniment.

Jimmy Smith begins to champion the use of the electric organ in rhythm and blues combos and jazz.

Art Blakey, Donald Byrd and The Jazz Messengers record the album *Hard Bop.*

Jazz pianist Cecil Taylor makes his first major recording, *Jazz Advance.*

Dizzy Gillespie's band undertakes a U.S. State Department goodwill tour, traveling through the Middle East and South America, becoming the first jazz band to be sent abroad by the U.S. Government.

Duke Ellington signs a contract with Columbia Records, and introduces his music to a younger audience by performing at the Newport Jazz Festival.

Jazz trombonist Melba Liston establishes an all-female band.

Jazz pianist/singer Nat King Cole is beaten by six white Citizens Council members at a concert in Birmingham, Alabama.

Gospel singer Mahalia Jackson appears at the Newport Jazz Festival in Rhode Island.

The Staple Singers release the gospel hit *Uncloudy Days,* with Mavis Staples on lead.

Singer Lena Horne appears in the film *Meet Me in Las Vegas.*

Entertainer Sammy Davis appears in the Broadway musical *Mr. Wonderful.*

Mattiwilda Dobbs makes her Metropolitan Opera debut, becoming the second black female to appear with this company.

Hale Smith composes *Five Songs for Mezzo Soprano and Violin.*

Lyric soprano Leontyne Price stars in the NBC-TV opera performance of *The Magic Flute.*

The autobiography of Marian Anderson is published, *My Lord, What a Morning.*

Actor/bass-baritone/political activist Paul Robeson is called to appear before the House Committee on American Activities. Committee members seek to label him a Communist subversive.

The United States State Department sends composer/conductor William Levi Dawson to Spain to conduct.

Conductor Everett Lee settles in Europe to find work.

Entertainer Josephine Baker retires to France to devote herself to her "rainbow family."

Geoffrey Holder joins the dance company of the Metropolitan Opera Company.

Martin Luther King, Jr.'s Montgomery, Alabama home is bombed.

A Prayer Pilgrimage takes 15,000 people to the Lincoln Memorial to draw attention to the need for the passage of civil rights legislation.

The Supreme Court rules Alabama's bus segregation to be unconstitutional.

The Post-Colonial era begins in Africa with the independence of Ghana.

Dwight D. Eisenhower is reelected president of the United States.

The first African American student at the University of Alabama, Autherine Lucy, enrolls.

Floyd Patterson becomes the youngest heavyweight boxing champion.

Althea Gibson wins the French Open, the first African American to win a Grand Slam tennis title.

Transatlantic telephone service begins.

Iku:

Jazz trumpeter Clifford Brown dies in a car accident.

Jazz pianist Art Tatum dies.

 **1957**

Agba:

R&B singer Stephanie Mills is born in New York.

Soul/pop singer Marlon David Jackson (of The Jackson Five) is born in Gary, Indiana.

Gospel singer Tremaine Hawkins is born in San Francisco, California.

Drummer Herlin Riley (of Wynton Marsalis Sextet) is born in New Orleans, Louisiana.

Kuumba:

Jazz educator/band conductor/arranger Gunther Schuller coins the phrase "Third Stream," for music that combines the jazz tradition with the European music tradition. The title assumes that the First Stream is concert-hall music, the Second Stream is jazz, and the Third Stream is the combination of one and two.

The soul/funk movement begins as a sub-genre of jazz, as exemplified by jazz organist Jimmy Smith and jazz guitarist Wes Montgomery.

Jazz bassist Charles Mingus records *Reincarnation of a Lovebird,* as tribute to Charlie Parker.

Miles Davis records the album *Miles Ahead.* He also improvises music for the Louis Malle film *Ascenseur pour l'echafaud.*

Jazz composer Duke Ellington writes a major work for a television special—*A Drum Is A Woman.*

Jazz vocal trio Lambert, Hendricks and Ross begin recording sophisticated scat interpretations of the music of Count Basie, John Coltrane, Miles Davis and others.

Jazz vocalist Ella Fitzgerald records the *Duke Ellington Song Book,* one of the series of albums she makes that are dedicated to a single composer.

Jazz vocalist Sarah Vaughn has hits with *Embraceable You* and *Summertime.*

Quincy Jones does an international tour with Lionel Hamptons band.

Julian "Cannonball" Adderley and Sonny Rollins join the Miles Davis ensemble. John Coltrane leaves the ensemble.

Singer Nat King Cole has a television show on NBC that is on the air for 64 weeks.

Pop/ballad singer Johnny Mathis has three major hits—*It's Not For Me To Say, Wonderful, Wonderful* and *Chances Are.* He acquires the title the *King of Necking Music.*

Singer Harry Belafonte has pop hits with *Banana Boat Song,* and *Day-O.*

Singer Lena Horne appears in the Broadway musical *Jamaica,* composed by Harold Arlen and produced by David Merrick. The show arrives on Broadway with a $1,300,000 advance ticket sale.

Singer Sam Cooke crosses over to the genre of R&B from the gospel group The Soul Stirrers. He first records *Lovable,* and subsequently has a hit with *You Send Me,* selling 1.7 million copies.

R&B group The Coasters have two number one recordings—*Searchin'* and *Young Blood.* It is typical of the songs they produce with lyrics that address the real life and times of teenage America.

The Chantels record their first R&B hits *He's Gone* and *The Plea.* They become the first of the successful girl groups, distinguished by their four-part, a cappela harmony.

Shirley Owens, Doris Coley, Addie Micki Harris and Beverly Lee begin singing together at Passaic High School in Passaic, New Jersey. They start using the name The Poquellos, and change to The Shirelles in 1958.

The R&B group, the Five Royales, records *Dedicated To The One I Love.*

R&B group The Dubs record *Could This Be Magic.*

R&B singer Jackie Wilson has a hit with *Reet Petite* (written by Berry Gordy).

R&B singers Huey (Piano) Smith and the Clowns record the hit *Rockin' Pneumonia and the Boogie Woogie Flu* for Ace Records.

R&B singer Fats Domino has a hit with *I'm Walkin'.* The song is later covered by Ricky Nelson.

The Drifters release the R&B hit *Fools Fall In Love.*

R&B singer Jimmy McCracklin has a hit with *The Walk.*

R&B group The Bobbettes record *Mr. Lee.*

Berry Gordy, Jr. begins to produce records in Detroit, Michigan.

The white participation in the rock and roll genre continues to expand and crosses over into the R&B charts when Jerry Lee Lewis has a hit with *Whole Lot of Shakin'.* He also has a hit with *Great Balls of Fire,* a song that was composed by black songwriter Otis Blackwell.

Hartley Peavey sees a performance by Bo Diddley and is so impressed that he decides to become a musician. His performance abilities are minimal, and instead, he becomes the CEO of Peavy Electronics, building musical equipment (amplifiers and other types of sound equipment). The company reaches a pinnacle in the 1990's when his company develops the Media Matrix System, a software-based sound system.

Bandstand becomes *American Bandstand,* a popular national show on the ABC television network, with Dick Clark as host communicating a clean-cut image for the rebellious music of R & R. The show becomes a primary vehicle for the promotion of popular music, particularly popular music by white performers.

The Clara Ward Singers participate in a national tour as part of the Big Gospel Cavalcade. They become the first gospel group to perform at the Newport Jazz Festival.

Gospel composer/conductor Doris Akers establishes the Los Angeles Sky Pilot Radio Choir, and composes *You Can't Beat God Giving.*

Composer/pianist George Walker writes *Sonata No. 2* for piano and *Concerto for Trombone and Orchestra.*

Lyric Soprano Leontyne Price stars in the NBC-TV opera performance of *Dialogues of the Carmelites.*

The Stroll becomes a popular dance.

Henry "Hank" Aaron is voted the most valuable player in the National League, and wins the home run title.

Tennis star Althea Gibson wins at Wimbledon.

President Eisenhower orders federal troops to Little Rock, Arkansas, as Central High School is desegregated.

The Civil Rights Act is passed by Congress - the first Civil Rights act since Reconstruction.

Television sets can be found in 80% of all U.S. homes (30 million sets).

Harry Belafonte and Dorothy Dandridge are featured in the film *Island in the Sun*, a movie that was the first to explore the theme of interracial love.

The Southern Christian Leadership Conference (SCLC) is organized.

Dorothy Height becomes the head of the National Council of Negro Women.

Russia launches Sputnik 1, the first space satellite.

Iku:

Jazz bassist Walter Sylvester Page dies.

 **1958**

Agba:

Singer Anita Baker is born in Toledo, Ohio.

Singer/composer Prince (Prince Roger Nelson) is born in Minneapolis, Minnesota.

Jazz drummer Kenny Washington is born.

Soul/Pop singer Michael Joseph Jackson is born in Gary, Indiana.

Jazz drummer Lewis Nash is born in Phoenix, Arizona.

Kuumba:

Curtis Mayfield, Jerry Butler, Sam Gooden, Richard Brooks and Arthur Brooks, friends from Chicagos Cabrini Housing Project, form the Soul group - The Impressions. They record what some identify as the first Soul hit, a song arranged in a ballad style that breaks away from the doo-wop concept—*For Your Precious Love*.

Eddie Levert, William Powell, Walter Williams, Bill Isles and Bob Massey form The Triumphs at McKinley High School in Canton, Ohio. The group eventually becomes The O'Jays.

R&B singer Clyde McPhatter achieves success for his solo career with the hit *A Lover's Question*.

James Brown starts his solo career with the R&B recording of *Try Me*.

R&B singer Lloyd Price records the popular *Stagger Lee*, a version of the country blues hit, *Stack O'Lee Blues* or *Stagolee*.

R&B singer/guitarist/composer Chuck Berry records *Sweet Little Sixteen, Reelin' and Rockin'*, and *Johnny B. Goode.*

Harvey and the Moonglows record the R&B hit *Ten Commandments of Love.*

Berry Gordy composes the R&B song *Lonely Teardrops* for Jackie Wilson.

R&B group The Chantels release *Maybe,* and record *I Love You So.*

The Shirelles record the R&B hit *I Met Him On A Sunday.*

R&B group Little Anthony & The Imperials have a hit with *Tears On My Pillow.*

The Platters release the R&B hits *Twilight Time* and *Smoke Gets in Your Eyes.*

White singer Peggy Lee has a hit with the Little Willie John song *Fever.*

Little Willie John records the R&B hit *Talk to Me, Talk to Me.*

Little Richard records *Good Golly, Miss Molly.*

The Coasters release the popular R&B hit *Yakety Yak* with *Zing Went the Strings of My Heart* on the flip side.

The Silhouettes have a hit with *Get a Job.*

White Citizens Councils describe rock 'n' roll as "sexualistic and unmoralistic."

Blues artist Muddy Waters tours Europe.

The stereo is introduced.

California's Monterey Jazz Festival is organized.

Art Blakey and the Jazz Messengers (with Lee Morgan, Benny Golson and Bobby Timmons) record the definitive hard bop album, *Moanin.*

Jazz trumpeter Miles Davis records the album *Milestones*, including the first example of melodic improvisations using modal scales.

Saxophonist Sonny Rollins composes and records the jazz suite *The Freedom Suite* (with Oscar Pettiford and Max Roach), an extended composition that celebrates the black experience. Its program notes explain: *America is deeply rooted in Negro culture: its colloquialisms, its humor, its music. How ironic that the Negro, who more than any other people can claim Americas culture as his own, is being persecuted and repressed, that the Negro, who has exemplified the humanities in his very existence, is being rewarded with inhumanity.*

Jazz drummer Cozy Cole records the solo record *Topsy,* the only drum solo record to sell more than a million copies.

Duke Ellington composes *Satin Doll.*

Jazz singer Billie Holiday records her last album, *Lady in Satin.*

Erroll Garner becomes the first jazz pianist to appear in concert at New York's Carnegie Hall.

St. Louis Blues, the film version of W. C. Handys life is released, starring balladeer Nat King Cole. It includes a cameo appearance by Ella Fitzgerald.

Gospel singer Mahalia Jackson performs at the Newport Jazz Festival.

Gospel singer Shirley Caesar joins the female group, the Caravans.

Singer Johnny Mathis performs the title song of the movie *A Certain Smile.*

Soprano Leontyne Price makes her debut with the Vienna State Opera, performing the title role in *Aida.*

Mezzo-soprano Betty Allen makes her concert debut at Town Hall in New York.

Mezzo-Soprano Shirley Verrett makes her concert debut at New York's Town Hall.

Marian Anderson is appointed by President Eisenhower as a delegate to the 13th General Assembly of the United Nations.

Classical composer Ulysses Kay serves as a cultural ambassador to Russia.

The film *The Defiant Ones* is released, featuring Sidney Poitier. He becomes the first black male to be nominated for an Academy Award.

Eartha Kitt and Sammy Davis, Jr. star in the film *Anna Lucasta.*

The National Aeronautics and Space Administration (NASA) is established.

The Alvin Ailey American Dance Theater is founded in New York

Dancer Arthur Mitchell becomes the first black member of a classical ballet company, the New York City Ballet.

Iku:

Blues composer W. C. Handy dies.

Blues singer Big Bill Bronzy dies of lung cancer.

 **1959**

Agba:

Soul singer Sade (Helen Folasade Adu) is born in Ibada, Nigeria.

R&B singer Freddie Jackson is born in New York City.

White jazz bassist John Patitucci is born in Brooklyn, New York.

Jazz bassist Marcus Miller is born in Brooklyn, New York.

Rap artist Kurtis Blow is born in New York City.

Kuumba:

Berry Gordy, Jr. becomes the founder of Detroit's Motown Records (originally called Hitsville, USA). He gradually signs Smokey Robinson and the Miracles, the Marvelettes, the Primes (the Temptations), Little Stevie Wonder, the Contours, Mary Wells, the Supremes, the Jackson Five, the songwriting team Holland-Dozier-Holland, and others, and their R&B sound reaches an even larger audience. This begins to transition into the Soul Music phase of the Blues.

R&B bassist James Jamerson joins Motown. He becomes part of the rhythm section that establishes the foundation for all the major hits of the label (with Benny Benjamin on drums, James Giddons on percussion, Earl Van Dyke on keyboards, and Joe Messina, Robert White, Eddie Willis and Dennis Coffey on guitar). He inspires the development of rock guitarist Paul McCartney and numerous others.

R&B ensemble The Drifters record *There Goes My Baby, This Magic Moment* and *Save the Last Dance For Me* with Ben E. King as lead singer. It utilizes more sophisticated arrangements, including strings and timpani, and studio production techniques.

R&B group The Flamingos record *I Only Have Eyes For You,* a classic doo-wop song.

The Clovers record the R&B hit *Love Potion #9.*

R&B group The Skyliners record *Since I Don't Have You.*

The Coasters record the R&B hits *Charlie Brown, Along Came Jones* and *Poison Ivy.*

R&B singer Brook Benton crosses over to the R&B genre from the gospel group The Jerusalem Stars. He has hits with *It's Just a Matter of Time* and *Thank You Pretty Baby.*

Ray Charles records *What'd I Say,* and *Georgia On My Mind.* He also begins to champion the use of the electric piano.

The Falcons release the R&B hit *You're So Fine.*

The Isley Brothers record the R&B hit *Shout,* Parts I and II.

Little Anthony and the Imperials release the novelty R&B hit *Shimmy Shimmy Ko-Ko Bop.*

The Olympics record the R&B hit *Hully Gully.*

The Marcels are formed as an R&B group in Pittsburgh, Pennsylvania.

Composer Margaret Bonds writes the song cycle *Three Dream Portraits*, using the poetry of Langston Hughes ("I, Too," "Dream Variation," and "Minstrel Man").

Martina Arroyo debuts at the Metropolitan Opera in *Don Carlos*.

Gospel singer Bessie Griffin performs at New Orleans Cabaret Concert Theatre.

A new gospel group is organized - The Mighty Clouds of Joy. They meet at Jefferson High School in Los Angeles and eventually become one of the most popular gospel groups of the 1960s and 1970s.

James Cleveland starts the gospel group The Gospel Chimes.

Singer/actor Harry Belafonte becomes the first black to have an hour-long television special. In this same year he is responsible for bringing South African singer Miriam Makeba to the United States.

Porgy & Bess is released as a film, starring Sidney Poitier, Dorothy Dandridge and Sammy Davis, Jr.

Congress completes its investigation of rigged television quiz shows and goes on to hold hearings about AM radio's "Top Forty" programming payola, focusing upon the practice of paying disc jockeys to get them to play a record.

Singer Ella Fitzgerald becomes the first black woman to win a Grammy Award - for *The Irving Berlin Songbook*. In this same year she records the five-record set *Gershwin Song Book* - another of the series of albums she makes that are dedicated to a single composer—including her popular rendition of "Oh, Lady Be Good."

Singer Della Reese records the hit *Not One Minute More*.

Jazz artist Nina Simone has a national hit with the recording of the Gershwin piece, *I Loves You Porgy*.

Jazz/Blues vocalist Dinah Washington has a hit with *What A Difference A Day Makes*.

Jazz singer Sarah Vaughn has a hit with *Broken-Hearted Melody*.

Third Stream jazz ensemble, The Modern Jazz Quartet, performs at the International Festival of Contemporary Music, a festival of European contemporary music.

The Dave Brubeck Quartet (with Paul Desmond, Joe Morello and Gene Wright) records *Time Out,* an album that includes the popular selections "Blue Rondo a la Turk" and "Take Five" (a piece distinguished by its use of 5/4 and 7/8 meter).

Jazz bassist Charles Mingus records *Blues and Roots.*

Jazz critic Leonard Feather composes *Twelve-Tone Blues,* a piece that he says was the first jazz composition to use serial compositional technique.

Ornette Coleman makes his New York debut at The Five Spot, performing an unpredictable "harmolodic" style that had a controversial impact upon the audience. He releases the album *The Shape of Jazz To Come.*

Miles Davis releases the album *Kind of Blue,* incorporating the use of modal scales in jazz.

Trumpeter Jazz band conductor/arranger Quincy Jones becomes musical director of the European tour of Harold Arlen's opera *Free and Easy.*

Otto Preminger's film *Anatomy of a Murder* features the music of Duke Ellington.

Brazilian Antonio Carlos Jobim is credited with originating the "bossa nova" style, using the term itself for the first time in the lyrics of the song *Desafinado.*

Centralto Marian Anderson is appointed to the Human Rights Committee as part of the U.S. Delegation to the United Nations.

The Cuban Revolution occurs, followed by a U.S. imposed cultural embargo and resulting in massive immigration into the United States (1959-1980). Afro-Cuban music and Afro-Cuban and Haitian religious practices are imported and/or revitalized (e.g. Santeria, Abakwa, Vodun) in the United States.

Poet/Playwright Derek Walcott founds the Trinidad Theatre Workshop.

Martin Luther King, Jr. spends time in India studying Gandhi's techniques of nonviolence.

W. E. B. DuBois wins the Lenin Peace Prize.

Ethel Waters appears in the film *The Sound and the Fury.*

Iku:

Jazz saxophonist Lester (Prez) Young.

Singer Billie Holiday dies.

Jazz saxophonist Sidney Bechet dies.

R&B singer Eddie Guitar Slim Jones dies.

Blues singer Blind Willie McTell dies of a brain hemorrhage.

Margaret Bonds

Mahalia Jackson

Leontyne Price

William Warfield

Buddy Collette

6

1960 - 1969
THE MUSIC OF CIVIL RIGHTS
AND CULTURAL REVOLUTION

Psychological and cultural transformation is generated within the African American community and within the nation as a whole by the politics of this era. The religious, popular and art musical forms of this period become the expression of the political movements of the era. Most significantly, the genres in these three categories interact with each other, driven by both the unifying search for social justice and cultural affirmation, and the quest for economic viability.

In this decade jazz reaches out to the church. The church reaches out to the popular R&B audience. African American performers and creators of Americanized music of the European classical tradition reach out to the black folk and popular musical voice. And increasingly, all the genres reach out to the musics of the African Diaspora.

The decade begins with a variety of jazz artists experimenting with new styles while articulating political protest through their music. It ends with Miles Davis and the Woodstock Festival opening the door to the Fusion style.

TRENDS
1960 - 1969

1960s

❧ A decade of political activism and a black cultural revolution that is sometimes called the Second Renaissance, with an over-arching theme of *Black Is Beautiful.*

❧ *We Shall Overcome* becomes the anthem of the Civil Rights movement, with verses being added: *1) We are not afraid; 2) We are not alone; 3) The Truth will make us free; 4) Well walk hand in hand; 5) The Lord will see us through; 6) Black and white together; 7) We will end Jim Crow; 8) We shall live in peace; 9) We shall all be free.*

❧ The avant-garde/"free jazz" movement emerges (centered in New York, Chicago and Los Angeles) with its controversial experiments in the practice of simultaneous improvisation. It is often described as being the musical voice of the Black Power movement. The use of 20th-century non-jazz techniques begins, including the use of modal, atonal and twelve-note methods. Some musicians begin to reject the use of the term "jazz" because they feel the term has become synonymous with the exploitation of black musicians and discrimination in popular music programming in the "cockroach capitalism" found in jazz clubs (as described by author Frank Kofsky).

❧ The Black Muslim Movement inspires an increasing interest in the music and performance practices of Africa, as reflected in the work of jazz and classical musicians.

❧ Louis Armstrong and his contemporaries start a New Orleans traditional jazz revival effort at Preservation Hall.

❧ A community of scholars work to define the Black aesthetic, as seen in the writings of Amiri Baraka, Rhonda Davis, Mari Evans, Hoyt Fuller, Addison Gayle, Maulana Karenga, Woodie King, Haki Madhubuti (Don L. Lee), Ron Milner, Larry Neal, Dudley Randall, and Sonia Sanchez. Artists whose work does not reflect the ideology of Black nationalism are often criticized.

꠶ A variety of "girl groups," emerge as the major popular artists of R&B, including The Chantels, The Shirelles, The Dixie Cups, Martha & The Vandellas, The Marvelettes, The Shangri-Las, The Chiffons, The Ronettes, The Blossoms, Patti LaBelle and the Blue Belles and The Supremes. This is a popular ensemble type from 1958 to 1965. Packaged in miniskirts, wigs, sequins and feathers, these groups give young black women a taste of glamour (most often as defined by white culture).

꠶ R&B transitions into Soul Music, as produced regionally in Detroit (Motown), Memphis (Stax), New York (Atlantic), Los Angeles (Warner Brothers/United Artists), Chicago (Curtom) and Philadelphia (The Philly Sound). As performed by Aretha Franklin, James Brown, Curtis Mayfield, Sam Cooke and others, this is music that gives popular voice to the political and social issues of the day. It also provides economic competition to the British invasion of the Beatles, The Rolling Stones and others. Additionally, a slick, pop/soul style evolves as performed by groups like the Delfonics, the O'Jays, and the Fifth Dimension.

꠶ Blues artists such as Lightnin' Hopkins, John Lee Hooker, B.B. King, Albert King, and Muddy Waters become international stars, achieving new popularity through their European tours.

꠶ The national profile of gospel music increases as gospel singers begin to perform in the gospel musical of the Broadway stage, in nightclubs and at the White House. At the same time, gospel music remains the music of the people, as sung by civil rights marchers, local church choirs, and by newly created college gospel choirs. The national commercial appeal is firmly established through the popular crossover recordings of The Edwin Hawkins Singers and others.

꠶ Black musicians gain national recognition for performance in the genre of Country Music.

꠶ The Reggae style originates in Jamaica, inspired by African music, R&B, the internationally popular Jamaican folk music known as Ska, and the Rastafarian religious movement.

꠶ Ragtime becomes the fun entertainment at commercial sites such as Shakey's Pizza Parlors.

ʖ The cultural practices of various Caribbean countries are imported to the United States via immigration.

ʖ African American composers of the Americanized classical genre increasingly express themselves in contemporary serial, atonal and electronic modes while often creating compositions that address aspects of African American culture and history. The black performers of music in the European classical tradition continue to build extraordinary careers as vocal and instrumental soloists. At the same time these performers battle barriers in some fields, particularly the talented musicians seeking to become orchestral conductors and orchestra members and males who seek to become opera singers.

ʖ The classical music notation system begins to change, removing the limitations imposed by the diatonic scale. This particularly facilitates the notation of microtonality.

ʖ The era of the Black Art Movement, as seen in the art of Jacob Lawrence, John Biggers, David Driskell, Murray DePillars, Bettye Ann Saar, Noah Purifoy, John Outterbridge, Varnette Honeywood, Jeff Donaldson, Ruth Waddy, Faith Ringgold, and many other artists who incorporate black themes into their creativity.

ʖ Steps are taken to dismantle Jim Crow laws and to implement equal opportunity laws for women and racial minorities. Multiple movements for equal rights are energized, e.g. women, Latinos.

ʖ The decade of white flight from the urban centers to the suburbs.

ʖ A period of urban riots.

ʖ The era of student protests that ultimately results in the development of Afro-American Studies curriculum for colleges across the country.

ʖ The age of protest music responding to issues that are part of the Vietnam War protest/The Age of Aquarius/The age of the flower child/The age of the Free Speech Movement.

ʖ The era of assassinations.

ʖ Television changes the speed and content of communications and drastically affects the social fabric of the United States.

ACHIEVEMENT DATELINE
1960 - 1969

 **1960**

Agba:

Jazz saxophonist Branford Marsalis is born in New Orleans.

Rap artist Afrika Bambaataa is born in New York City.

Kuumba:

Ornette Coleman (together with Eric Dolphy, Don Cherry, Freddie Hubbard, Scott LaFaro, Charlie Haden, Billy Higgins, and Ed Blackwell) releases the album *Free Jazz*, using two quartets and providing an example of free group improvisation (recorded on an album that is released with a Jackson Pollock album cover). Free jazz (improvisation without the restrictions of harmonic patterns and regularized rhythm) becomes the controversial musical expression of the Black Power movement. A *Downbeat* Double View review presents the competing viewpoints regarding this new musical style. Critic Pete Welding gives the album a rating of five stars:

> *In first hearing, Free Jazz strikes one as a sprawling, discursive,*
> *chaotic jumble of jagged rhythms and pointless cacophonies, among*
> *which however are interlarded a number of striking solo segments...*
> *On repeated listening, however, the form of the work gradually reveals*
> *itself, and it is seen that the piece is far less unconventional than it*
> *might at first appear. It does not break with jazz tradition; rather, it*
> *restores to currency an element that has been absent in most jazz since*
> *the onset of the swing orchestra—-spontaneous group improvisation...*
> *It is a powerful and challenging work of real conviction and honest*
> *emotion.*

Whereas critic John A. Tynan gives the album a rating of no stars:

> *It's every man-jack for himself in an eight-man emotional regurgita-*
> *tion...Where does neurosis end and psychosis begin? The answer must*
> *lie somewhere within this malestrom. If nothing else, this witch's brew*

*is the logical end product of a bankrupt philosophy of ultraindividual-
ism in music. "Collective improvisation?" Nonsense. The only
semblance of collectivity lies in the fact that these eight nihilists were
collected together in one studio at one time and with one common
cause: to destroy the music that gave them birth. Give them top marks
for the attempt. DownBeat, February 1, 1962.*

Jazz performers Max Roach and Abbey Lincoln collaborate on the
recording *We Insist! Freedom Now!,* reflecting a heightened political
awareness.

Alto saxophonist Eric Dolphy releases his first records, *Outward Bound*
and *Out There.*

The Modern Jazz Quartet releases the album *Third Stream Music,*
incorporating the use of European musical forms and instrumentation.

Saxophonist John Coltrane forms his own group (with McCoy Tyner,
Jimmy Garrison, Elvin Jones, Steve Davis, and, sometimes, Eric Dolphy), recording his first popular hit, *My Favorite Things* (with Coltrane
performing polytonality on the soprano saxophone).

Bassist Charles Mingus records *Fables of Faubus,* inspired by his con-
tempt for Arkansas Governor Orville Faubus.

Duke Ellington does an arrangement for jazz orchestra of Russian composer Tchaikovsky's *Nutcracker Suite.*

Ella Fitzgerald appears in the film *Let No Man Write My Epitaph.*

Jazz band conductor/arranger Quincy Jones forms a big band which
tours Europe and the United States.

South African trumpeter Hugh Masekela comes to New York to study
at the Manhattan School of Music.

The Hall Johnson Choir gives its last public performance.

Gospel singer James Cleveland has a hit with *The Love of God.*

Alex Bradford conducts and records with the Abyssinian Baptist
Gospel Choir.

Stax Records is established in Memphis, Tennessee, by white owners

Jim Stewart and Estelle Axton and goes on to record several Soul music acts, including Rufus Thomas, Carla Thomas, and Booker T. & the M.G.s.

Soprano Grace Bumbry makes her debut with the Paris Opera Company.

Lyric Soprano Leontyne Price stars in the NBC-TV performance of *Don Giovanni.*

The House of Representatives holds hearings to investigate potential commercial bribery and disc jockey Alan Freed is indicted for accepting payola.

The Ike and Tina Turner R&B Revue begins touring.

R&B (DooWop) artists The Satintones have the first Motown hit—*My Beloved/Sugar Daddy.*

Smokey Robinson and the Miracles record *Shop Around*, Motown's first Top 10 hit.

The Drifters release the hits *This Magic Moment* and *Save The Last Dance For Me.*

Harold Melvin and the Blue Notes release the R&B hit *My Hero.*

R&B singer James Brown has a hit with *Do The Mashed Potatoes.*

The Platters release the R&B hit *Harbor Lights.*

R&B singer Fats Domino has a hit with *Walking to New Orleans.*

Paul Williams, Otis Williams, Melvin Franklin, Eddie Kendricks & Elbridge Bryant form The Temptations.

Creadel Jones, Clarence Johnson, Robert (Squirrel) Lester, Eugene Record and Marshall Thompson form The Chi-Lites.

Chubby Checker records *The Twist*, starting a national dance craze with his appearance on Dick Clark's *American Bandstand.*

Sam Cooke has a hit, *Chain Gang.* He also establishes the Sar/Derby Recording Company.

R&B singer Jackie Wilson has a hit with *Doggin' Around.*

Ray Charles records the R&B hit *Georgia On My Mind.*

R&B group The Shirelles record *Will You Still Love Me Tomorrow.*

R&B artists Dinah Washington and Brook Benton release the duet *Baby, You've Got What It Takes.*

Harry Belafonte wins an Emmy Award for the television special *Tonight With Harry Belafonte.*

73.2% of the black population live in urban areas, while 26.8% live in rural areas.

Comedian Jackie "Moms" Mabley makes her first album.

Martin Luther King, Jr., is arrested at a sit-in at an Atlanta department store and sentenced to four months of hard labor. He is released after presidential candidate John F. Kennedy posts bail.

Wilma Rudolph becomes a triple Olympic gold medalist (winning the 100-meter, the 200-meter and the 400-meter relays).

Floyd Patterson becomes the first boxer to regain the heavyweight title, defeating Ingemar Johansson.

Student sit-ins at an F. W. Woolworth lunch counter in Greensboro, North Carolina begin wide-scale student involvement in the Civil Rights Movement.

President Dwight Eisenhower signs the Civil Rights Act of 1960.

John F. Kennedy is elected president of the United States.

Iku:

Jazz bassist Oscar Pettiford dies.

R&B singer/songwriter Jesse Belvin dies in a car crash.

Composer Clarence Cameron White dies.

 **1961**

Agba:

Jazz trumpeter Wynton Marsalis is born in New Orleans, Louisiana.

Soul/pop singer Steven Randall (Randy) Jackson (of The Jackson Five) is born in Gary, Indiana.

Classical composer Gregory T. S. Walker is born in Northhampton, Massachusetts.

Kuumba:

A very active year for the Freedom Riders who ride into Alabama singing songs adapted to familiar melodies such as *Yankee Doodle:*

> *Freedom Riders came to town; Riding on the railway; Mississippi locked them up; Said you can't even use Trailways; Mississippi, you are wrong; You've gone against the nation; We'll keep coming big and strong; And we'll end segregation.*

Jazz artist John Coltrane records the album *Live at the Village Vanguard,* including the tribute "Song of the Underground Railroad."

The Modern Jazz Quartet appears with a symphony for the first time, the Cincinnati Symphony.

Singer Carmen McRae releases the album *Yesterdays*, a collection of songs associated with Billie Holiday.

Singer Nat King Cole records *Unforgettable.* The song becomes a hit again a quarter of a century later when his daughter Natalie Cole releases it as a technologically-produced duet.

Jazz stars Louis Armstrong and Duke Ellington appear in the Martin Ritt film *Paris Blues.*

The Gospel musical, *Black Nativity*, opens in an off-Broadway production (script by Langston Hughes, music by Alex Bradford and Marion Williams' new ensemble, The Stars of Faith).

Mahalia Jackson sings at an inauguration party for President John F. Kennedy, a precedent-setting activity in the field of gospel music.

The number of radio stations in the country that provide programming for African American audiences expands to 310.

Leontyne Price debuts with New York's Metropolitan Opera production of *Il Trovatore*.

George Shirley wins the Metropolitan Opera auditions and makes his debut with the company.

Grace Bumbry becomes the first African American to perform a principal role at the Bayreuth Festival, chosen for this role by the grandson of composer Richard Wagner, despite considerable protest. She sings the role of Venus in *Tannhauser.*

Henry Lewis makes his debut conducting the Los Angeles Philharmonic.

Composer Margaret Bonds writes the cantata *Ballad of the Brown King,* with text by Langston Hughes.

Symphony conductor Dean Dixon serves as musical director of the Hesse Radio Symphony Orchestra in Frankfurt, West Germany, until 1974.

Conductor Jester Hairston begins to make State Department tours to Europe. He first tours Germany.

The Marvelettes record the R&B hit *Please, Mr. Postman.*

The Chantels record the R&B hit *Look In My Eyes.*

R&B singer Carla Thomas has a hit with *Gee Whiz (Look at His Eyes).*

The Shirelles have a hit with the songs *Dedicated To The One I Love,* and *Will You Love Me Tomorrow?*

Soul group The Impressions have a hit record with *Gypsy Woman* with Curtis Mayfield as lead singer.

The Drifters release the hit *Some Kind of Wonderful.*

Soul singer Solomon Burke has a hit with *Just Out of Reach of My Two Open Arms.*

R&B singer Ben E. King has a hit with *Stand By Me,* an adaptation of the Soul Stirrers gospel hit *Stand By My Father.*

R&B group The Marcels record *Blue Moon,* with its distinctive intro-duction: *Bomp baba bomp, ba bomp ba bomp bomp, baba bomp baba bomp, da dang da dang dang, da ding a dong ding Blue Moon.*

The Platters release the R&B hit *If I Didn't Care.*

Patricia Holt, Cindy Birdsong, Sarah dash and Nona Henryx form the Blue Belles in Philadelphia. They then change the name to Patti LaBelle and The Blue Belles. They have a hit with *I Sold My Heart To The Junkman.*

Gladys Knight and the Pips record the R&B hit *Every Beat Of My Heart.*

R&B singer Marvin Gaye makes his debut record *Let Your Conscience Be Your Guide.*

The Moonglows release the R&B hit *Blue Velvet.*

R&B singer Lee Dorsey has a hit with *Ya Ya—("Sittin in la la/Waitin' for my ya ya").*

Chubby Checker continues the dance craze with his hit *Let's Twist Again.*

The Vibrations have a hit with *The Watusi.*

R&B singer Gene Chandler records *Duke of Earl.*

Aretha Franklin releases her first album for Columbia Records, *Aretha.*

R&B singer Ray Charles has a hit with *Hit The Road Jack.*

White rock and roll begins to focus upon California surfing songs, as performed by the Beach Boys.

Manned space flights begin in the USSR.

In a split from the National Baptist Convention, U.S.A., Inc., and in support of the Civil Rights Movement and Dr. Martin Luther King, Jr., the Progressive Baptist Convention of America is founded in Cincinnati, Ohio.

CORE, SCLC and other civil rights groups begin Freedom Rides through the South, often encountering violence.

The Ebony Museum of African American History is founded in Chicago by Margaret Taylor Goss Burroughs, later to become the DuSable Museum of African American History.

Raisin In The Sun is released as a film.

Dancer/choreographer Alvin Ailey creates his best known work, *Revelations,* utilizing the music of a group of spirituals.

The Berlin Wall divides the city of Berlin into two halves.

The aborted Bay of Pigs invasion of Cuba occurs.

The Ossie Davis play, *Purlie Victorious* opens on Broadway, costarring Ossie Davis and Ruby Dee.

Iku:

Jazz bassist Scott LaFaro dies in a car crash.

 **1962**

Kuumba:

Rev. Ralph Abernathy introduces the freedom song *Ain't Gonna Let Nobody Turn Me Round* to the demonstrators in Albany, Georgia; and protestors who find themselves in jail, sustain themselves by adapting the spiritual *Oh Mary, Oh Martha* into *Oh Pritchett, Oh Kelly, Oh Pritchett, Open them Cells.*

Motown becomes the new name for Berry Gordy's company, and the decade of Detroit produces sounds for young America.

R&B singer James Brown releases his hit album *Live At The Apollo,*

Vol. 1, an album that remains on the charts for sixty-six weeks. It is a performance that reflects his irresistible funk, precision controlled band, and the flamboyant, screaming showmanship that causes him to be known as the "Hardest-Working Man in Show Business." It is a style that is very influential on Michael Jackson and numerous others.

R&B singers The Isley Brothers record *Twist and Shout* in response to the current dance craze.

R&B artist Sam Cooke records *Twist the Night Away* in response to the current dance craze, covered by The Beatles in 1964.

The Drifters record the R&B hit *There Goes My Baby.*

The Miracles release the hit *You Really Got A Hold On Me.*

The Marvelettes release the hit *Beechwood 4-5789.*

Jerry Butler releases the hits *Moon River* and *Make It Easy On Yourself.*

R&B singer Ray Charles releases the album *Moving Sounds In Country and Western.* He also has a crossover country & western hit with *I Can't Stop Loving You.*

R&B singer Marvin Gaye writes and records *Stubborn Kind of Fella.*

Future R&B artist Martha Reeves becomes a secretary at Motown.

The soul group The Temptations is formed.

Mary Wells records the R&B hit *You Beat Me To The Punch.*

R&B girl group - The Jaynettes, record *Sally Go Round the Roses.*

R&B girl group - The Supremes record their first major record, *Your Heart Belongs To Me.*

The Contours record *Do You Love Me.*

R&B girl group - The Marvelettes record *Please, Mr. Postman* and release the hit *Beechwood 4-5789.*

R&B girl group - The Shirelles record *Soldier Boy.*

R&B artists Booker T. & the MG's record *Green Onions,* Stax first hit.

R&B girl group - The Crystals record *He's a Rebel.*

R&B girl group - The Chiffons, record *He's So Fine* and *One Fine Day.*

Willie Dixon, John Lee Hooker, Shakey Jake, Brownie McGhee, Memphis Slim, Sonny Terry and T-Bone Walker tour western Europe as part of The American Folk Blues Festival. The tour is very successful, stimulating the continuing development of the European blues audience. The Festival becomes an annual event for the next ten years.

Urban blues singer B.B. King continues to tour the country, playing one-night stands in such places as the Rhythm Club of Baton Rouge, Louisiana, Club Handy of Memphis, Tennessee, Club Ebony of Indianola, Mississippi, Cobra Club of Midland, Texas, Club 66 of Shreveport, Louisiana, and the Moulin Rouge Club of Gladwater, Texas.

Quincy Jones produces an album with Little Richard performing gospel music, *It's Real.*

Jazz composer David Baker receives the *Down Beat* New Star award in trombone.

Jazz saxophonist Sonny Rollins returns from retirement and records *What's New.*

Alto saxophonist Eric Dolphy performs the Edgard Varese composition *Density 21.5* at the Ojai Music Festival.

Art Blakey records an album that explores African rhythm/percussion, *The African Beat.*

Trumpeter Miles Davis records the album *Quiet Nights.*

Ella Fitzgerald wins the Grammy Award for best female jazz vocalist of the year.

Gospel singer James Cleveland has a hit with *Peace Be Still.*

Gospel composer Doris Akers composes *Sweet, Sweet Spirit.*

Singer Diahann Carroll appears on Broadway in the Richard Rodgers musical, *No Strings.*

Pop vocalist Nat King Cole has a hit with *Ramblin' Rose.*

Grace Bumbry makes her debut with the Paris Opera Company and at New York's Town Hall. She also performs at the White House at the request of First Lady Jacqueline Kennedy.

Tenor Roland Hayes goes into retirement after giving his last concert at Carnegie Hall.

Hale Smith composes *Contours*, supported by a commission from BMI. It is performed by the Louisville Symphony Orchestra.

Violinist Sanford Allen becomes the first black to hold a permanent position with the New York Philharmonic.

Conductor James Anderson DePreist tours Asia on a State Department cultural exchange. This includes his debut as conductor of the Bangkok Symphony of Thailand. While on the tour he contracts polio.

James Meredith breaks the color line at the University of Mississippi.

SNCC establishes the Free Southern Theatre in Atlanta.

SNCC, CORE and NAACP continue protest marches and sit-ins.

Sammy Davis and Woody Strode are featured in *Sergents Three.*

The United States launches the first communications satellite, Telstar.

Iku:

Opera director Mary Cardwell Dawson dies.

Pianist/singer Carl Rossini Diton dies.

 **1963**

Agba:

Singer Whitney Houston is born in Newark, New Jersey.

Rapper M.C. Hammer is born in Oakland, California.

Bassist Reginald Veal (of Wynton Marsalis Sextet) is born in New Orleans.

Jazz pianist Gonzalo Rubalcaba is born in Havana, Cuba.

Singer/actress Vanessa Williams is born in Tarrytown, New York.

Kuumba:

Nina Simone records the protest song *Mississippi Goddam*! after a church bombing in Birmingham,

> *Alabama: Alabama's got me so upset*
> *Tennessee made me lose my rest*
> *And everybody knows about*
> *Mississippi–Goddam!*

Martin Luther King, Jr., leads more than 500,000 people in the March on Washington, the largest civil rights demonstration in history giving his "I Have a Dream" speech at the Lincoln Memorial. The speech is preceded by a Mahalia Jackson performance of the spiritual *I Been Buked and I Been Scorned.* The Eva Jessye choir is the official choir for the march.

The Roberta Martin Singers (gospel music ensemble) are invited by Gian Carlo Menotti to perform at the Spoleto Festival.

The Ward Singers become the first gospel music group to perform at New York's Radio City Music Hall.

The Langston Hughes musical, *Tambourines To Glory*, opens on Broadway (starring Clara Ward).

Four-track tape cassette becomes available, thereby improving recording technology.

Reverberation becomes an essential technology for guitars in combos, with the production of the Vibro-Verb, the Deluxe Reverb, the Super Reverb and the Twin Reverb.

Martha Reeves and the Vandellas record the R&B hits *Heat Wave* and *Come and Get These Memories*.

The Drifters release the R&B hit *On Broadway.*

The Impressions release the soul hit *It's All Right.*

Soul singer Marvin Gaye records a gospel-blues hit, *Can I Get A Witness?*

Eddie Levert, Walter Williams, Bobby Massey and William Powell form The O'Jays and record their first hit, *Lonely Drifter.*

Major Lance releases the R&B hit *Monkey Time.*

Patti LaBelle and the Blue Belles record their hit *Down The Aisle.*

The Miracles record the hit *Mickey's Monkey.*

The Chiffons record the hit *He's So Fine.*

R&B singer James Brown establishes his own production company.

Country blues singer Mississippi John Hurt is rediscovered and becomes a favorite performer at folk festivals.

Flutist Herbie Mann fuses jazz with Brazilian music in the album *Do the Bossa Nova.*

Jazz musicians begin to exhibit an interest in World music (the music of Asia, Africa and South America).

Stan Getz records the album *The Girl from Ipanema* with bossa nova artists Joao and Astrud Gilberto.

Duke Ellington's *My People* is presented in Chicago on the occasion of the one hundredth anniversary of the Emancipation Proclamation. Also, the Duke Ellington Orchestra tours Africa, Asia, and the Middle East for the U.S. State Department.

White ragtime pianist Max Morath performs with a ragtime quartet at New York's Blue Angel.

William Grant Still's opera, *Highway 1, USA*, premieres at the University of Miami.

Pianist Andre Watts makes a debut performance with the New York Philharmonic.

Soprano Grace Bumbry makes her American opera debut at the Chicago Lyric Opera.

Soprano Adele Addison tours the Soviet Union.

Marian Anderson is given the Presidential Medal of Freedom, by President Lyndon Johnson, becoming the first black woman to receive this award.

Composer/conductor Jester Hairston tours Sweden, Finland, Norway and Denmark for the U.S. State Department.

Lilies of the Field is released as a film. Sidney Poitier, becomes the first black to win an Oscar Award for a starring role. The film includes the performance of Jester Hairstons *Amen* as a musical leitmotiv.

Quincy Jones writes the score for *The Pawnbroker.*

Actress Cicely Tyson becomes a regular on the television series *East Side, West Side.*

The Museum of African Art/Frederick Douglass Institute is founded in Washington, D.C.

Black Scholar magazine is founded.

During demonstrations to protest segregation in Birmingham, Alabama, Martin Luther King, Jr., is arrested and placed in solitary confinement. He writes his famous "Letter from Birmingham Jail," explaining his support for nonviolent civil disobedience.

Medgar Evers is assassinated in Jackson, Mississippi.

President John F. Kennedy is assassinated in Dallas, Texas.

W.E.B. DuBois dies in Accra, Ghana.

Iku:

Blues singer Dinah Washington dies.

Blues artist Elmore James dies.

Gospel composer Lucie Eddie Campbell Williams dies

 **1964**

Agba:

Alto saxophonist Wes Anderson (of Wynton Marsalis Sextet) is born in Brooklyn, New York.

Rap artist Eric Wright (Eazy-E) is born.

Kuumba:

The SCLC develops a massive voter registration effort in Selma Alabama, with protestors singing songs such as *We're Gonna Do What the Spirit Says Do.*

R&B singer Sam Cooke records the R&B civil rights theme song - *A Change is Gonna Come.*

Curtis Mayfield and The Impressions record sermon R&B/civil rights-themed songs - *Keep on Pushing* and *Amen.*

English groups (the Beatles/Rolling Stones) are influenced by blues and rhythm & blues singers, and begin to tour the United States, with the Beatles having a tremendous hit with *I Want to Hold Your Hand.*

The Rolling Stones appear in their U.S. television debut on *Shindig,* requiring the inclusion of blues singer Howlin' Wolf on the same broadcast.

The Supremes record their first national hit, *Where Did Our Love Go,* followed by a series of hits - *Baby, I Need Your Loving - Baby Love-Stop in the Name of Love - Come See About Me.*

The Temptations release the hits *The Way You Do The Things You Do, The Girl's Alright With Me,* and *My Girl (Talking 'Bout).*

The Coasters release the R&B hit *Wild One.*

The Drifters release the R&B hits *Under The Boardwalk* and *Do The Jerk.*

R&B singer Mary Wells has a hit with *My Guy.*

Jerry Butler and Betty Everette record the R&B duet *Let It Be Me.*

Martha and the Vandellas release the hit *Dancing In The Street.*

The Dixie Cups record the R&B hit *Chapel Of Love.*

R&B singer Marvin Gaye has a hit with *How Sweet It Is to be Loved by You.*

The Four Tops have a debut hit with *Baby I Need Your Loving.*

Louis Armstrong challenges the Beatles' number one pop status with his hit recording of *Hello Dolly.*

The Jazz Composers' Guild is established in New York.

Jazz band conductor/arranger Quincy Jones becomes vice president of Mercury Records, the first black to hold a top administrative position in a white-owned record company.

John Coltrane (with Elvin Jones, McCoy Tyner, and Jimmy Garrison) releases the album, *A Love Supreme.* The album, which sells 250,000 copies, celebrates the spiritual principles of Eastern religions (and incorporates vocal chanting). It is structured into four sections, Acknowledgement, Resolution, Pursuance, and Psalm. The album inspires the formation of a church in California.

Jazz saxophonist Albert Alyer forms the Albert Ayler Quintet, a group that performs in the free jazz tradition.

Jazz vocalist Ella Fitzgerald records the *Johnny Mercer Songbook,* one of the series of albums she makes that are dedicated to a single composer.

Jazz vocalist Nancy Wilson has a hit with *How Glad I Am.*

Gospel artist Sister Rosetta Tharpe performs at the Paris Jazz Festival.

The Symphony of the New World is founded in New York to give orchestral experience to black professional musicians.

James DePreist wins the Dimitri Mitropoulos International Music Competition for Conductors.

An elementary school in Chicago, Illinois is named for classical composer Florence Price.

Sammy Davis, Jr., stars in the Broadway musical *Golden Boy.*

Actress/Jazz vocalist Abbey Lincoln appears in the film *Nothing But A Man.*

Pop singer Shirley Bassey performs the theme song of the film *Goldfinger.*

Visual artist Romare Bearden creates the collage *The Prevalence of Ritual: Baptism.*

Malcolm X withdraws from Elijah Muhammads Nation of Islam.

The bodies of civil rights workers James Cheney, Michael Schwerner and Andrew Goodman are discovered in Philadelphia, Mississippi.

Thirty-four black Mississippi churches are burned.

The Mississippi Freedom Democratic Party (MFDP) is established.

Martin Luther King, Jr. is awarded the Nobel Peace Prize.

Lyndon B. Johnson is elected president of the United States.

The U.S. Congress passes the Economic Opportunity Act, starting the War on Poverty, with programs such as Head Start and Upward Bound. It also passes the Civil Rights Act, barring discrimination based on race.

The Free Speech Movement is born at UC Berkeley, led by Mario Savio.

Boxer Cassius Clay changes his name to Muhammad Ali, and knocks out Sonny Liston.

Arthur Ashe wins the American singles tennis championships.

Racial riots break out in Harlem, New York, Chicago, Illinois and Philadelphia, Pennsylvania.

The use of blackface by white comedians finally comes to an end with the death of Eddie Cantor.

Iku:

R&B singer Sam Cooke dies from a gunshot wound.

Jazz clarinetist Eric Dolphy dies.

Jazz trombonist Jack Teagarden dies.

Jazz saxophonist/arranger Don Redman dies.

 **1965**

Agba:

Jazz trombonist Delfeayo Marsalis is born.

Jazz saxophonist Mark Turner is born.

Kuumba:

Civil rights activists continue to use the spiritual as a source for inspiration, such as:

> *Gonna lay down my burden,*
> *Down by the riverside*
> *Down by the riverside*
> *Down by the riverside*
> *Gonna lay down my burden,*
> *Down by the riverside*
> *To study war no more.*

Saxophonist Archie Shepp releases the album *Fire Music,* with its tribute to Malcolm X, Malcolm, Malcolm Semper Malcolm.

John Coltrane releases a free-jazz style album, *Ascension,* featuring his quartet and Marion Brown, Freddie Hubbard, Dewey Johnson, Pharoah Sanders, Archie Shepp and John Tchicai. He is voted top tenor saxophonist and Jazz Man of the Year, and is elected to the Hall of Fame in the annual *Downbeat* magazine readers poll.

Duke Ellington begins to produce sacred jazz concerts (multi-movement cantata-like works for voice, orchestra and dance), beginning with a concert at the Grace Cathedral Church of San Francisco in September, repeated and recorded at Fifth Avenue Presbyterian Church in New York.

Sun Ra releases the mystical jazz album, *The Heliocentric Worlds of Sun Ra*.

Billy Taylor establishes Harlem's Jazzmobile, an organization that gives free concerts.

Jazz pianist Herbie Hancock releases the jazz suite album *Maiden Voyage*, a celebration of the sea.

Don Ellis and Hari Har Rao form the Hindustani Jazz Sextet, a group that fuses jazz with the music of India.

Stan Kenton establishes the Los Angeles Neophonic Orchestra group of studio musicians that performs in the big-band tradition.

The Association for the Advancement of Creative Musicians (a jazz collective) is formed in Chicago, Illinois to sponsor open rehearsals and free concerts featuring original compositions that explored free jazz in a setting that released the artists from commercial pressure. It consisted of over three dozen musicians, including Fred Anderson, Thurman Barker, Anthony Braxton, Charles Clark, Steve McCall, and Leo Smith. Similar groups were created in other areas of the country, including the Black Artists Group of St. Louis and Strata of Detroit.

Jazz band conductor/arranger Quincy Jones composes the score for the film *Mirage*.

Lewis Gilbert's film *Alfie* features the music of jazz saxophonist Sonny Rollins.

Roman Polanski's film *Repulsion* features the music of jazz artist Chico Hamilton.

Thomas Reichman makes a documentary on the life of bassist Charles Mingus - *Mingus*.

Country singer Charley Pride makes his first record, *The Snakes Crawl at Night*. (After RCA executives complete a blind review of the demonstration tape brought to them by Chet Atkins, they learn that the performer is black. There is a pause and they all look back at each other. But they all concur, "We're gonna sign him anyway.") The explanation of the marketing strategy for this first record is interesting, as reported in the <u>Journal of Country Music,</u> vol. 14, no. 2: *In those days, the market in country records was primarily for singles, which were normally shipped with plain white sleeves, so the decision was made not to send out publicity photos until Pride had a hit.* It takes two more records, but Pride finally has a hit in 1966 with *Just Between You and Me* and goes on to have twenty-nine #1 records on the *Billboard* country singles chart between 1966 and 1986, earning twelve gold albums and one gold single.

The eight-track tape cartridge is invented.

R&B singer Otis Redding has a hit song *Respect*, reaching #4 on the R&B charts.

Soul singer Curtis Mayfield and The Impressions record *People Get Ready* and *Meeting Over Yonder.*

WOL Radio in Washington, D.C., begins to advertise itself as "Soul Radio."

R&B singer James Brown takes a forty-piece ensemble on a 340-day tour of the country. He records the hit *Papa's Got a Brand New Bag.*

The Four Tops have R&B hits, *I Can't Help Myself (Sugar Pie, Honey Bunch)* and *The Same Old Song.*

R&B artists Smokey Robinson and the Miracles have their first number one hit - *My Girl.* They also record *Ooo Baby Baby* and *The Tracks Of My Tears.*

The Supremes release the hits *Back In My Arms Again, I Hear A Symphony* and *My World Is Empty Without You.* They become a headliner act at the Copacabana in New York.

Wilson Pickett records the crossover hit *In The Midnight Hour* for Stax Records. The song is perfect for the dance known as the Jerk.

The Dells release the soul/R&B hit *Stay In My Corner.*

Martha and the Vandellas release the hit *Nowhere To Run.*

The Marvelettes release the hit *Don't Mess With Bill.*

Memphis establishes an annual Country Blues Festival.

Henry Lewis is named musical director of the Los Angeles Opera Company.

Grace Bumbry makes her Metropolitan Opera debut.

Soprano Martina Arroyo performs *Aida* at the Metropolitan Opera.

Soprano Leontyne Price receives the Presidential Medal of Freedom.

Contralto Marian Anderson retires, and her nephew, conductor James DePreist, conducts her farewell concert.

Composer/conductor Jester Hairston tours Ghana, Mali, Ivory Coast and Nigeria for the U.S. State Department.

Dorothy Maynor founds the Harlem School of the Arts.

LeRoi Jones (Amiri Baraka) establishes the Black Arts Theatre and School in Harlem.

Gospel singer/songwriter Andrae Crouch forms a gospel/soul band, The Disciples.

The first college-based gospel choir is established at Howard University.

The Alvin Ailey American Dance Theatre tours Europe. They are held over for six weeks on their London stop to meet ticket demand. Judith Jamison makes her debut with the troupe.

Malcolm X (El Malik El Shabazz) is assassinated at the Audobon Ballroom in New York City.

Thurgood Marshall becomes Solicitor General of the United States.

Rioting breaks out in the Los Angeles Watts area, leaving 35 dead.

The Us organization is established through the leadership of Maulana Karenga.

Claude Brown is the author of *Manchild in the Promised Land.*

Ivan Dixon and Abbey Lincoln star in the film *Nothing But a Man.*

The National Endowment for the Arts (NEA) and the National Endowment for the Humanities (NEH) are established.

By this year, legal apartheid in the South has been destroyed.

Bill Cosbys weekly television show *I Spy,* debuts.

Demonstrators are beaten by police while marching from Selma to Montgomery, Alabama.

Student protests (via teach-ins) against the Vietnam war begin at the University of Michigan, as the living room war reaches Americans on television.

Alex Haley serves as the ghostwriter of *The Autobiography of Malcolm X.*

The Voting Rights Act is signed by President Johnson, and major voter registration drives start throughout the South. He also outlines many of the ideas behind affirmative action in a speech at Howard University: *You do not take a person who, for years, has been hobbled by chains and liberate him, bring him up to the starting line of a race, and then say, `You are free to compete with all the others, and still justly believe that you have been completely fair.*

Iku:

Jazz saxophonist Earl O. Bostic dies in Rochester, New York.

Composer/publisher Clarence Williams dies.

Composer Asadata Dafora Horton dies.

Jazz pianist/composer Tadd Dameron dies.

Jazz pianist/singer-balladeer Nat King Cole dies of lung cancer.

 **1966**

Agba:

Singer Janet Damita Jackson is born in Gary, Indiana.

Kuumba:

Leontyne Price opens the Metropolitan Opera season at the new Opera House at Lincoln Center, performing the role of Cleopatra in an opera written especially for her by Samuel Barber, *Anthony and Cleopatra.*

Ulysses Kay composes *Markings*, written in memory of United Nations Secretary-General Dag Hammerskjold.

Composer Hale Smith becomes composer-in-residence for the year with the Symphony of the New World.

Pianist Andre Watts is featured as the principal soloist at New York's Stravinsky Festival.

Nina Simone writes and records the protest song *Four Women*, describing the life styles and attitudes of black women with varying skin color.

R&B singer Stevie Wonder records the Bob Dylan antiwar song *Blowin' in the Wind.*

R&B singer Otis Redding has a hit song with a cover version of The Rolling Stones hit, *Satisfaction* (#31 on the pop charts and #4 on the R&B charts).

R&B singer Aretha Franklin signs with Atlantic Records.

Soul singer Lou Rawls releases the hit *Love Is A Hurtin' Thing.* He had crossed over to the popular music field from the gospel group The Pilgrim Travelers.

The Miracles release *Going To A Go-Go.*

Soul singer Percy Sledge has a hit with *When a Man Loves a Woman,* (a song that was improvised on the stage as the singer responded to his own broken affair), and *Warm and Tender Love.*

R&B singer Ray Charles has hits with *Crying Time* and *Let's Go Get Stoned* (written by Ashford & Simpson).

The Supremes release the hits *You Can't Hurry Love*, and *Love Is Like An Itching In My Heart.*

The Four Tops have a hit with *Reach Out, I'll Be There,* noted for the James Jamerson electric bass line. They also record *Standing In The Shadows (Of Love).*

Joe Jackson forms The Jackson Five with his children, Michael, Jermaine, Marlon, Jackie and Tito.

Soul singer Wilson Pickett has a hit with *Mustang Sally.*

Soul singer Curtis Mayfield founds his own recording company in Chicago, Windy C Records, the company that becomes the outlet for the Five Stairsteps.

R&B singer Aaron Neville has a major hit, *Tell It Like It Is.*

Vee Jay Records goes out of business.

Blues singer Sippie Wallace tours Europe.

Duke Ellington and Billy Strayhorn compose a nine-movement jazz suite, *Far East Suite,* inspired by the bands recent U.S. State Department tour. Ellington also composes music for the film *Assault On A Queen.*

John Coltrane releases the album *Meditations* (unusual because of its use of two drummers).

Sonny Stitt begins to champion the use of electronically amplified wind instruments in jazz.

Cecil Taylor records *Unit Structures.*

Gospel singer Shirley Caesar leaves the Caravans and organizes her own group, the Caesar Singers. They perform in a rock-gospel style.

Mahalia Jackson publishes her autobiography, *Movin' On Up.*

Poet Margaret Walker publishes the historical novel, *Jubilee.*

Actor Bill Cosby becomes first black to win an Emmy for best actor in a dramatic series.

The National Organization For Women is established.

Bill Russell becomes the first black to coach a major professional athletic team, the Boston Celtics.

The Black Panther Party is founded in Oakland, California by Huey Newton and Bobby Seale.

The Supreme Court declares the poll tax unconstitutional.

The First World Festival of Black Arts is held in Dakar, Senegal.

Steps are taken towards the establishment of the discipline of Black Studies, with the development of a Black Student Union and a Black Arts and Culture series at San Francisco State University.

Activist/scholar Maulana Karenga establishes the African American holiday of *Kwanzaa* combining elements from many African harvest festivals. It is built upon the *Nguzo Saba,* Seven Principles which emphasize the heritage, values and hopes of African Americans: *Umoja* (Unity), *Kujichagulia* (Self-Determination), *Ujima* (Collective Work and Responsibility), *Imani* (Faith), *Kuumba* (Creativity), *Nia* (Purpose), and *Ujamaa* (Cooperative Economics). It is a celebration of family, community and culture that begins on December 26 and ends New Year's Day.

Iku:

Jazz pianist Earl (Bud) Powell dies.

Blues singer Mississippi John Hurt dies.

 **1967**

Agba:

Tenor saxophonist Todd Williams (of Wynton Marsalis Sextet) is born in St. Louis, Missouri.

Kuumba:

R&B singer Aretha Franklin records the Otis Redding hit *Respect* and *I Never Loved A Man* - her first hits for Atlantic records, and makes her first European tour.

Gladys Knight and the Pips record the hit *I Heard It Through The Grapevine.*

Smokey Robinson and the Miracles record the hits *The Love I Saw In You Was Just A Mirage, More Love* and *I Second That Emotion.*

Fortune magazine reports that Motown Records is grossing thirty million dollars annually.

The Supremes become Diana Ross & The Supremes, and Florence Ballard leaves the group.

The psychedelic rock/soul group Sly and the Family Stone is formed in the San Francisco Bay area.

Dionne Warwick attains special popularity with the Bachrach/David songs *Walk On By,* and *What the World Needs Now.*

Over one hundred radio stations in the country play music primarily for the black audience.

The Four Tops release the soul hit *Bernadette.*

R&B singer Isaac Hayes makes his debut with the album *Presenting Isaac Hayes.*

Blues singer Etta James records the classic *I'd Rather Go Blind.*

Soul singers Sam and Dave have a hit with *Soul Man.*

R&B singer Kim Weston records *It Takes Two.*

Martha and the Vandellas release the hit *Jimmy Mack.*

Ray Charles records the blues theme song for the film *In the Heat of the Night.*

Louis Armstrong releases *What a Wonderful World*, a song that becomes a #1 hit in Great Britain.

The Roberta Martin Singers perform gospel music at the Spoleto Festival of Two Worlds in Italy.

Country singer Charley Pride becomes the first African American to appear on Nashville's Grand Ole Opry.

Composer Frederick C. Tillis writes *Freedom* for mixed chorus. The work is recorded by the University of Massachusetts Chorale in 1973.

Opera singer Shirley Verrett makes her debut at Londons Covent Garden.

Cab Calloway and Pearl Bailey star in the all-black revival of *Hello Dolly!* (for which Pearl Bailey wins a Tony Award).

Leslie Uggams stars in the Broadway musical *Hallelujah Baby,* winning a Tony Award for her performance.

The John Coltrane Quartet records the album *Expression.*

Ornette Coleman becomes the first jazz artist to receive a Guggenheim Fellowship for composition.

Quincy Jones writes the score for *In Cold Blood.*

Visual artist Faith Ringgold produces the work *Die*, a study of ethnic struggle.

The Negro Ensemble Theater of New York is founded.

Dancer/anthropologist Katherine Dunham founds the performing Arts Centre at Southern Illinois University's East St. Louis Campus.

Sidney Poitier, Katharine Hepburn and Spencer Tracy star in *Guess Who's Coming To Dinner?*

Stokely Carmichael becomes leader of the SNCC and develops the "Black Power" slogan.

Martin Luther King, Jr. announces his opposition to the Vietnam War.

Riots erupt in more than 30 cities, including Newark, New Jersey, Detroit, Michigan, New York City, Cleveland, Ohio, Washington, D.C., Chicago, Illinois, and Atlanta, Georgia.

President Lyndon Baines Johnson appoints the Kerner Commission to study the cause of the riots.

A group of Chicago visual artists create a mural of black heroes, The Wall of Respect, thus beginning the Public Arts Movement.

Thurgood Marshall is appointed to the U.S. Supreme Court.

The Public Broadcasting Act of 1967 passes Congress, establishing the Corporation for Public Broadcasting (CPB), which, in turn, established the Public Broadcasting System (PBS) and National Public Radio (NPR).

Iku:

Opera singer Lillian Evanti dies.

Jazz composer/arranger Billy Strayhorn dies.

Classical pianist Philippa Duke Schuyler dies.

Pop singer John Mills, Sr. dies.

Soul singer Otis Redding dies in a private airplane crash. Prior to his death, he is voted most popular male vocalist in England, per the *Melody Maker* magazine poll. Three days prior to his death he records *Sittin' On The Dock Of The Bay*.

Jazz artist John Coltrane dies of liver cancer.

Composer/educator/conductor John Wesley Work III dies.

Author/poet/librettist Langston Hughes dies.

Blues singer Ida Cox dies of cancer.

 **1968**

Agba:

Rap artist L. L. Cool Jay (James Todd Smith) is born in New York City.

Kuumba:

The Edwin Hawkins Singers record *Oh Happy Day*, the first commercially successful, crossover gospel piece. This is the song that opens the modern era of contemporary gospel music.

James Cleveland organizes the Gospel Music Workshop of America to train and introduce people to the gospel tradition.

Gospel artist Margaret Pleasant Dourox composes *Give Me a Clean Heart.*

James Brown, the Godfather of Soul, records *Say It Loud, I'm Black and I'm Proud,* an exciting example of the use of call and response. He is called Soul Brother No. 1 or Mr. Dynamite. Poet LeRoi Jones describes him as being the No. 1 black poet. At the same time, he publicly meets with Richard Nixon, and thereby becomes a symbol of both black rage and black conservatism.

Aretha Franklin, the Queen of Soul, sings the national anthem at the Democratic National Convention. Her album, *Lady Soul,* includes the hit single *Chain of Fools.* She is featured in a *Time* magazine cover story, "Lady Soul: Singing It Like It Is."

Jose Feliciano sings the national anthem at the World Series, using the melismatic melodic style associated with soul music and accompanying himself on acoustic guitar

R&B singer Marvin Gaye has a hit with *I Heard It Through The Grapevine.* He also records duets with Tammi Terrell, *You're All I Need to Get By,* and *Ain't Nothing Like The Real Thing.*

R&B singer Curtis Mayfield establishes Curtom Records in Chicago, the company that becomes the outlet for The Five Stairsteps, The Impressions and Major Lance.

The Delfonics release their first pop/R&B hit, *La-La Means I Love You.*

The Temptations release the hit *I Wish It Would Rain.*

The Stylistics are formed by Russell Thomkins, Aaron Love, James Smith, Herbie Murrell and James Dunn. The group becomes one of the most commercially successful performers of the Philly Soul sound.

The Commodores are established by Lionel Richie, Milan Williams, William King and Thomas McClary.

Pop/Soul group The Fifth Dimension win five Grammys for the Jimmy Webb song *Up, Up and Away.* This includes Record of the Year and Best Contemporary Group of the Year. They also release the hit *Stoned Soul Picnic.* The group is distinguished by its use of sophisticated arrangements.

Soul Singer Ray Charles has a hit with a cover version of the John Lennon/Paul McCartney song *Eleanor Rigby* (the first example of "reverse covering.") He establishes his own recording label, *Tangerine.*

R&B singer Fats Domino has a hit with a cover of the Beatles' *Lady Madonna.*

Soul singer O. C. Smith releases the hit *Little Green Apples.*

Jerry Butler releases the hit *Hey Western Union Man.*

The recording industry takes in a total of $1.1 billion in gross income, per the year-end assessment of *Billboard* magazine.

White blues singer Janis Joplin begins her recording career in Texas.

The Jazz-rock band Chicago records its debut hit, *Chicago Transit Authority.*

Psychedelic rock/soul group Sly and the Family Stone release their first hit *Dance To The Music.*

Walter Carlos introduces the Moog synthesizer to a wide audience with his album *Switched-on Bach.*

Composer Olly Wilson's composition *Cetus* wins the Dartmouth Arts Council Prize, the first international competition for electronic music compositions.

The Society of Black Composers is organized in New York and begins to sponsor a series of concerts featuring the works of black composers.

Paul Freeman becomes an associate conductor of the Dallas Symphony.

Henry Lewis becomes musical director of the New Jersey Symphony Orchestra - the first African American director of a major U.S. orchestra.

Duke Ellington produces a Jazz Concert of Sacred Music at the Cathedral of St. John the Divine in New York. He also composes the *Latin American Suite* for jazz orchestra.

The Miles Davis Quintet records the album *Miles In The Sky,* featuring Herbie Hancock on electric piano.

The International Association of Jazz Educators is founded (an organization that helps to establish jazz studies programs in colleges and high schools across the country).

Composer/conductor Jester Hairston tours the Ivory Coast, Senegal, and Ghana.

Diahann Carroll stars in the weekly television series *Julia.*

Martin Luther King, Jr. announces plans to lead a Poor Peoples Campaign in Washington, D.C.

The BSU is established at Holy Cross College in Worcester, Massachusetts, by a group of students led by Clarence Thomas.

The terms Afro-American or black become the primary replacement for the term Negro.

Visual artist Elizabeth Catlett produces a sculptural symbol of Pan-Africanism, *Black Unity.*

The First National Conference of Black Museum and Museum Professionals is held in Detroit, Michigan.

At the Olympics (in Mexico City) John Carlos and Tommie Smith raise black-gloved fists to protest the treatment of African Americans in the United States.

Alabama governor George Wallace launches a white backlash presidential candidacy.

Richard Nixon is elected President of the United States.

Shirley Chisholm becomes the first black woman to serve in Congress.

The first Miss Black America pageant is held.

Abbey Lincoln and Sidney Poitier star in the film *For Love Of Ivy.*

Ralph David Abernathy is named successor to Martin Luther King, Jr., to lead the SCLC.

The Kerner Commission report is released.

Martin Luther King, Jr. is assassinated in Memphis, Tennessee.

Gwendolyn Brooks becomes Poet Laureate of Illinois.

The film *Sounder* is released.

Black Panther leader Huey P. Newton is convicted of manslaughter.

Iku:

R&B singer Little Willie John dies of pneumonia in the Washington State Penitentiary.

Jazz guitarist Wes Montgomery dies.

Jazz pianist Charles Luckey Roberts dies.

 **1969**

Agba:

R&B singer Bobby Brown is born in Boston, Massachusetts.

Jazz trumpeter Roy Hargrove is born near Dallas, Texas.

Kuumba:

The Miles Davis Quintet records the albums *In A Silent Way* (with Herbie Hancock, Chick Corea and Josef Zawinul on keyboards) and *Bitches Brew.* Both albums reflect his interest in electronic instruments and the emerging fusion style that blends rock and soul with jazz.

The Vatican commissions jazz pianist Mary Lou Williams to compose *Mary Lou's Mass.*

Jazz composer/educator David Baker composes one of his first classical works - *Song Cycle*, a cycle of five songs.

Duke Ellington receives the Presidential Medal of Freedom from President Nixon at a White House celebration of his 70th birthday.

Flutist Herbie Mann has a hit with the album *Memphis Underground.*

The Beatles sign the Modern Jazz Quartet to their Apple label.

Rufus Harley gains national recognition as a performer of jazz bagpipe.

Jazz artist Pharaoh Sanders records the Indian-inspired album, *Karma,* with Leon Thomas featured as the singer on the cut "The Creator Has A Master Plan."

Singer Nina Simone composes and records *To Be Young, Gifted and Black.*

Billboard magazine changes the term "rhythm and blues" to "soul", thus catching up with both the professional and the general community. At the same time, the categorization continues to have economic impact, facilitating the restricting practices of radio station play lists.

Songwriting team Holland-Dozier-Holland organize Invictur Records and Gold Forever Music.

The Woodstock Festival is held in New York featuring folk, rock, soul and blues music. Jimi Hendrix causes a sensation when he performs *The Star Spangled Banner.*

Psychedelic rock/soul group Sly and the Family Stone release the hits *Everyday People* and *I Want To Take You Higher.*

Pop/soul group The Fifth Dimension have a hit with a medley from the musical *Hair - Aquarius/Let The Sunshine In* and *Walking On A Groovy Thing.*

R&B singer Marvin Gaye has a hit with *Too Busy Thinking About My Baby.*

Jerry Butler releases the soul hit *Only The Strong Survive.* (Note that in the 1990s Jerry Butler becomes a Cook County Commissioner.)

The Impressions release the Curtis Mayfield soul hit *Choice of Colors.*

Soul group Gladys Knight and the Pips have a hit with *The Nitty Gritty* and with *Friendship Train.*

Robert "Kool" Bell and Ronald Bell form the Soul group Kool and The Gang.

Lionel Richie, William King, Walter Clyde Orange, Milan Williams, Ronald LaPread and Thomas McClary form the Soul group - The Commodores.

Soul singer Isaac Hayes records the album *Hot Buttered Soul.*

The Jackson Five record *I Want You Back.*

Motown star Diana Ross leaves The Supremes to go solo.

Berry Gordy, Jr. begins to relocate Motown to Los Angeles.

Soul singer James Brown opens WRDW radio in Augusta, Georgia.

Gospel singer/composer/conductor James Cleveland organizes the Southern California Community Choir.

The Afro-American Music Opportunities Association (AAMOA) is founded by C. Edward Thomas - "to promote the involvement of black musicians in the varied fields of classical music."

Composer/educator Undine Smith Moore becomes co-director of the Virginia State College Black Music Center. She also composes *Afro-American Suite* for flute, cello and piano.

A five-day seminar, "Black Music in College and University Curricula," is held at Indiana University, chaired by Dominique-Rene de Lerma.

Singer Jessye Norman makes her opera debut by the Deutsche Opera.

Denis de Coteau wins the Pierre Monteau Conducting Prize.

The Della Reese Show, a television variety show, premieres.

Soul food restaurants emerge in white communities, e.g. Player's Choice in Hollywood.

The U. S. Post Office issues a commemorative stamp in honor of W. C. Handy.

The First Pan-African Cultural Festival is held in Algiers.

The Dance Theater of Harlem is organized by choreographer/dancer Arthur Mitchell.

Lena Horne appears in the film *Death of A Gunfighter*, her first dramatic film role.

Artist Romare Bearden establishes the Cinque Gallery in New York City.

Racial rioting occurs in Asbury Park, New Jersey New Bedford, Massachusetts Trenton, New Jersey Henderson, North Carolina Cairo, Illinois and Hartford, Connecticut (mostly generated by reactions to busing/school desegregation policies).

Huey P. Newton's conviction for manslaughter is reversed by the California Court of Appeals.

Harvard University completes a study and moves to establish an Afro-American Studies program.

A Black Studies program is established at Cornell University.

The Department of Afro-American Studies and the Afro-American Resource Center are created at Howard University.

Photographer Gordon Park's autobiography, *The Learning Tree*, is made into a movie.

New York's Metropolitan Museum of Art exhibits *Harlem On My Mind*.

The City University of New York adopts an open-admissions policy, effective in 1970.

New York's IBM Gallery exhibits *30 Contemporary Black Artists*.

Visual artist Elizabeth Catlett produces *Malcolm Speaks for Us*.

Iku:

Concert pianist Hazel Harrison dies.

Blues singer Nehemiah (Skip) James dies of cancer.

Blues/folk singer Josh White dies.

Pop singer Roy Hamilton dies.

Jazz saxophonist Coleman Hawkins dies.

Gospel singer Roberta Martin dies.

7

1970 - 1980
THE MUSIC OF
COMMERCIALISM AND FUSION

Musicians from previous eras continue to produce in styles that have historical roots. However, a new commercial vitality is achieved with the development of jazz-rock fusion and disco. The vitality is accompanied with considerable controversy. The commercialism is also balanced by the organized interest in the study and preservation of black music.

The period begins with the formation of two of the major vehicles for the development and distribution of fusion: The Weather Report Band and the ECM jazz/fusion recording label. It ends with the beginning of Michael Jackson's mega-stardom.

TRENDS
1970 - 1980

1970s

◊ The current status of the economic base for jazz is indeed precarious. Record sales are inadequate; major record companies begin to abandon the production of straight-ahead jazz; concert and club attendance is diminishing. The popular world of soul, R&B, and Rock has taken over. Some jazz musicians recognize this and move to incorporate aspects of the more popular styles into their music. The result is Fusion, music that combines rocking rhythms, repetitive harmonies and electronic instrumentation with jazz. The Latin sound is also often present.

◊ The style is exemplified in the work of Chick Corea, Freddie Hubbard, Weather Report, George Benson, Herbie Hancock, Blood, Sweat and Tears, Chicago and Miles Davis. Some jazz artists assert that the term Fusion becomes popular only as a merchandising appeal. As a result of the popularity of Fusion, mainstream, acoustic players turn increasingly to Europe and Japan for live audience and recording. Others worked in collectives or perform in lofts that allow them to be more experimental on acoustic instruments.

◊ At the same time, a wider spectrum of Fusion is occurring, one that is not just limited to the blend of rock and jazz. Specifically, performers in all genres begin crossing over to other genres. The repertoire and styles of all genres becomes available to all performers. The concept of genre specialization fades.

◊ The era of black awareness stimulates renewed interest in gospel music, and the era of contemporary gospel music begins to flourish, led by the work of Andrae and Saundra Crouch and Edwin and Walter Hawkins.

◊ Motown continues reaching the popular audience, even though it relocates to Los Angeles. Soul singers continue releasing socially conscious songs that address various urban issues. A number of the lead singers of soul/pop groups launch solo career, often achieving the celebrity superstardom that requires them to hold their shows in

296

stadiums and open air amphitheaters. The top singers sell millions of records, and the recording industry recognizes this success by issuing first Gold records and than Platinum records.

♮ Popular music is increasingly dependent upon the proficiency of the recording engineer, often a non-musician who is adept in the use of the multiple track tape recorder.

♮ Disc jockeys become a staple of the dance clubs of New York City, and their work (mixing their own music) leads to the development of Disco. African Americans begin performing this popular music, drum machine driven dance genre characterized by its throbbing beat, synthesized accompaniment, and sexually overt texts. Critics suggest that the emphasis upon a technologically produced sound eliminates the creative spontaneity of music. The style is seriously disliked by many musicians.

♮ A response to the popularity of Disco is the emergence of revivalism. This leads to the phenomenon of the Oldies but Goodies movement.

♮ The general public rediscovers Ragtime and the music of Scott Joplin.

♮ Reggae, a style of Jamaican popular music, becomes an influential voice in the evolving field of world music.

♮ Rap (street poetry improvised over music) becomes a fad in New York City. The form is also known as hip-hop.

♮ Breakdancing emerges as a technically demanding style performed originally in street gang challenge contests in Manhattan and the Bronx. The form evolves from the street to the dance floor to the stage.

♮ The era of the blaxploitation movie, a genre that often romanticizes the negative parts of ghetto culture. A number of these films have soundtracks written by black composers and R&B artists.

♮ Charley Pride is named Country Artist of the Decade by *Cashbox* magazine.

♮ Composers of music in the Americanized European classical tradition write music that reflects the folk and popular musical tradition of black culture.

♮ The era of the Watergate scandal.

ACHIEVEMENT DATELINE
1970 - 1980

 **1970**

Kuumba:

Robert L. Watt joins the Los Angeles Philharmonic, becoming the first African American french horn player employed by a major U.S. symphony.

Sister Elise, of the Catholic order of the Sisters of the Blessed Sacrament, becomes co-founder of Opera/South. She builds a company that stages operas by black composers with outstanding African American guest artists and exceptional students from the black-college members of the Mississippi Inter-Collegiate Opera Guild (Jackson State University, Utica Junior College and Tougaloo College).

Olly Wilson joins the music faculty of the University of California at Berkeley campus. He also composes *Voices* for full orchestra, with a large and varied percussion section that includes wood drums, brake shoes, suspended bottles, West African Talking Drums, large West African Master Drums, and African gourd rattles. The work is the result of a commission by the Boston Symphony Orchestra and The Fromm Foundation.

Tania Leon becomes the musical director for the Harlem Dance Theater.

Paul Freeman becomes an associate conductor of the Detroit Symphony.

New recordings of Scott Joplin ragtime compositions are issued and a resurgence of Ragtime popularity begins.

George Wein commissions Duke Ellington to compose *New Orleans Suite*, an eight-movement jazz suite that depicts the musical history of New Orleans (performed at the 1970 New Orleans Jazz Festival and recorded in 1971). Duke Ellington also conducts a sacred jazz concert at Harlem's St. Sulpice Church.

Frank Kofsky reports the views of jazz artist Archie Shepp in the continuing dialogue about the black aesthetic and the general place of black music and musicians within current culture:

> *The Negro musician is a reflection of the Negro people as a social phenomenon. His purpose ought to be to liberate America aesthetically and socially from its inhumanity....I think the Negro people through the force of their struggles are the only hope of saving America, the political or cultural America.*

Wayne Shorter, Joe Zawinul and Miroslav Vitous establish the fusion band Weather Report.

The ECM jazz/fusion label is established by Manfred Eicher, doing much of its recording of avant-garde musicians (e.g. Sam Rivers, Miroslav Vitous, Dave Holland, Keith Jarrett, Gary Burton, Chick Corea and Jack DeJohnette) in Oslo and Munich.

Trumpeter Miles Davis releases the jazz-rock fusion album *Miles At The Fillmore*.

Jazz pianist Herbie Hancock and his sextet release the fusion album *Mwandishi*.

Psychedelic rock/soul stars Sly and The Family Stone release the hit *Hot Fun In The Summertime*.

Soul singer Curtis Mayfield begins a solo career.

Teddy Pendergrass joins the soul group Harold Melvin and the Blue Notes, soon becoming their lead singer.

The Jackson Five win their first Grammy Award for the record *ABC* and have a hit with *I Want You Back*. They also sell over four million copies of *I'll Be There*.

Soul singer Marvin Gaye records *What's Going On*.

Soul group Smokey Robinson and the Miracles have a hit with *The Tears of a Clown*.

Soul singer Stevie Wonder has hits, *Signed, Sealed, Delivered I'm Yours* and *Heaven Help Us All*.

Jean Terrell replaces Diana Ross in The Supremes. The group has a hit with *Up the Ladder to the Roof* and with *Stoned Love.*

Soul singer Diana Ross has a hit with *Reach Out and Touch (Somebody's Hand)* and with *Ain't No Mountain High Enough.*

The Four Tops have a hit with *It's All in the Game.*

The Supremes and The Four Tops combine to release the album *The Magnificent Seven* with its hit "River Deep, Mountain High."

Soul singer Brook Benton has a hit with *Rainy Day in Georgia.*

The Ike and Tina Turner Revue tours the country.

Several black artists begin recording in Muscle Shoals, Alabama, including Aretha Franklin, Wilson Pickett and Percy Sledge.

Pop/soul group The Delfonics release the hit *Didn't I Blow Your Mind.*

Pop/Soul group The Fifth Dimension release the hit *One Less Bell To Answer.*

The Five Stairsteps release the pop/soul hit *O-o-h Child.*

Soul group the Temptations have a hit with *Psychedelic Shack.*

The Impressions release the hit *Check Out Your Mind.*

Soul singer Edwin Starr has a hit with *Stop the War Now.*

Soul group Gladys Knight and the Pips have a hit with *If I Were Your Woman.*

Blues guitarist Buddy Guy tours with the Rolling Stones.

Blues singer/guitarist John Lee Hooker records a double album with white California blues group, Canned Heat.

Blues singer B. B. King has a major hit with *The Thrill Is Gone.* He becomes the Ambassador of the blues.

Maurice White, Verdine White and Philip Bailey form the Soul group, Earth, Wind and Fire.

The Chess recording company is sold to MCA, an early indicator of the coming trend of corporate consolidation.

Washington, D.C.'s Howard Theatre closes, affected by desegregation, television, neighborhood deterioration and the accelerating costs of live performances.

Boston's Museum of Fine Arts exhibits Afro-American Artists, New York and Boston.

Art historian Samella Lewis establishes the *International Quarterly.*

Essence Magazine debuts as a national publication with the mission of serving African American women.

Black Enterprise Magazine debuts.

The *Flip Wilson Show* debuts on NBC television.

Writer Maya Angelou publishes *I Know Why The Caged Bird Sings* (nominated for the 1970 National Book Award).

The Martin Luther King, Jr., Center is dedicated in Atlanta (becoming part of the three-block King National Historic Site on Auburn Avenue).

Angela Davis is apprehended in New York by the FBI.

Iku:

Jazz saxophonist Johnny Hodges dies.

Jazz saxophonist Albert Ayler dies.

Pop singer/organist Earl Grant dies in a car crash.

Blues singer/guitarist Earl Hooker dies.

Blues singer/pianist Otis Spann dies.

Blues/jazz pianist/composer Perry Bradford dies.

Acid Rock guitarist Jimi Hendrix dies.

Choral conductor Hall Johnson dies.

 **1971**

Kuumba:

The box-office boom in black movies begins. This includes *Shaft,* directed by Gordon Parks with an Academy Award-winning score by Issac Hayes.

The film *Sweet Sweetbacks Baadass Song* is released, produced and distributed by Melvin Van Peebles, featuring Earth, Wind and Fire in the soundtrack.

Singer Roberta Flack's hit song, *The First Time Ever I Saw Your Face* is featured in the Clint Eastwood movie *Play Misty for Me.* The Monterey Jazz Festival (with Cannonball Adderley and the Johnny Otis Show) is featured in the same film.

Jazz band arranger/conductor Quincy Jones arranges and conducts the music for the Academy Awards Show. In this same year he wins the Grammy for best instrumental pop, rock, or folk performance for his album *Smackwater Jack.*

Duke Ellington and his orchestra tour the Soviet Union.

Thelonious Monk, Art Blakey, Dizzy Gillespie and Sonny Stitt go on an international tour with The Giants of Jazz.

The Herbie Hancock Sextet release the Fusion album *Crossings.*

Saxophonist Sam Rivers opens his home as a performing loft in New York. Studio Rivbea helps make Manhattan's Soho District a home for avant-garde jazz.

The annual Bix Beiderbecke Memorial Jazz Festival begins in Iowa.

Vera Brodsky Lawrence edits and The New York Public Library publishes *The Collected Works of Scott Joplin.*

Eileen Southern's *The Music of Black Americans* is published, the first scholarly documentation of the entire history of black music in the U.S. Joseph and Eileen Southern establish the Foundation for Research in the Afro-American Creative Arts.

Composer Dorothy Rudd Moore writes *Dirge and Deliverance* for cello and piano.

Composer Adolphus Hailstork receives the Ernest Bloch Award for the choral composition *Mourn Not The Dead.*

New York's Lincoln Center for the Performing Arts, Inc., appoints Leonard DePaur Director of Community Relations, an example of the outreach efforts urban cultural centers are making to connect with the Black community.

Soul singer Marvin Gaye records the ground-breaking album *Whats Going On.*

Soul singers George Clinton and the Parliaments release the album *Maggot Brain.*

The Temptations release the hit *Just My Imagination.*

The Chi-Lites record the pop/R&B hit *Have You Seen Her.*

The Jackson Five have a hit with *Never Can Say Goodbye.* They are featured in an animated television series.

Michael Jackson goes solo, with the hit *Got To Be There.*

Gospel singer Shirley Caesar wins the Grammy Award for *Put Your Hand In The Hand of The Man.*

Charley Pride becomes the first black to be named Entertainer of the Year and Male Vocalist of the Year in the field of country music.

Harvard University adopts an affirmative-action program for the hiring of women and members of minority groups, and creates an office of minority affairs.

The U.S. Supreme Court overturns the conviction of boxer Muhammad Ali for evading the draft.

Operation PUSH (People United to Save Humanity) is established in Chicago, Illinois by Jesse Jackson.

Visual artist Raymond Saunders produces a contemporary portrait of black boxer *Jack Johnson.*

Activist Angela Davis is arraigned on charges of murder, kidnapping and criminal conspiracy in Marin County, California.

The Congressional Black Caucus is formed.

Joe Frazier defeats Muhammad Ali, winning the world heavyweight boxing championship.

Pitcher Satchel Paige is given full membership into the Cooperstown Baseball Hall of Fame.

Henry Aaron hits his 600th career home run.

Iku:

Blues singer/harmonica player Little Junior Parker dies.

Jazz trumpeter Louis Armstrong dies.

Jazz pianist/composer/band leader Lillian (Lil) Hardin Armstrong dies.

 **1972**

Kuumba:

Addison Gayle, Jr. serves as the editor of *The Black Aesthetic*, including a chapter by Ron Wellburn that attempts to define the future for African American musicians:

> *Black music in the 1970s must incorporate a world of non-white musics if black people in America hold the key to the worlds survival. All kinds of percussion instruments can be used (and you can do the popcorn to the merengue). Saxophones and other horns, or even pianos, do not necessarily have to be amplified as Miles Davis prefers now. Afro-Asian music has done without it for centuries, but if it must be done it must be done wisely. It was inevitable with the guitar and the organ; but the varitone gimmick for saxophone muddles the feeling and sound. Electronic music can make the black man blind from the sight of money and the white man rich on his deathbed, laughing absurdly at having fooled the niggers this last go-round. Black musi-*

cians should re-evaluate the technological intrusions now threatening our music; times may come when that technology will be useless. Our music is our key to survival (141-142).

A cultural debate permeates the decade regarding the pigeonholing impact of a philosophy that requires political and sociological values to be expressed through works of art.

Jazz bassist Ray Brown establishes the L. A. Four (with Shelly Manne, drums, Bud Shank, reeds, and Laurindo Almeida, guitar).

Jazz pianist Chick Corea forms the jazz-rock fusion ensemble Return To Forever with Stanley Clarke on bass, Joe Farrell on saxophone, Airto Moreira on percussion and Flora Purim on vocals.

Ornette Coleman records *Skies Of America* with the London Symphony.

Jazz vocalist Carmen McRae releases the album *The Great American Song Book.*

The Smithsonian Institution establishes the African Diaspora Program of the Festival of American Folklife, and initiates the Jazz Oral History Project.

Yale University establishes the Duke Ellington Fellowship Program.

Ragtime pianist/composer Eubie Blake appears at the Newport Jazz Festival and at the Berlin Jazz Festival.

The opera of ragtime composer Scott Joplin, *Treemonisha*, premieres in Atlanta, with new orchestration by T. J. Anderson, and is performed later in the year at Wolf Trap Park.

William Grant Still's opera, *Highway 1, USA*, and Ulysses Kay's opera, *The Juggler of Our Lady*, are performed by Opera/South in Jackson, Mississippi with Margaret Harris, conductor.

Henry Lewis becomes the first African American to conduct the Metropolitan Opera Orchestra.

Soprano Kathleen Battle makes her solo debut at Spoleto.

Composer Dorothy Rudd Moore composes *Weary Blues* for baritone, cello and piano on a text of Langston Hughes.

Akwan is composed by Olly Wilson. It is a work that is commissioned by pianist Richard Bunger.

Composer/conductor Eva Jessye directs her *Paradise Lost* and *Regained* at the Washington Cathedral.

Classical composer Julia Amanda Perry completes the *Soul Symphony.*

Ebony Magazine proclaims actor/bass-baritone/political activist Paul Robeson as one of the "ten most important black men in American history."

Motown moves to Los Angeles.

Soul group The Temptations have a hit with *Papa Was A Rolling Stone.*

Soul singer Marvin Gaye records the album *Trouble Man.*

Soul singers Harold Melvin and The Blue Notes (Teddy Pendergrass, Dwight Johnson, Jerry Cummings and William Spratley) are signed by the Philadelphia International label. They have a hit with *If You Don't Know Me By Now.*

Soul singer Stevie Wonder has a hit with the album *Music Of My Mind*, on which he performs on every instrument.

Michael Jackson has a hit with *Ben.*

Jermaine Jackson goes solo with the hit *That's How Love Goes.* He follows that with *Daddy's Home.*

The Chi-Lites record the pop/R&B hit *Oh Girl.*

The Stylistics have pop/R&B hits *Betch By Golly, Wow—I'm Stone In Love With You,* and *Break Up To Make Up.*

The 5th Dimension release the pop/soul hit *(Last Night) I Didn't Get To Sleep At All.* They subsequently perform for president Nixon at the White House.

The Main Ingredient has a pop/soul hit *Everybody Plays The Fool.*

Pop/soul singer Bill Withers releases the hit *Use Me.*

Sammy Davis, Jr. releases the pop hit *Candy Man.*

Soul Train, a black television show, premieres.

The gospel/soul group, The Staples Singers, have a hit with the message song *Respect Yourself.*

Rev. James Cleveland, the Southern California Community Choir and Aretha Franklin record a double-album, *Amazing Grace*. It becomes the first gospel album to sell more than five hundred thousand copies.

The gospel musical *Don't Bother Me, I Can't Cope* (composed by Micki Grant and Alex Bradford) opens on Broadway. It wins the Obie Award and a Grammy Award for Best Broadway Cast Album.

Oliver Nelson composes the score for the film *Last Tango In Paris.*

Quincy Jones writes the score for *The Getaway.*

Diana Ross and Richard Pryor star in the film, *Lady Sings The Blues*, an autobiographical study of singer Billie Holiday.

Curtis Mayfield composes the soundtrack of *Superfly*, and the soundtrack album goes platinum.

Cicely Tyson and Paul Winfield star in the film *Sounder.*

The Coalition Against Blaxploitation (CAB) is established in Los Angeles.

Maya Angelou becomes the first African American woman to direct a major movie, *Georgia, Georgia.*

Visual artist Charles Young produces the work *Musicians*, a celebration of music and musicians on canvas.

African American and Hispanic young people develop the graffiti art form in New York.

Visual artist David Driskell produces a work reflecting African influence, *Shango Gone.*

Visual artist Betye Saar produces the mixed media work *The Liberation of Aunt Jemima.*

Iku:

Composer Margaret Bonds dies.

Blues/Gospel artist Rev. "Blind" Gary Davis dies of a heart attack.

Mahalia Jackson dies in Evergreen Park, Illinois.

Jazz/blues singer Jimmy Rushing dies.

R&B artist Clyde McPhatter dies.

R&B singer Mabel (Big Maybelle) Smith dies.

 **1973**

Kuumba:

Barry White sells sixteen million dollars in records with the hits *I'm Gonna Love You Just A Little More, Baby—Never, Never Gonna Give Ya Up,* and *You're The First, The Last, My Everything.* He and Isaac Hayes become leaders in producing the popular disco/soul sound that uses lush production techniques, fuller orchestrations and extended, longer pieces. In describing the 1970s, Barry White suggests *Disco deserved a better name, a beautiful name because it was a beautiful art form. It was beautiful, you see, because it made the consumer beautiful. The consumer was the star. There were Barry White contests in discos everywhere—who looked the prettiest, who dressed the sharpest. This was the beginning of designer jeans; it was designer disco.* "The Long Days Night of Barry White" by David Ritz in *Essence,* April 1992, p. 109.

Singer Roberta Flack has a hit song with *Killing Me Softly.*

Diana Ross releases the hit *Touch Me In The Morning.*

Smokey Robinson releases his first solo album, *Smokey.*

Soul singer Marvin Gaye records the soundtrack album *Let's Get It On.*

Singer-songwriter Stevie Wonder records *You Are the Sunshine of My Life, All in Love is Fair,* and *Living For The City,* a musical examination of crime, violence and urban life.

The Dramatics release the R&B/pop hit *Me and Mrs. Jones.*

Gladys Knight and the Pips have hits with *Midnight Train To Georgia* and *Neither One Of Us (Wants To Be The First To Say Goodbye).*

Blues singer Esther Phillips is nominated for a Grammy Award for the album *From a Whisper to a Scream.*

The Pointer Sisters release their first hit album, *The Pointer Sisters.*

The band Graham Central Station releases its debut pop/R&B album.

Entertainer Josephine Baker launches a comeback with a performance at Carnegie Hall.

Bernice Johnson Reagon establishes Sweet Honey In The Rock, an African American women's a cappella quintet, performing a repertoire of songs and styles that spans two centuries of African and African American music.

Gospel singer/composer Andrae Crouch writes *Bless His Holy Name,* a song that eventually becomes a popular musical response for Sunday services: *Bless the Lord, O my soul, and all that is within me, Bless His holy Name.*

Everett Lee becomes the conductor of the Symphony of the New World.

Primous Fountain III composes *Ritual Dances of the Amaks* for symphony orchestra, performed by the Buffalo Philharmonic Orchestra, Michael Tilson Thomas conducting, and by the Minnesota Orchestra, Paul Freeman conducting.

The scholarly journal, *The Black Perspective in Music*, begins publication.

The Afro-American Music Opportunities Association (AAMOA) begins to sponsor a series of Black Composer Symposia, presenting concerts, recitals and workshops on the music of the African American community.

Sam Rivers serves as composer-in-residence for the Harlem Opera Company, and composes the jazz-improvisational opera *Solomon and Sheba.*

Composer David Baker is nominated for a Pulitzer Prize.

Duke Ellington produces his third Jazz Concert of Sacred Music at Westminister Abbey in London.

Jazz trombonist Melba Liston starts the African American Division of the Jamaica School of Music.

Jazz arranger Gil Evans mixes rock, funk & free jazz in the album *Svengali.*

Jazz pianist Herbie Hancock *Headhunters,* a Fusion album that reflects his interest in the music of Sly Stone. He then composes the soundtrack of the Charles Bronson movie *Death Wish.* He becomes a real specialist in performing on electronic instruments, using synthesizers and the electric piano.

Jazz pianist Chick Corea records the fusion album *Light as a Feather,* featuring Brazilian music performed with Airto Moreira and singer Flora Purim.

The Yusef Lateef Quartet publishes a group of writings by the individual members of the Quartet, entitled *Something Else,* including a poem, Change Reality by Albert Heath (Kuumba) that expresses the concerns of many black musicians:

> *Smoking grass, dropping pills, shooting dope,*
> *drinking alcohol or sniffing cocaine,*
> *These things temporarily release the pain of*
> *reality. They don't do a thing to help.*
> *How can we love our fellowman? We are*
> *killing ourselves as fast as we can.*
> *Youth of today hear my plea. You are the ones*
> *to change reality.*
> *The reality of greed is taking care of wants*
> *and not needs.*
> *Suffering is a family of four living in a two room*
> *apartment through a winter without heat.*
> *War takes our brothers and sons away and destroys*
> *their minds and values while it conditions them to kill.*
> *Racism is denying a child a chance for an education.*
> *Poverty is Harlem, East New York, the lower East*
> *side of Manhattan and Newark, N.J.*

> *Hate is to dislike intensely.*
> *And lastly—ignorance is not knowing or not understanding*
> *your fellowman or his problems.*
> *To change these realities to a future of harmony and*
> *peace, there is a lot of work to be done by both*
> *old and young.*

Raisin In The Sun is revived on Broadway as the musical *Raisin*, starring Debbie Allen. It wins a Tony Award for Best Musical.

The sound track for the film *American Graffiti* features the use of R&B/soul songs.

The films *The Spook Who Sat by the Door*, and *Five on the Blackhand Side* are released as films.

Vice President Spiro Agnew resigns and Gerald Ford becomes vice president of the United States.

The Children's Defense Fund is established by Marian Wright Edelman.

Iku:

Blues singer Minnie (Memphis Minnie) Douglas dies.

Gospel/blues Sister Rosetta Tharpe dies of a stroke.

New Orleans Traditional jazz trombonist Kid Ory dies.

Jazz saxophonist Benjamin (Ben) Webster dies.

Gospel singer Clara Ward dies.

 **1974**

Kuumba:

The Afro-American Music Opportunities Association (AAMOA) and Columbia Records launch a Black Composer Series, with Paul Freeman as artistic director and conductor, and ethnomusicologist Dominique-Rene de Lerma as chief consultant. A recorded repository of symphonic and operatic works by black composers is created for the first time.

Mezzo-soprano Hilda Harris joins the New York City Opera.

Soprano Barbara Hendricks makes her operatic debut with the San Francisco Opera.

Frederick C. Tillis composes *Ring Shout Concerto* for percussion, brass and orchestra.

George Walker composes *Spirituals* for orchestra.

Carman Moore composes *Gospel Fuse,* a work for symphony orchestra and gospel quartet, commissioned and performed by the San Francisco Symphony.

William Grant Still's 1941 opera, *A Bayou Legend*, receives its world premiere performance by Opera/South in Jackson, Mississippi, conducted by Leonard DePaur.

Classical composer Olly Wilson has a composition premiered by the Oakland Symphony, *Spiritsong*. It is composed for orchestra and womens voices as an exploration of the evolution of the spiritual.

The Albert McNeil Jubilee Singers tour Africa, performing spirituals in Morocco, Tunisia, Sierre Leone, Ivory Coast, Ghana, Afghanistan, Pakistan, Lebanon and Egypt.

Opera Ebony is founded in Philadelphia, Pennsylvania.

The *Journal of Jazz Studies* is founded, a scholarly journal devoted to the study of jazz.

The New York Jazz Repertory Orchestra is established.

Ellis Marsalis helps to establish the New Orleans Center for the Creative Arts. It is an arts public high school that helps stimulate interest in jazz performance.

The University of Maryland builds the Ella Fitzgerald Center For The Performing Arts.

Return To Forever receives a Grammy for the best jazz performance by a group for the album *No Mystery.* It reflects the evolution of jazz-rock fusion.

Jazz bassist Monk Montgomery and the All-Stars and singer Lovelace Watkins become the first jazz band to tour South Africa.

Ragtime composer Scott Joplin's *The Entertainer* is used in the sound-track of the Paul Newman movie *The Sting.*

Stevie Wonder wins five Grammy Awards: best-engineered recording, best R&B single, and best pop vocal performance for *Superstition,* best pop vocal performance by a male singer for *You Are the Sunshine of My Life,* and album of the year for *Innervisions.*

R&B singer Roberta Flack has a hit with *Feel Like Makin' Love.*

R&B singer Barry White has a disco hit with *Can't Get Enough of Your Love, Babe.* He is known as the "icon of love" because of the deep quality of his voice.

NBC-TV produces the Emmy-award winning musical television series, *The Nancy Wilson Show.*

Diane Carroll and James Earl Jones are featured in the film *Claudine,* for which she receives an Academy Award Best Actress nomination. Gladys Knight and the Pips perform on the soundtrack for the film.

Visual artist Romare Bearden completes two collages: *New Orleans Farewell,* and *Carolina Shout.* Both are celebrations of black music, musicians, and musical practice.

Visual artist Varnette Honeywood produces the acrylic work *Gossip in the Sanctuary.*

Cicely Tyson stars in the TV drama *The Autobiography of Miss Jane Pittman.*

President Richard Nixon resigns because of the Watergate scandal, and Gerald Ford becomes president.

Henry "Hank" Aaron breaks Babe Ruths record when he hits his 715th home run.

Frank Robinson becomes the first African American manager in base-ball, as the manager of the Cleveland Indians.

Boxer Muhammad Ali defeats George Foreman for the heavyweight championship.

Iku:

Blues singer "Ivory" Joe Hunter dies.

Jazz saxophonist Eugene (Gene) Ammons dies.

Composer Mark Fax dies.

Music critic Nora Holt dies.

Ethnomusicologist John Lovell, Jr. dies.

Pianist/composer/bandleader Duke Ellington dies of lung cancer.

 **1975**

Kuumba:

An all-black version of the musical, *The Wiz*, opens on Broadway with Geoffrey Holder as director. An interesting *Time* Magazine article describes the dynamics of the response to this production:

> *Despite all the gains financing remains an Excedrin-proof headache for most would-be black producers. Some black impresarios have gone directly to the black community and drafted preachers and teachers to get out the audience and plug shows as if they were the last revival meeting. So, in a way, they are. Between black performers and black audiences, linked by subtle nuances of black language and black experience, there is a crackling communion that often electrifies white audiences as well. There is also the question of black pride. When a white New York critic panned Wiz, suggesting that black is not all that beautiful, Harlem's Amsterdam News ran an outraged front-page editorial ordering readers to get on down to the Majestic Theater. The crucial Friday night box-office take rose from an anemic pre-pan $2,500 to $90,000 the next week and $120,000 the week after.* ("Welcome to the Great Black Way!," November 1, 1976)

Pearl Bailey and Billy Daniels appear in the all-black version of *Hello Dolly.*

The musical *Me and Bessie*, a celebration of the blues as sung by Bessie Smith, opens on Broadway.

Scott Joplin's opera *Treemonisha* opens in a production by the Houston Grand Opera Company and on Broadway with Carmen Balthrop in the title role.

Violinist Itzhak Perlman and pianist Andre Previn record an album of Scott Joplin rags, *The Easy Winners.*

Opera singer Clamma Dale makes her debut with the New York City Opera.

Singer Dorothy Maynor is appointed to the board of directors of the Metropolitan Opera.

Stax Records declares bankruptcy.

Gladys Knight and The Pips release the hit *The Way We Were.* They also star in an NBC-TV summer replacement variety show.

The Staple Singers release the hit *Let's Do It Again.*

Singer Minnie Riperton has a major hit with the song *Loving You.*

Singer Natalie Cole has a hit with *This Will Be.*

Singer Donna Summers, the Queen of Disco, records the album, *Love to Love You, Baby.*

Gospel singer Shirley Caesar has a hit with an adaptation of the country song *No Charge.*

Gospel singer/composer Walter Hawkins records the album *Love Alive 1* (including the popular songs "Changed" and "Going Up Yonder" with Tremaine Hawkins as soloist).

Conductor Calvin Simmons makes his American debut with the Los Angeles Philharmonic.

Raoul Abdul becomes music critic for the *Amsterdam News* in New York.

Cellist Norman Johns becomes the first black member of the Cincinnati Symphony Orchestra.

Composer/arranger/conductor/educator William Levi Dawson is honored by the American Choral Directors Association.

Carman Moore composes *Wild Fires and Field Songs*, commissioned and performed by the New York Philharmonic.

Jazz bassist Stanley Clarke releases the hit album *Journey To Love*.

Saxophonist Ornette Coleman establishes an electric band that he calls Prime Time.

The film *Leadbelly* is released, directed by Gordon Parks.

Diana Ross stars in the film *Mahogany*.

Heavyweight boxer Ken Norton stars in the Dino DeLaurentiis film *Mandingo*.

Artist Elizabeth Catlett creates a ten-foot bronze of Louis Armstrong for the Bicentennial celebration of the city of New Orleans.

The first black-owned television station, WGPR-TV, goes on the air in Detroit, Michigan.

HBO is established as the first satellite cable network.

Betamax is introduced as the first home video cassette recording (VCR) system, using half-inch tape. JVC pioneers the more popular VHS (Video Home System) 1/2 inch video cassette format in 1976. This establishes the technology needed for the music video.

Racial violence erupts in Boston, Massachusetts over the issue of busing.

Saigon falls.

Iku:

Texas blues artist Aaron "T-Bone" Walker dies.

Composer Shelton Brooks dies.

Entertainer Josephine Baker dies.

Jazz/R&B singer/bandleader Louis Jordan dies.

Bandleader Noble Sissle dies.

Jazz saxophonist/composer/arranger Oliver Nelson dies.

Jazz saxophonist Julian "Cannonball" Adderley dies.

 **1976**

Kuumba:

Ragtime composer Scott Joplin is posthumously awarded a Pulitzer Prize for his opera *Treemonisha.*

Billy Dee Williams stars in the film, *Scott Joplin.*

The bicentennial production of *Porgy & Bess* by the Houston Grand Opera Company opens on Broadway, featuring Clamma Dale in the role of Bess.

Bubbling Brown Sugar opens on Broadway, featuring the music of Eubie Blake, Cab Calloway and Duke Ellington.

The gospel musical *Your Arm's Too Short to Box With God* opens on Broadway.

Guys and Dolls opens on Broadway with a predominantly black cast.

Paul Freeman becomes the musical director of the Victoria Symphony in British Columbia.

The Detroit Symphony records *Celebration,* a work composed by Adolphus Hailstork, commissioned by J. C. Penney as part of the bicentennial package of music distributed throughout the nation.

Conductor James A. DePreist debuts as musical director of the Quebec Symphony.

Primous Fountain, III composes a *Cello Concerto*, performed by the Minnesota Orchestra.

R&B singer Tina Turner breaks up with Ike Turner.

Soul singer Teddy Pendergrass begins his solo career.

Soul singer Marvin Gaye records the album *I Want You.*

The Jackson Five leave Motown and lose the right to their name, becoming known as The Jacksons.

Jermaine Jackson stays with Motown, and records the album *My Name Is Jermaine.*

Soul singer/composer Stevie Wonder celebrates the birth of his daughter Aisha by writing the hit song *Isn't She Lovely.*

The Pointer Sisters appear in the film *Car Wash.*

Soul singer Gladys Knight begins her acting career, starring in the film *Pipe Dreams.*

Jazz bassist Stanley Clarke releases the hit album *School Days,* reflecting the evolution of jazz-rock fusion.

Weather Report releases the jazz-fusion hit album *Heavy Weather* with its hit song "Birdland."

The World Saxophone Quartet is established in Chicago. It is one of the first jazz ensembles not to have a rhythm section.

Jazz vocalist Betty Carter releases the album *Now It's My Turn.*

Jimmy Carter is elected president of the United States

Bicentennial celebration of the Declaration of Independence.

David C. Driskell serves as curator for the 1976 Bicentennial Exhibition for the Los Angeles County Museum of Art - *Two Centuries of Black American Art: 1750-1950.*

Dr. Mary Frances Berry is named Chancellor of the University of Colorado.

The National Council For Black Studies (NCBS) is established, the professional organization whose mission is the institutionalization and perpetuation of the discipline of Africana Studies.

Pearl Bailey stars with Redd Foxx in the film *Norman...Is That You?*

Iku:

Tenor Roland Hayes dies.

Singer/actor/activist Paul Robeson dies.

Conductor Dean Dixon dies.

Blues singer Howlin Wolf dies.

Blues singer Mance Lipscomb dies.

Classic blues singer Victoria Spivey dies.

R&B singer Florence Ballard dies.

 **1977**

Agba:

Jazz drummer Jason Marsalis is born.

Kuumba:

The National Baptist Publishing Board produces *The New National Baptist Hymnal,* a compilation that becomes the most widely used hymnal since the *Gospel Pearls* of 1921.

Alex Haley receives the Pulitzer Prize for the book *Roots.* The book is dramatized and airs on national television to record audiences. Quincy Jones wins an Emmy for the musical score.

Jazz pianist Chick Corea releases the Fusion album *Musicmagic.*

Jazz saxophonist Archie Shepp records a collection of spirituals *Goin Home.*

Jazz vocalist Sarah Vaughan releases the album *I Love Brazil.*

Jazz saxophonist Ornette Coleman releases the album *Dancing in Your Head.*

Symphony conductor Paul Freeman conducts the New York Philharmonic Chamber Orchestra in series of concerts that celebrates the works of black composers, *Two Centuries of Black Music.*

The Holman United Methodist Choir performs an Advent Concert with the Los Angeles Philharmonic Orchestra conducted by Calvin Simmons.

Soprano Kathleen Battle makes her Metropolitan Opera debut in Wagners *Tannhauser.*

Ethnomusicologist Samuel Floyd begins publishing the *Black Music Research Newsletter.*

Willis Patterson publishes a collection, *Anthology of Art Songs By Black American Composers.*

Soul singer Jermaine Jackson records the album *Feel the Fire.*

Soul singer Patti LaBelle becomes a solo singer.

The National Afro-American Historical and Genealogical Society is established in Washington, D.C.

The Junior Black Academy of Arts and Letters, Inc. (JBAAL) is established in Dallas, Texas, Curtis L. King, Founder/President.

The Second World Black and African Festival of Arts and Culture is held in Lagos, Nigeria.

The Personal Computer (PC) is developed, helping to fuel the coming information revolution.

Iku:

Shirley Graham DuBois dies.

Jazz saxophonist Roland Rahsaan Kirk dies.

Jazz pianist Erroll Garner dies.

Singer/actress Ethel Waters dies of cancer.

Jazz pianist/composer Hampton Hawes dies.

Jazz saxophonist Paul Desmond dies.

Blues singer/guitarist Sleepy John Estes dies.

 **1978**

Kuumba:

Soprano Leontyne Price performs a nationally televised recital in the White House, for which she receives an Emmy Award.

Opera singer Carmen Balthrop gives her debut performance with the Metropolitan Opera.

Opera singer Simon Estes performs in Wagner's *The Flying Dutchman*, becoming first black male to sing at the Bayreuth Festival.

Classical composer Primous Fountain, III, writes *Caprice* for full orchestra, performed by the American Composers Orchestra, Gunther Schuller conducting, and *Poem for Wind Instruments* for wind and brass players.

Classical composer Frederick C. Tillis composes *Three Symphonic Spirituals* for symphony orchestra.

The Dominguez Hills Jubilee choir is established at California State University Dominguez Hills by conductor Hansonia Caldwell.

The National Afro-American Philharmonic is established in Philadelphia, Pennsylvania by James Frazier.

Prince releases his debut album *For You.*

Disco singer Barry White signs an eight million dollar contract with CBS records.

Singers Johnny Mathis and Deniece record the R&B hit duets *Too Much Too Little Too Late* and *You're All I Need To Get By.*

Jazz pianist/composer Hazel Scott is inducted into the Black Filmmakers Hall of Fame.

The annual Playboy Jazz Festival begins. It is an annual weekend of jazz performances at the Los Angeles Hollywood Bowl.

Weather Report releases the jazz-rock Fusion album *Mr. Gone.*

Chick Corea composes the Fusion suite *The Mad Hatter.*

The musical *Ain't Misbehavin* (with the music of Fats Waller) opens on Broadway.

Eartha Kitt performs in the Broadway musical *Timbuktu!*

Michael Jackson, Diana Ross and Richard Pryor star in the film *The Wiz.*

Big Al Downing becomes a popular country music star, with three hits: *Touch Me; Mr. Jones;* and *Bring It On Home.*

The United States Postal Service establishes the Black Heritage series of stamps, to be issued annually in recognition of Black History Month.

The Supreme Court rules in *Regents of the U. of California v. Bakke* that colleges may use race as a factor in admissions decisions, but may not set aside a specific proportion of their entering classes for minority students.

Iku:

Gospel singer/composer Alex Bradford dies.

Jazz trumpeter Don Ellis dies.

Composer Howard Swanson dies

Composer William Grant Still dies.

Entertainer Blanche Calloway dies.

 **1979**

Kuumba:

Disco singer Donna Summer performs the song *Last Dance* that wins the Academy Award for best song in a motion picture, *Thank God It's Friday.*

Singer Johnny Mathis has a hit with the disco song *Gone, Gone, Gone.*

Prince records the album *Prince.*

Singer/composer Stevie Wonder creates the soundtrack for the movie *Journey Through The Secret Life of Plants.*

Soul singer Marvin Gaye records the album *Here My Dear,* a musical representation of his divorce.

The first two rap recordings are released to an international audience, *King Tim III*, by the Fatback Band, and *Rapper's Delight*, by the New Jersey-based Sugar Hill Gang. The lyrics of *Rapper's Delight* contain the phrase "hip-hop", and its popularity gives a name to the genre.

Sister Sledge records the hit *We Are Family.*

Gospel group The Edwin Hawkins Singers have a hit album, *Love Alive II.*

Gospel group The Mighty Clouds of Joy win a Grammy for the album *Changing Times.*

Singer Ella Fitzgerald receives the Kennedy Center Honors for lifetime achievement in the performing arts.

The Smithsonian Institution establishes a permanent black music concert series.

Calvin Simmons becomes musical director of the Oakland Symphony.

Paul Freeman becomes musical director of the Victoria (British Columbia) Symphony.

Frederick C. Tillis composes *Concerto for Piano, Jazz Trio and Symphony Orchestra,* commissioned by the Springfield Symphony Orchestra.

The Art Ensemble of Chicago records the avant-garde jazz album *Nice Guys.*

The musical *Eubie* opens on Broadway.

Franklin Thomas becomes the first black president of the Ford Foundation.

Donald McHenry is named U.S. ambassador to the United Nations, replacing Andrew Young.

Ted Turner starts CNN, the first 24-hour-a-day TV news channel.

Willie Mays is elected to the National Baseball Hall of Fame.

Iku:

Composer Julia Amanda Perry dies.

Jazz bassist Charles Mingus dies.

R&B singer/composer Donny Hathaway dies.

Jazz pianist/composer/arranger Stan Kenton dies.

 **1980**

Kuumba:

Michael Jackson's album *Off the Wall*, produced by Quincy Jones, becomes historically significant as the first solo record album to produce four top 10 hits. It is nominated for a Grammy in the R&B category. It is reported that Michael Jackson felt that because his music is not "black music," this album should have been nominated in the pop category. In protest, he refuses to sing at future Grammy Awards shows.

Diana Ross signs a $2.52 million contract with Atlantic City's Resorts International Casino.

Singer/composer Stevie Wonder creates *Happy Birthday* as a tribute song to Martin Luther King, Jr. as part of his lobbying effort to turn Martin Luther King, Jr.'s birthday into a national holiday.

The Queen of Soul, Aretha Franklin, Cab Calloway and James Brown appear in the film *The Blues Brothers*.

Disco Queen Donna Summer releases the hits *Hot Soul* and *Bad Girls*. She subsequently becomes a born-again-Christian and stops performing disco.

The Robert Cray Band records its first blues album, *Who's Been Talking*.

The Blues Foundation establishes the annual W. C. Handy Blues Awards in Memphis, Tennessee.

Fifth Dimension member Marilyn McCoo becomes the host of the *Solid Gold* television show.

Soprano Leontyne Price receives the Kennedy Center Honors Award in recognition of "great achievement in the performing arts."

Opera singer Betty Allen becomes the director of the Harlem School of the Arts.

Jazz singer Ella Fitzgerald wins her first Grammy Award.

Jazz trumpeter Wynton Marsalis joins Art Blakey and his Jazz Messengers.

Jazz singer Al Jarreau has a hit with the album *This Time.*

The Institute of Jazz Studies at Rutgers University becomes the administrator and repository of the resources (tapes and transcribed interviews) from the Smithsonian Institution's Jazz Oral History Project.

White actress Bo Derek receives substantial publicity for her appearance in the movie *10,* wherein her hair is styled in African cornrows. This is viewed as being another example of the appropriation of black culture.

Visual artist Synthia Saint James receives the Prix de Paris award for her animal paintings.

Norma Sklarek becomes the first black woman fellow of the American Institute of Architects.

BET (Black Entertainment Television) is founded by Robert L. Johnson, beginning as a two-hour-a-week cable television service.

Ronald Reagan is elected president of the U.S.

Sixteen people are killed in a major race riot in Miami, Florida.

Iku:

Jazz pianist/composer/flutist William (Bill) Evans dies.

Jazz clarinetist Leon Albany (Barney) Bigard dies.

8

1981 - 1995
THE MUSIC OF NEW MEDIA
AND CONTEMPORARY GRIOTS

The communications revolution contributes to continuous musical innovation. The African griot emerges in a contemporary African American form—as performers of rap music, and as cultural spokespersons (e.g. Wynton Marsalis).

The period begins with two communications/technological developments: the creation of MTV, the communications medium for which the music video becomes a major product, and the development of the "sampling" technique, a practice that becomes integral to the Rap industry. The period ends with the release of several "homage albums" by contemporary griots.

Throughout the era, the preservation and celebration of the history of African American music becomes a focus for organizations and artists, and maintaining the economic control of the contemporary musical product becomes a primary goal of the African American community.

TRENDS
1981 - 1995

1980s

ℓ The era of the jazz renaissance, featuring the work of Wynton Marsalis and other young jazz artists.

ℓ A style known as New Age emerges, combining jazz and classical genres and, at the same time, creating a "mood music" sound by fully eliminating the swing feel of jazz—performed by Paul Winter and George Winston and other white musicians.

ℓ R&B seems to lose creative energy. Very little new music makes an impact on the charts. At the same time audiences reconnect with the music of their youth through the growth of Oldies But Goodies R&B party and radio programming. The music of the 1950s and 1960s is becoming the new popular music standard repertoire, often with the original versions being used for movie and television soundtracks.

ℓ Rap music grows in popularity with black and brown youth. Additionally it becomes popular with the white teenagers of middle America. Its creators develop lyrics that are often performed over a technologically developed accompaniment using the borrowing technology known as "sampling."

ℓ Stereophonic sound becomes mobile with the growing popularity of ghetto blasters (later known as boom boxes).

ℓ Disco evolves into "House Music," or "Underground Dance Music," attracting urban gay black, white and Latino male patrons to the gay black clubs of New York and Chicago.

ℓ The Zydeco music (formerly known as zodico) from the black/French community of Louisiana's bayous gains in popularity, as performed by Buckwheat Zydeco, Zachary Richard and others.

ℓ African Americans are major contributors to establishing the market trends of the country, with Michael Jackson being paid $6 mil-

328

lion for Pepsi commercials, Ray Charles and the "Uh-huh" girls selling Diet Pepsi, Bill Cosby selling Kodak film, and Aretha Franklin's *Natural Woman* helping to sell Chic jeans.

℔ MTV emerges, featuring 3-minute video clips that are used to market recordings.

℔ Gospel music and spirituals become a regular feature of the hymn and anthem repertoire in churches of all denominations. Contemporary gospel groups begin to broaden their appeal.

℔ A plethora of national awards organizations and shows emerge to give recognition to outstanding artists in every genre.

℔ Video games proliferate.

℔ Opera attendance begins to flourish in the United States, spurred by audiences reached by television. African Americans continue developing distinguished opera performance careers. Additionally, an increasing number of African American composers write operas, often using librettos that depict aspects of Black history.

℔ The intellectual concept of Afrocentricity begins to emerge as the framework for the discipline of Black/Africana Studies, led by the writings of Molefi Asante, Cheikh Anta Diop, and Martin Bernal.

℔ A focus on Black women studies begins to emerge in the disciplines of literature and history, as seen in the work of Barbara Christian, Angela Davis, Paula Giddings, Darlene Clark Hine, bell hooks, La Frances Rodgers-Rose.

℔ The cellular telephone technology evolves.

℔ The U.S. Hispanic population grows 67.7% - from 14 million to almost 25 million, reaching 10% of the U.S. population.

1990s

℔ The era of the youthful renaissance of the jazz tradition continues, as performed by a group of young artists known as the "young lions" including Wynton Marsalis, Branford Marsalis, Delfeayo Marsalis, Marcus Roberts, Terence Blanchard, Roy Hargrove, Wes

Anderson, Todd Williams, Wycliffe Gordon, Philip Harper, Marlon Jordan, Eric Reid, Kevin Eubanks, Geoff Keezer, Benny Green, Cristopher Hollyday, Vincent Herring, Mark Whitfield, Howard Alden, Winard Harper, Joey DeFrancesco, Mark Turner, and Harry Connick Jr.

◊ Major record companies establish jazz divisions. Numerous classic jazz recordings are reissued.

◊ Rap continues as the contemporary communication style of African American urban griots, mixing storytelling and music. Often the lyrics express contemporary Black rage in a style known as gangsta rap. At the same time the texts generate substantial legal difficulty for various performers, philosophical controversy pitting advocates against dissenters, and economic boycotting of the companies that disseminate this product. Contemporary griots include Snoop Doggy Dogg, Dr. Dre, Geto Boys, Tupac Shakur, Ice Cube, N.W.A., 2 Live Crew, and Biggie Smalls and Crew.

◊ Rap is commercialized, emerging in television advertising that is targeted for teenagers.

◊ Rap also develops as a multicultural/international art form, emerging in England, France, Japan, Mexico, Russia, in various African countries, and continuing to flourish in performances by Latinos and whites of the United States.

◊ The rap genre is fused with other genres, creating Hip-hop gospel and symphonic rap.

◊ The electronically engineered duet becomes a popular component of recording.

◊ A decade that includes serious economic recession, hard-hitting budget cuts, and particularly severe federal defense-spending cutbacks along with the parallel emergence of the Information Age economy/technology revolution, all contributing to a social transformation.

◊ The communications industry burgeons, with over 8000 commercial radio stations, 350 million radios at home, and 125 million car radios.

◊ Black nationalism is reflected in music, in the visual arts, in film and in fashion.

◊ Numerous social problems are discussed via public, often video-taped spectacle with the spotlight on the black male, e.g., sports figure Arthur Ashe, Mayor Marion Barry, sports figure Magic Johnson, citizen Rodney King, Judge Clarence Thomas, football star/actor O. J. Simpson, and boxer Mike Tyson.

◊ A multi-dimensional male character begins to emerge on film, as seen in the work of Laurence Fishburne, Danny Glover, Morgan Freeman, Samuel L. Jackson and Denzel Washington. At the same time, several African American male movie directors are emerging as film griots, including Matty Rich, Bill Duke, Mario Van Peebles, Ernest Dickerson, Reginald and Warrington Hudlin, Charles Lane, John Singleton, Spike Lee and Charles Burnett.

ACHIEVEMENT DATELINE
1981 - 1995

 **1981**

Kuumba:

MTV is created by Warner Communications and the American Express Company originally to provide an album-oriented rock station for television using videos supplied by record companies. The earliest products primarily feature white, hard rock musicians. As a result of the potential economic impact of MTV, almost all popular music performers eventually produce at least one video as a marketing device. MTV becomes a competitor to radio. At the same time, it is sometimes criticized as being "empty-vee." Its success generates clones with USA Cable Network launching *Night Flite* in 1982 and MTV launching a second channel, Video Hits-1 (VH-1) in 1985.

Grandmaster Flash (Joseph Saddler) and the Furious Five release *Wheels of Steel*. It is the first Rap record to use sampling and scratching techniques. Grandmaster Flash is known as the godfather of hip-hop DJing.

R&B singer Tina Turner tours with the Rolling Stones.

As a part of Mississippi's efforts to reclaim and celebrate the Blues as a positive aspect of the States culture, the governor holds a reception at the governor's mansion in Jackson to honor Muddy Waters. This reflects the concern of some about the fact that cities like Memphis, Chicago and Los Angeles had become centers for the production of the Blues. Mississippi wants the public to remember that it is the Home of the Blues. This event provides the occasion for Muddy Waters' first trip back to Mississippi since he left for Chicago almost thirty years before.

R&B singers Diana Ross and Lionel Richie record *Endless Love,* the song that has become the most-requested song for wedding receptions.

Singers Johnny Mathis and Gladys Knight record the hit duet *When A Child Is Born*.

Soul singer Jermaine Jackson records two albums *Jermaine*, and *I Like Your Style*.

Arranger/conductor/producer Quincy Jones releases an album that reaches platinum sales levels, *The Dude*. The album receives five Grammys in 1982.

The Gospel Mass is composed by Robert Ray, including six movements: Kyrie, Gloria, Credo, Acclamation, Sanctus and Agnus Dei.

The United Methodist supplemental hymnal is published - *Songs of Zion*, providing general access to religious music in the black tradition (spirituals/gospel). The book contains a preface that explains and defines the gospel song:

> *The gospel song expresses theology. Not the theology of the academy or the university, not formalistic theology or the theology of the seminary, but a theology of experience—the theology of a God who sends the sunshine and the rain, the theology of a God who is very much alive and active and who has not forsaken those who are poor and oppressed and unemployed. It is a theology of imagination—-it grew out of fire shut up in the bones, of words painted on the canvas of the mind. Fear is turned to hope in the sanctuaries and storefronts, and bursts forth in songs of celebration. It is a theology of grace that allows the faithful to see the sunshine of His face—even through their tears. Even the words of an ex-slave trader become a song of liberation and an expression of God's amazing grace. It is a theology of survival that allows a people to celebrate the ability to continue the journey in spite of the insidious tentacles of racism and oppression and to sing, 'It's another days journey, and I'm glad about it.'*

Gospel composer Margaret Pleasant Dourox establishes the Heritage Music Foundation to nurture and preserve gospel music by building a monument, hall of fame and museum in Los Angeles.

Jazz trumpeter Wynton Marsalis, who forms his own band this year with his brother Branford, Kenny Kirkland, Jeff Watts, Phil Bowler and Ray Drummond, is voted "the talent most deserving of wider recognition" on the *Down Beat* magazine poll.

The Duke Ellington musical *Sophisticated Ladies* opens on Broadway.

Lena Horne stars in and wins a Tony Award for *Lena Horne: The Lady and Her Music*,—the longest running one-woman show on Broadway.

Entertainer Ben Vereen is criticized for performing a tribute to Bert Williams at Ronald Reagan's first inaugural.

The William Grant Still opera, *A Bayou Legend*, gains nationwide attention through its Public Television premiere, becoming the first opera by a black composer to be telecast on a national network.

Trumpeter Miles Davis marries actress Cicely Tyson.

Actress Marla Gibbs and Angela Mills co-found the Crossroads National Education and Arts Center - to provide viable arts and education programs to the communities within Los Angeles, California.

Members of Delta Sigma Theta Sorority march on Washington, D.C. in support of extending the Voting Rights Act, and in opposition to the Reagan Administration's position.

Iku:

Reggae singer Robert (Bob) Marley dies.

Jazz pianist/composer Hazel Scott dies.

Composer Edward H. Boatner dies.

R&B singer David Lynch dies.

Jazz trumpeter William Alonzo (Cat) Anderson dies.

Jazz pianist/composer Mary Lou Williams dies.

 **1982**

Kuumba:

The compact disc (CD) is introduced, an audio technology that uses a laser to read sound that has been encoded as digital information on a five-inch metal disc. The phonograph and magnetic tape technologies are eventually superseded by CDs that are played on mini-audio systems. This technology evolves into CD-Rom (CD-Read Only Memory) for computer data.

Grandmaster Flash (Joseph Saddler) and the Furious Five release *Flash To The Beat*. This is the first Rap record to contain singing. They also release *The Message*, an example of a Rap record that addresses social problems.

The Pointer Sisters have a hit with *I'm So Excited*.

Soul singer Jermaine Jackson records the album *Let Me Tickle Your Fancy*.

The Temptations have a hit with their *Reunion* album, featuring both David Ruffin and Eddie Kendricks.

Lionel Richie leaves the Commodores, becoming a solo act. He releases the album *Lionel Richie*, selling 4.9 million copies.

Billy Ocean releases the R&B hit *Night (Feel Like Getting Down)*.

The *Billboard* magazine Soul Music chart is renamed Black Music.

Dream Girls opens on Broadway, starring Jennifer Holliday. The show uses a storyline about a girl-group that is similar to the real-life world of The Supremes.

Leslie Uggams stars in the Broadway show *Blues in the Night*.

Jazz vocalist Sarah Vaughn makes major appearances on the pops concerts of several orchestras, including the Los Angeles Philharmonic.

The annual Village Jazz Festival begins in New York City.

Simon Estes makes his Metropolitan Opera debut in Wagner's *Tannhauser*.

Undine Smith Moore's cantata, *Scenes from the Life of a Martyr (to the memory of Martin Luther King, Jr.)* premieres, and is subsequently nominated for a Pulitzer Prize.

Composer T. J. Anderson writes the opera *Soldier Boy, Soldier,* premiered at Indiana University.

Isaiah Jackson becomes the musical director of the Anchorage (Alaska) Symphony.

August Wilson writes the play *Ma Rainey's Black Bottom.* The play starts a series of decade-by-decade explorations into the experience of twentieth century African Americans. Music often plays a central role in defining the spirit of his plays.

James Earl Jones stars in a Broadway production of *Othello.*

Val James becomes the first African American to play in the National Hockey League.

Jku:

Blues artist Sam "Lightnin" Hopkins dies.

R&B singer Addie Micky Harris (of The Shirelles) dies on stage of a heart attack.

Conductor Calvin Simmons drowns.

Pop singer Harry Mills (of the Mills Brothers) dies.

Jazz pianist/composer Thelonious Monk dies.

Jazz vibraphonist Cal Tjader dies.

Jazz saxophonist Sonny Stitt dies.

 **1983**

Kuumba:

Michael Jackson's album, *Thriller,* becomes the first album to produce five top singles (Quincy Jones, producer). The album remains in the Top 10 from March 1983 through June, 1984, selling over 25 million copies worldwide. It subsequently sells a record forty-one million copies. In the same year, his video *Billie Jean* is released and played constantly on MTV.

Lionel Richie releases the album *Can't Slow Down*. It eventually sells 11.2 million copies.

Soul singer Anita Baker releases her first album *The Songstress*.

Singers Roberta Flack and Peabo Bryson record the duet album *Born To Love*, including the hit "Tonight I Celebrate My Love."

Rap artists Bambaataa and the Soulsonic Force release the hit record *Planet Rock*.

The Houston Grand Opera produces a revival of the 1927 musical *Show Boat*, starring Donald O'Connor, Sheryl Woods, Ron Raines, Lonette McKee and Bruce Hubbard.

Tenor George Shirley makes his opera debut in Germany.

Soprano Jessye Norman makes her Metropolitan Opera debut in the Berlioz *Les Troyens*.

Soprano Leontyne Price receives a second Emmy Award for her televised *Live From Lincoln Center* performance with the New York Philharmonic.

Composer Adolphus Hailstork is awarded first prize in a national contest sponsored by the Virginia College Band Directors for the composition *American Guernica*.

Jazz critic Leonard Feather receives the *Down Beat* Lifetime Achievement Award.

New York's Apollo Theatre closes.

The Supreme Court rejects a plea from Bob Jones University, ruling that a non-profit tax exemption cannot be granted to schools and colleges that violate "fundamental public policy" by practicing racial discrimination.

The Smithsonian Institution establishes the Program in Black American Culture within the National Museum of American History.

Gloria Naylor wins the American Book Award in fiction for *The Women of Brewster Place*.

337

Jesse Jackson declares his candidacy for President.

Guion "Guy" Buford becomes the first African American in space.

The Martin Luther King, Jr. holiday is signed into law by president Ronald Reagan.

Jku:

Ragtime/Broadway composer/pianist Eubie Blake dies.

Blues artist Muddy Waters dies.

Gospel singer Gertrude Ward dies.

Jazz pianist Earl Fatha Hines dies.

 **1984**

Kuumba:

Wynton Marsalis becomes the first artist to be nominated for and win Grammy Awards in both the jazz and classical music categories in a single year, for the album *Think of One*, and *Trumpet Concertos* respectively. He also records *Hot House Flowers* with a string ensemble.

Jazz pianist/composer/educator Billy Taylor receives the *Down Beat* Lifetime Achievement Award.

Singer Lena Horne receives the Kennedy Center lifetime achievement award.

Anthony Davis composes *X, The Life and Times of Malcolm X*, an opera that combines jazz, gospel and blues techniques with Classical/Romantic music traditions.

Primous Fountain, III composes *Symphony No. I (Epitome of the Oppressed)*, performed by the Milwaukee Symphony Orchestra with Lukas Foss conducting, and by the Oregon Symphony, James DePreist conducting.

The New American Orchestra of Los Angeles commissions Ed Bland to write *Let Peace Be Free*.

Gospel singer/composer Andrae Crouch wins a Grammy for the album *No Time To Lose.*

Essence magazine reports that rap music is being used as a teaching device by teachers of elementary and junior high school students. The three R's become reading, riting, and rapping.

Run-DMC records the first gold rap record - *Run DMC.*

The Us Girls rap group is established.

Roxanne Shante becomes the first female rap artist to have a hit.

Motown Records celebrates its 25th anniversary with a television special featuring its previous artists.

Michael Jackson's album, *Thriller,* is certified by the *Guinness Book of Records* as the best-selling album of all time. It wins eight Grammy Awards and the MTV Video Music Awards.

The Jacksons record their reunion album, *Victory.* They go on a Victory concert tour that grosses $5.5 million.

Singer Whitney Houston is signed to Arista Records. Her debut album *Whitney Houston* sells over 18 million copies worldwide. It becomes the all-time best-selling solo artist debut album.

Soul singer Aretha Franklin has a hit album, *Who's Zoomin' Who?,* and a hit single, *Freeway of Love.*

R&B pioneer Chuck Berry receives a Grammy for Lifetime Achievement.

R&B group the New Edition reach platinum with their debut album, *New Edition.*

Soul/pop singer Billy Ocean has a hit with *Caribbean Queen.*

Tina Turner records the pop-soul album *Private Dancer,* with its hit single "What's Love Got to Do With It." She wins a 1985 Grammy for the song.

Singer/composer Stevie Wonder creates the soundtrack for the movie

The Woman In Red, containing the hit song, *I Just Called to Say I Love You*.

Denzel Washington, Adolph Caesar and Howard Rollins star in the film *A Soldier's Story*, with a soundtrack composed by Herbie Hancock.

Elaborate home entertainment centers become popular. It usually includes a compact disk player, one or more video cassette players, a laser-disc video machine, a 45" or 60" projection television, noise reduction units, patch bays for switching between components, and remote control units.

African Americans begin to make a real impact upon television; Oprah Winfrey becomes host of the Chicago show, *A.M. Chicago*, renamed *The Oprah Winfrey Show* in 1985, and Bill Cosby stimulates the revival of the prime-time sitcom with *The Cosby Show*.

Olympic athlete Carl Lewis becomes the second person to win four gold medals in track and field.

The first Black Family Summit is held at Fisk University.

Ronald Reagan is reelected president of the United States.

The AIDS virus is identified.

New York's Museum of Modern Art exhibits "Primitivism In 20th Century Art/Affinity of The Tribal and The Modern."

The National Conference of Artists, the oldest organization of African American visual artists, holds its first international meeting in Dakar, Senegal.

Eddie Murphy stars in *Beverly Hills Cop*.

Vanessa Williams becomes the first African American woman to be crowned Miss America.

Leontine T. C. Kelly becomes the first black female bishop of a major U. S. religious denomination (United Methodist Church).

Iku:

Jazz/Composer/Arranger/Conductor Count Basie dies.

Jazz drummer Shelly Manne dies.

R&B singer Jackie Wilson dies after spending eight years in a coma.

Blues Pioneer Willie Mae (Big Mama) Thornton dies.

Blues singer Alberta Hunter dies.

R&B singer Percy Mayfield dies from a heart attack.

Singer Marvin Gaye is murdered.

 **1985**

Kuumba:

Quincy Jones produces *We Are The World,* a song co-written by Michael Jackson and Lionel Richie. It is performed by a large cast of top entertainers, with the income designated for African famine relief.

The Burt Bacharach/Carole Bayer Sager song *That's What Friends Are For* is recorded by Dionne Warwick, Gladys Knight, Stevie Wonder and Elton John, to generate funds for the American Foundation for AIDS Research.

Prince wins a Grammy for best original film score for *Purple Rain.* The album sells seventeen million copies.

Jazz saxophonist Branford Marsalis joins the Sting rock group.

Jeffrey Osborne and Joyce Kennedy have a hit with their duet *The Last Time I Made Love.*

Pop singer Michael Jackson buys the rights to the Beatles catalogue.

The Black American Music Symposium is held at the University of Michigan, Ann Arbor campus.

The Metropolitan Opera gives its premiere performance of Gershwin's

Porgy and Bess, featuring Simon Estes as Porgy and Grace Bumbry as Bess.

Opera Ebony premieres *Frederick Douglass*, an opera by Dorothy Rudd Moore.

Opera star Leontyne Price receives the first National Medal of the Arts, and gives her farewell operatic performance at the Metropolitan Opera.

Oprah Winfrey is nominated for an Academy Award for her role in the film *The Color Purple*. The soundtrack of this film, composed by Quincy Jones, portrays the values conflict inherent in the juxtaposition of blues and gospel music.

Joe Morton stars in *The Brother From Another Planet*, a film distinguished by its Caribbean/reggae music soundtrack.

Tina Turner co-stars with Mel Gibson in the film *Mad Max: Beyond Thunderdome*.

August Coppola produces the film *Cotton Club*.

Gregory Hines and Mikhail Baryshnikov star in the film *White Nights*, a film that spotlights both tap dancing and ballet.

Julius Erving and J. Bruce Llewellyn purchase the franchise for the Philadelphia Coca-Cola Bottling Company.

Poet Rita Dove wins the Pulitzer Prize for the book *Thomas and Beulah*.

Iku:

Jazz trumpeter Cootie Williams dies.

Jazz drummer Kenny Clarke dies.

Blues/R&B singer Big Joe Turner dies.

 **1986**

Kuumba:

Anthony Davis' opera *X, The Life and Times of Malcolm X*, is performed by the New York City Opera.

Soprano Leontyne Price is named a Commandeur of the French Order of Arts and Letters.

Composer David Baker writes *Through This Vale of Tears*, a song cycle for tenor, string quartet and piano, composed as a tribute and commentary on the death of Dr. Martin Luther King, Jr.

The William Grant Still Performing Arts Society is organized in Los Angeles by Fannie Benjamin and Jane Taylor as a branch of the National Association of Negro Musicians.

The Afro-American Chamber Music Society is founded in Los Angeles. It is dedicated to preserving and performing the works of international composers of African descent.

Marian Anderson receives National Medal of Arts.

The Rock and Roll Hall of Fame opens in Cleveland, Ohio, and inducts Chuck Berry, James Brown, Ray Charles, Sam Cooke, Fats Domino, The Everly Brothers, Buddy Holly, Jerry Lee Lewis, Elvis Presley, Little Richard, Robert Johnson, Jimmie Rodgers, Jimmy Yancey, Alan Freed and John Hammond.

Soul singer James Ingram records the album *Never Felt So Good.*

Pop/soul singer Janet Jackson releases the debut album *Control,* selling four million copies. It contains the hits "Nasty," "What Have You Done For Me Lately?" and "Funny How Time Flies." The album is aimed at eliminating her "child star" image.

R&B group the New Edition have a platinum hit with the album *All For Love.*

R&B singer Bobby Brown starts his solo career with the album *King of Stage.*

R&B/soul singer James Brown records the hit *Living in America.*

The soul group Levert (Gerald and Sean Levert, the sons of Eddie Levert of the O'Jays, joined by Marc Gordon) signs with Atlantic Records and records the album *Bloodline* with its popular single "(Pop Pop Pop Pop) Goes My Mind."

White pop singer/composer Paul Simon has a hit with the antiapartheid album *Graceland,* reintroducing the music of South Africa to mainstream America by combining it with popular rock.

Billy Ocean releases the hit album *Love Zone,* including the hit "When the Going Gets Tough, the Tough Get Going."

The female rap group, Salt-N-Peppa record a platinum gold album, *Hot, Cool, and Vicious.* They are a part of a second era of all-girl groups. Their popularity is followed by En Vogue, Sisters With Voices (SWV), TLC, Brownstone, Jade and others.

R&B singer Little Richard has a supporting actor role in the film *Down and Out in Beverly Hills.*

Prince stars in the film *Under The Cherry Moon.*

Levi Stubbs of the Four Tops provides the voice of the flesh-eating green plant in the film *Little Shop Of Horrors.*

The film *Stand By Me* is released, using the R&B hit as the center of its soundtrack. The song is reissued and reaches the *Billboard* magazine charts once again.

Singer/dancer Debbie Allen stars in the Broadway musical *Sweet Charity.*

Jazz singer Al Jarreau records the album *L Is For Love.*

Jazz artist Lester Young's career is celebrated in the film *'Round Midnight,* with tenor saxophonist Dexter Gordon in the leading role (nominated for an Oscar Award).

The U. S. Post Office issues a commemorative stamp in honor of Duke Ellington.

Dr. Martin Luther King, Jr.s birthday is observed as a federal holiday for the first time.

Debi Thomas becomes the first African American to win the U.S. Figure Skating and the World Figure Skating Championship senior titles.

Nigeria's Wole Soyinka is awarded the Nobel Prize in Literature.

James Earl Jones stars in the August Wilson Pulitzer prize winning play *Fences.*

Spike Lee directs the film *She's Gotta Have It,* and goes on to build a career that inspires a new generation of black filmmakers.

Visual artist Synthia Saint James completes the painting *Ensemble,* a work that becomes the cover art for the Terry McMillan best selling-book *Waiting to Exhale.*

The year of the Challenger space shuttle launching disaster.

Iku:

Blues singer Sippie Wallace dies

Blues singer Sonny Terry dies.

R&B singer O'Kelly Isley dies of a heart attack.

Jazz pianist Teddy Wilson dies.

Jazz trumpeter/composer Thad Jones dies.

Soprano Caterina Jarboro dies.

 **1987**

Kuumba:

The U.S. Congress (with the leadership of Congressman John Conyers) passes a resolution declaring jazz "a rare and valuable national treasure":

> *Whereas, jazz has achieved preeminence throughout the world as an indigenous American music and art form, bringing to this country and the world a uniquely American musical synthesis and culture through the African American experience and —*

> *(1) makes evident to the world an outstanding artistic model of individual expression and democratic cooperation within the creative process, thus fulfilling the highest ideals and aspirations of our republic;*

*(2) is a unifying force, bridging cultural, religious, ethnic and age dif-
ferences in our diverse society;*

*(3) is a true music of the people, finding its inspiration in the cultures
and most personal experiences of the diverse peoples that consti-
tute our Nation;*

*(4) has evolved into a multifaceted art form which continues to birth
and nurture new stylistic idioms and cultural fusions;*

*(5) has had a historic, pervasive, and continuing influence on other
genres of music both here and abroad; and*

*(6) has become a true international language adopted by musicians
around the world as a music best able to express contemporary
realities from a personal perspective; and*

*Whereas, this great American musical art form has not yet been prop-
erly recognized nor accorded the institutional status commensu-
rate with its value and importance;*

*Whereas, it is important for the youth of America to recognize and
understand jazz as a significant part of their cultural and intellectual heritage;*

*Whereas, in as much as there exists no effective national infrastruc-
ture to support and to preserve jazz;*

*Whereas, documentation and archival support required by such a
great art form has yet to be systematically applied to the jazz field;
and*

*Whereas, it is in the best interest of the national welfare and all of
our citizens to preserve and celebrate this unique art form;*

Now, therefore be it

*Resolved by the House of Representatives (the Senate concurring),
that it is the sense of the Congress that Jazz is hereby designated
as a rare and valuable national American treasure to which we
should devote our attention, support and resources to make certain
it is preserved, understood and promulgated.*

Composer David Baker receives the *DownBeat* Lifetime Achievement
Award. He also composes *Concerto for Cello and Jazz Band*, juxtapos-

ing the classically oriented cello with the contemporary jazz band, including a 12-bar blues in the 2nd movement.

Jazz pianist Marcus Roberts wins the Thelonious Monk International Jazz Competition.

A Catholic church hymnal is published - *Lead Me, Guide Me,* a collection that reflects African American culture.

Aretha Franklin releases *One Lord, One Faith, One Baptism,* a double album of gospel music.

The Winans release the album *Decisions,* featuring a variety of styles and artists, thus pushing gospel music to the very cutting edge.

M. C. Hammer borrows twenty thousand dollars each from two former Oakland A's players to start Bust It Productions and, subsequently, his independent label, Bustin' Records. Oakland, California becomes a center of hip hop culture.

Arsenio Hall receives a thirteen-week commitment from Fox to replace Joan Rivers as the host of *The Late Show.* Subsequently he syndicates his show through Paramount, explaining his belief in the importance of African Americans maintaining control over their products: *White America has always let us entertain them, but we've never had any real control, any real power. So many of our greatest performers died broke. Me and my boys— Hammer, Magic (Johnson)—would sit around and talk about that for hours before all of this materialized. It's a new day, you know, and it's time for us to stop shooting the ball and start owning the court.* (From *Essence,* November 1993, page 74.) The show becomes a very significant performance venue for African American musicians–particularly for the Rap musicians who are systematically excluded in the programming decisions at the other network late-night television shows.

Rap group Public Enemy helps change the direction of rap texts with *Yo! Bum Rush the Show.*

Prince establishes his own recording label, Paisley Park.

Michael Jackson has a hit with the album *Bad.*

R&B singer Anita Baker receives the Grammy for her album *Rapture.*

B. B. King receives the Grammy Lifetime Achievement Award.

Aretha Franklin, the Coasters, Eddie Cochran, Bo Diddley, Marvin Gaye, Bill Haley, B. B. King, Clyde McPhatter, Ricky Nelson, Roy Orbison, Carl Perkins, Smokey Robinson, Joe Turner, Muddy Waters, Jackie Wilson, Louis Jordan, T-Bone Walker and Hank Williams are inducted into the Rock and Roll Hall of Fame.

The Black Music Repertory Ensemble is established by Samuel Floyd, director of Chicago's Columbia College Center For Black Music Research. It is a fifteen-member ensemble that includes Kenneth Adams on woodwinds; Donnie Ray Albert, bass baritone; George Blanchet, percussion; Nathaniel Brickens, trombone; Lyman Brodie, trumpet; William A. Brown, tenor; Winterton Garvey, violin; Elaine Mack, cello; Toni-Marie Montgomery, piano; Michael Morgan, conductor; Sylvia Morris, violin; Bernadine Oliphint, soprano; Walter Payton, double bass and tuba; and George Taylor, viola. The purpose of the group is to promote appreciation for music written by black composers between 1800 and the present.

Leslie B. Dunner is appointed assistant conductor of the Detroit Symphony Orchestra.

Classical composer Ed Bland writes *Romantic Synergy* for symphony orchestra.

Opera star Barbara Hendricks debuts at the Metropolitan Opera in *Der Rosenkavalier*. She also becomes Goodwill Ambassador for the United Nations High Commission for Refugees.

David C. Driskell and Mary Schmidt-Campbell serve as co-curators of *Harlem Renaissance: Art of Black America.*

Toni Morrison's novel, *Beloved*, is awarded the Pulitzer Prize.

Blackside Productions produces the award-winning documentary *Eyes on the Prize.*

Robert Townsend directs *Hollywood Shuffle.*

Playwright August Wilson wins a Pulitzer Prize in drama for *Fences.*

He and Lloyd Richards, James Earl Jones and Mary Alice win Tony awards for the Broadway production of the play.

Artist Romare Bearden is awarded the Presidents National Medal of Arts.

Lt. General Colin L. Powell becomes National Security Advisor.

The Camcorder emerges, facilitating home video movie-making.

Iku:

Classical pianist Natalie Hinderas dies.

Gospel music composer William Herbert Brewster dies.

 **1988**

Kuumba:

Rap group Public Enemy records the classic activist song *It Takes a Nation of Millions to Hold Us Back.* They refer to this art form as "black America's CNN."

Rap artist Eazy-E records his debut album *Eazy-Duz-It.*

Rap artist Ice-T performs the theme song for the movie *Colors.*

Nathan (Alex Vanderpool) Morris, Michael (Bass) McCary, Wanya (Squirt) Morris, and Shawn (Slim) Stockman form the Soul group Boyz II Men.

R&B group the New Edition have a platinum hit with the album *Heart Break.*

R&B singer Bobby Brown has a hit with the album *Don't Be Cruel.*

Dawn Robinson, Terry Ellis, Cindy Herron and Maxine Jones form En Vogue—a soul/pop girl group.

R&B group The Four Tops record the album *Indestructible.*

R&B/soul singer James Brown is given two concurrent six-year jail sentences for assault and weapons charges in South Carolina.

The Rock and Roll Hall of Fame inducts The Beach Boys, the Beatles, the Drifters, Bob Dylan, The Supremes, Berry Gordy, Jr., Woody Guthrie, Leadbelly and Les Paul.

Singer Bobby McFerrin releases a smash hit with the song *Don't Worry, Be Happy*. The song wins a Grammy in 1989.

Louis Armstrong's hit, *What a Wonderful World*, is released again as part of the film *Good Morning, Vietnam*, once again becoming a Billboard chart hit.

Jazz saxophonist Charlie "Yardbird" Parker's career is celebrated in the Clint Eastwood film, *Bird*.

The Wynton Marsalis sextet records the CD *The Majesty Of The Blues*—a celebration of the musical heritage of New Orleans, a declaration regarding the premature autopsies of various styles of jazz, and an effort to help *remove the supposed generation gaps that have bedeviled jazz since musicians began to emerge who were able to play with authority in only one style.*

New York's Lincoln Center begins a Classical Jazz Festival.

Jazz drummer Max Roach receives a MacArthur Foundation award.

Congressman John Conyers, Jr. receives the *Down Beat* Lifetime Achievement Award.

President Ronald Reagan awards the Presidential Medal of Freedom to Pearl Bailey.

Classical composer Alvin Singleton writes *Shadows and After Fallen Crumbs*, premiered by the Atlanta Symphony Orchestra, and *String Quartet No. 2*, performed by the Kronos Quartet.

Adolphus Hailstork composes *Symphony No. 1,* a four-movement work scored for a classical-size orchestra. It is written for a summer music festival in Ocean Grove, New Jersey, with the composer conducting the first performance.

Composer Tania Leon writes *Kabiosile*, commissioned by the American Composers Orchestra.

Classical composer Ed Bland composes *Atalantas Challenge*, a three-movement work for symphony orchestra.

The New Brass Ensemble, five internationally respected black brass instrumentalists (Bob Watt, French horn James Tinsley, trumpet Leonard Foy, trumpet Gordon Simms, trombone and William Roper, tuba) complete a concert tour of Europe.

Poet Gwendolyn Brooks writes *Gottschalk and the Grande Tarantelle* in honor of the Creole pianist/composer Louis Moreau Gottschalk.

Atlanta, Georgia holds the first National Black Arts Festival.

August Wilson writes the play *Joe Turner's Come And Gone.*

Atlanta University and Clark College merge to create Clark-Atlanta University.

Figure skater Debi Thomas wins the bronze medal in the Calgary winter Olympics.

The National Missionary Baptist Convention (in Dallas, Texas) is created after another split in the National Baptist Convention of America.

Olympian Anita DeFrantz becomes first black woman to serve on the International Olympic Committee.

The Ku Klux Klan loses a court battle and is ordered to pay one million dollars to the African Americans who were attacked in Forsyth County, Georgia.

Reverend Jesse Jackson runs for President of the United States.

George Bush is elected President of the United States.

Iku:

Gospel singer/composer Sallie Martin dies.

Jazz/blues singer/saxophonist Eddie (Cleanhead) Vinson dies.

Soul Singer Brook Benton dies.

Jazz arranger/bandleader Gil Evans dies.

Jazz singer/entertainer Billy Daniels dies.

Blues singer Son House dies.

 **1989**

Kuumba:

MTV begins playing rap music videos on a relatively regular basis (on the show "Yo! MTV Raps"), and black artists in general begin to appear on MTV.

Los Angeles rap group N.W.A. (Niggas with Attitude) have a hit with the album *Straight Outta Compton,* including the song "F... tha Police." Some critics describe the album as "demonic" because of its celebration of violence and sexism.

Rapper Anthony Smith takes the name Tone-Loc and records the hit *Wild Thing,* a recording that is erroneously cited as the entertainment enjoyed by the teenage attackers of the Central Park jogger.

Rap's activist artists Public Enemy has a hit with *Fight the Power,* and in the same year generates a national scandal because of statements made by its Minister of Information that are characterized as anti-Semitic.

Singer Ruth Brown receives a Tony Award for her performance in the Broadway musical *Black and Blue*, and a Grammy Award for the album *Blues On Broadway*.

The Rock and Roll Hall of Fame inducts Dion, Otis Redding, The Rolling Stones, The Temptations, Stevie Wonder, The Ink Spots, Bessie Smith, The Soul Stirrers, and Phil Spector.

The Jazz-Blues-Gospel Hall of Fame, in Chicago, induct their first honorees: Ella Fitzgerald, Louis Armstrong, Willie Dixon, Muddy Waters, Mahalia Jackson and Thomas A. Dorsey.

Jazz pianist Marcus Roberts records the album *The Truth Is Spoken Here,* his first recording as a leader.

Clint Eastwood produces the documentary *Thelonious Monk: Straight No Chaser.*

Quincy Jones produces the album *Back On The Block.*

Soul singer James Ingram records the album *It's Real.*

Soul singer Jermaine Jackson records the album *2300 Jackson Street.*

R&B singer Janet Jackson has a major hit album, *Rhythm Nation 1814*, becoming the first singer to have seven Top Five singles from one album on the Billboard chart.

Radio researcher Gary Corbitt develops an analysis of the African American radio audience, identifying two groups—Urban Underclass and Affluent Middle Class. It is an audience analysis to help programmers develop target audience programming.

Leslie B. Dunner is appointed music director of the Dearborn Symphony Orchestra and music advisor for the Harlem Festival Orchestra.

Anthony Davis composes *Under the Double Moon*, a science-fiction opera. It is premiered at the Opera Theatre of St. Louis.

Soprano Jessye Norman performs the French national anthem for the bicentennial of the French Revolution. She also stars in the Metropolitan Opera production of Schoenberg's *Erwartung.*

Soprano Leontyne Price performs for the first State Dinner of President and Mrs. Bush at the White House.

Opera singer Mattiwilda Dobbs joins the Board of Directors of the Metropolitan Opera Association.

Gregory Hines and Sammy Davis, Jr., appear in the film *Tap.*

Spike Lee directs the film *Do the Right Thing.*

Judith Jamison becomes the director of the Alvin Ailey American Dance Theater.

Barbara Harris becomes the first woman bishop in the Episcopal

Church. Joan Salmon Campbell becomes the first black woman elected moderator of the Presbyterian Church, U.S.A..

The biennial National Black Theatre Festival is started in Winston-Salem, North Carolina.

The Civil Rights Memorial is dedicated in Montgomery, Alabama.

David C. Driskell and Henry Drewall serve as co-curators of the California Afro-American Museum exhibit *Introspective: Contemporary Art by Americans and Brazilians of African Descent.*

Emerge magazine publishes its first issue.

General Colin Powell becomes chairman of the U. S. Joint Chiefs of Staff.

Bill White becomes the first black to serve as president of the National Baseball League.

Iku:

Gospel singer Bessie Griffin dies.

Pop singer Herbert Mills (of the Mills Brothers) dies.

Jazz trumpeter David Roy Eldridge dies.

Jazz pianist Phineas Newborn, Jr., dies.

Composer/educator Undine Smith Moore dies.

 **1990**

Kuumba:

Rapper Luther Campbell, the "Hugh Hefner of hip-hop," and 2 Live Crew challenge women and the 1st Amendment with the Luke Records album *Nasty As They Wanna Be.* His performances result in an obscenity trial in Miami, Florida. Among other things, they are charged with presenting a performance that simulates "deviate sexual intercourse," as defined by Florida Statute 847.0011. The defense includes expert witness Henry Louis Gates, Jr., who in his testimony defines rap as a continuation of the black oral tradition with its use of hyperbole, parody and signifying. The trial results in a not guilty verdict. Subsequent debate rages in newspapers and magazines (e.g. *Village Voice*) as well as in scholarly publications. Of special interest is the journal article *Beyond Racism and Misogyny: Black Feminism and 2 Live Crew* by Kimberle Crenshaw, *Boston Review,* December 1991. (Interestingly, this legal battle is being waged at the same time that the Cincinnati Contemporary Art Center is being tried on obscenity charges because of the Robert Mapplethorpe photography exhibit.)

Vanilla Ice becomes the first white act to have a popular Rap record, *Ice Ice Baby.*

Rap artist M. C. Hammer releases the album *Please Hammer Don't Hurt 'Em,* selling 15 million copies.

Rap artist Queen Latifah records the hit *Ladies First.*

Kenny "Babyface" Edmonds releases the hit album *Tender Love.*

The Rock and Roll Hall of Fame inducts Hank Ballard, Bobby Darin, The Four Seasons, The Four Tops, The Kinks, The Platters, Simon & Garfunkel, The Who, Louis Armstrong, Charlie Christian, "Ma" Rainey, Gerry Goffin & Carole King, and Holland, Dozier & Holland.

Spike Lee produces a syndicated television special *Do It A Cappella,* featuring The Persuasions and Take 6.

R&B singer Aaron Neville returns to the national spotlight with the Grammy Award-winning duet recorded with Linda Ronstadt, *I Don't Know Much.*

B. B. King receives the Presidential Medal of Freedom.

Time Magazine publishes a cover article on "The New Jazz Age" (October 22nd) featuring trumpeter Wynton Marsalis on the cover and profiles of the instrumentalists who are contributing to a jazz renaissance.

Jazz pianist Marcus Roberts releases his second and third albums, *Deep in the Shed* and *Alone With Three Giants.*

Jazz singer Jon Hendricks (of Lambert, Hendricks and Ross) has a hit album with *Jon Hendricks and Friends.*

Singer Bobby McFerrin begins to develop a career as an orchestra conductor, leading the San Francisco Symphony in a performance of Beethoven's *Seventh Symphony.*

Classical composer Alvin Singleton serves as the music director of the Music Alive concert series of Atlanta's National Black Arts Festival.

Classical composer Regina A. Harris Baiocchi composes *Miles Per Hour,* a fanfare/sonatina inspired by Miles Davis, fusing jazz and concert idioms—premiered by the Chicago Symphony Orchestra in 1991.

Classical composer Olly Wilson writes a song cycle for baritone, tenor and soprano voices, *Of Visions of Truth,* including the use of the spiritual "I've Been Buked and I've Been Scorned" as the first movement.

Margaret Harris appears as guest conductor of the Bronx Arts Symphony in New York.

Ovation Magazine reports that 14% of the singers hired by the Metropolitan Opera are African American.

Singer/actor/activist Harry Belafonte becomes the first person to receive the TransAfrica Forum Nelson Mandela Courage Award.

Quincy Jones wins the Grammy Legend Award, and receives the French Legion of Honor in recognition of his work as a trumpeter, composer, arranger and record producer.

Charles Burnett's film *To Sleep With Anger* features a blues soundtrack with performances by Jimmy Witherspoon, Little Milton, Bobby Blue Bland and Z. Z. Hill.

Rev. George Stallings becomes the first bishop of the African American Catholic Church.

The census counts 31 million African Americans, 12.1% of the U.S. population—the largest minority group—a group that spends more than $170 billion in the consumer market.

The nation's savings and loan companies face a significant financial crisis.

Boxer Mike Tyson loses his title to James Buster Douglas.

The National Council of African American Men, Inc. is founded and headquartered at the University of Kansas Center for Black Leadership.

South African freedom fighter Nelson Mandela is released after twenty-seven years in prison. He then makes his first visit to the United States.

President Bush vetoes the Civil Rights Act of 1990.

Charles Johnsons novel, *Middle Passage*, wins the National Book Award for fiction.

Multimedia artist Lorna Simpson becomes the first African American woman artist to represent the United States at the Venice Biennal. She also has a solo exhibition at Manhattan's Museum of Modern Art.

Dancer-choreographer Judith Jamison continues the Alvin Ailey tradition, leading the Alvin Ailey American Dance Theatre in a season featuring five premieres,including *Forgotten Time* by Judith Jamison, *Impinyuza* by Pearl Primus.

Playwright August Wilson wins the Pulitzer Prize for *The Piano Lesson*.

I Dream A World: Portraits of Black Women Who Changed America, a collection of seventy-six photos of African American women, is published.

Iku:

Singer/dancer Sammy Davis, Jr. dies of cancer.

Composer William Levi Dawson dies.

Jazz artist Dexter Gordon dies.

Jazz drummer/bandleader Art Blakey dies.

Singer Pearl Bailey dies.

Singer Sarah Vaughan dies.

 **1991**

Kuumba:

School systems across the country continue to eliminate music from the curriculum of elementary and secondary schools, causing increased alarm among professional musicians. Wynton Marsalis becomes more active as an advocate for arts education, and his concern is cited in the National Commission on Music Education's publication, *Growing Up Complete: The Imperative For Music Education*: *Our nation really suffers from a cultural problem more than a scientific one. Whether we're behind the Japanese people is secondary. Our culture is dying from the inside.*

Alvin Singleton composes *Even Tomorrow*, an orchestral composition created as an homage to Thurgood Marshall, commissioned by the Northwest Indiana Symphony and the Alabama Symphony. He also composes *Sinfonia Diaspora*, commissioned by the Oregon Symphony.

The Baltimore Symphony Orchestra and the American Symphony Orchestra League initiate a "Live, Gifted and Black" music reading program, featuring the works of black composers. They commission composer Hannibal Peterson to write *African Portraits*, premiered in November at Carnegie Hall and performed a second time in Baltimore. *African Portraits* is a two-act work for orchestra, the Hannibal Peterson quintet, a blues singer, a gospel singer, a griot, African percussionists, narration and chorus.

Tania Leon composes *Carabali*, commissioned by the Cincinnati Symphony and recorded by the Louisville Symphony.

Jazz vocalist Bobby McFerrin (son of baritone Robert McFerrin) appears with the New Jersey Symphony, conducting a variety of classical pieces (often while singing one of the instrumental lines).

Composer David Baker writes *Suite for Cello and Jazz Trio*, combining the traditional jazz combo with the cello as lead instrument.

The Jazz at Lincoln Center series is inaugurated, with a Randy Weston African Rhythms Orchestra concert "Blues to Africa."

Quincy Jones becomes the first black to win six Grammy awards in one year, for the album *Back On The Block.* He also has a hit with the album *Secret Garden.*

The Rock and Roll Hall of Fame inducts LaVern Baker, The Byrds, John Lee Hooker, The Impressions, Wilson Pickett, Jimmy Reed, Ike & Tina Turner, Howlin Wolf, Dave Bartholomew and Ralph Bass.

Boyz II Men release *Cooleyhigharmony,* an album that sells 9 million copies.

Pop singer Michael Jackson signs a sixty-five million dollar multimedia contract with Sony Records. This is the year he also releases the album *Dangerous,* selling twenty-three million worldwide.

The *Forbes* magazine list of the forty richest people in the entertainment business includes the following musicians: New Kids on the Block producer and manager Maurice Starr ($115 million); Michael Jackson ($60 million); Janet Jackson ($43 million); M. C. Hammer ($33 million) and Prince ($25 million).

Singer Roberta Flack releases the hit album *Set the Night to Music.*

Singer/composer Stevie Wonder creates the soundtrack for the Spike Lee movie *Jungle Fever.*

The film *Good Fellas* features the Moonglows R&B hit *Sincerely* in its soundtrack.

Singer Whitney Houston sings the National Anthem at the Super Bowl.

Singer Aaron Neville releases the album *Warm Your Heart,* continuing as an example of the continuing vitality in the music of New Orleans.

Rap artist Yo-Yo records the popular album *Make Way for the Motherlode.*

The Mario Van Peebles film *New Jack City* stars rapper Ice-T and uses a rap soundtrack.

Los Angeles rap group N.W.A. (Niggas with Attitude) record a pop chart hit with *Efil4zaggin* (Niggaz 4 Life backward), selling one million copies in fifteen days.

James Brown is paroled.

Soul singer Gerald Levert starts a solo career recording the album *Private Line.*

The Audio Home Recording Act (S.1623) is proposed to implement both a royalty payment system and a serial copy management system for digital audio recording, while at the same time insulating consumers from infringement suits for home copying. It attempts to address the issue of unauthorized home taping of copyrighted works and its potential impact on the economics of the recording industry.

The Soviet Union breaks up.

Denzel Washington is awarded an Oscar Award for his performance in *Glory.*

Whoopi Goldberg wins Academy Award for best actress in a supporting role for *Ghost.*

Dancer/producer Debbie Allen serves as choreographer for the Academy Awards show.

National Football League owners vote to move the 1993 Super Bowl from Phoenix to protest Arizonas failure to pass a paid state Martin Luther King, Jr. holiday.

Magic Johnson retires from professional basketball because of a positive HIV virus test.

The National Civil Rights Museum opens in Memphis, Tennessee.

Black law professor Anita Hill ignites a national debate by appearing before Congress to charge Supreme Court nominee Judge Clarence Thomas with sexual harassment.

BET (Black Entertainment Television) becomes the first black-owned company to be traded on the New York Stock Exchange

Iku:

Gospel singer/composer/conductor James Cleveland dies.

Trumpeter Miles Davis dies of pneumonia and a stroke.

Soul singer David Ruffin dies.

 **1992**

Kuumba:

The album *Handel's Messiah, A Soulful Celebration* is recorded. It features parts of the *Messiah,* arranged in the various genres of African American music. The instrumental Overture is produced by Mervyn Warren as "A Partial History of Black Music." Other individual pieces are performed by various outstanding African American artists: "Comfort Ye My People," performed in duet by Vanessa Bell Armstrong and Daryl Coley; "Every Valley Shall Be Exalted," performed in duet by Lizz Lee and Chris Willis, with Rap lyrics by Mike E.; "And The Glory Of The Lord" performed by Dianne Reeves and produced by George Duke; "And He Shall Purify" performed by Tremaine Hawkins; "O Thou That Tellest Good Tidings To Zion" performed by Stevie Wonder and Take 6; "Why Do The Nations So Furiously Rage?" performed by Al Jarreau; and the "Hallelujah!" Chorus with Quincy Jones conducting a Choir that includes Vannessa Bell Armstrong, Patti Austin, Andrae Crouch, Sandra Crouch, Clifton Davis, Charles Dutton, Kim Fields, Larnelle Harris, Edwin Hawkins, Tramaine Hawkins, Linda Hopkins, Al Jarreau, Chaka Khan, Gladys Knight, Johnny Mathis, Marilyn McCoo, Stephanie Mills, Jeffrey Osborne, Phylicia Rashad, Joe Sample, Sounds of Blackness, Take 6 and Mike E.

Gospel choir Sounds of Blackness win a Grammy for the album *The Evolution of Gospel.* The Minneapolis-based ensemble consists of forty-plus voices.

Singer Natalie Cole wins a Grammy Award for *Unforgettable,* the electronically engineered musical tribute to her late father, Nat King Cole.

Jazz artist Branford Marsalis becomes the musical director for the *Tonight Show.*

The Smithsonian Institution's Jazz Oral History Program is reactivated in partnership with The Lila Wallace-Reader's Digest Fund, relocated at the National Museum of American History, and expanded to support a ten-year national jazz celebration of touring exhibitions, performances, educational programs, recordings, special events, publications, radio programs, and the continuing oral interview program.

The annual Charlie Parker Jazz Festival begins in New York City.

Jazz vocalist Ella Fitzgerald receives the Magnum Opus Award for lifetime achievement from the University of Southern California School of Music.

Jazz vocalist Abbey Lincoln releases a hit album *You Gotta Pay The Band.*

Rap artist M. C. Hammer releases the album *Too Legit To Quit.* It includes *Do Not Pass Me By* with Tremaine Hawkins and a gospel choir, a record that fuses a traditional gospel hymn with the rap genre.

Rap artist Sister Souljah is verbally attacked by Bill Clinton at a presidential campaign meeting of the Rainbow Coalition.

The Atlanta-based cross-gender rap group Arrested Development (AD) releases their debut album *3 Years, 5 Months and 2 Days in the Life of...* It is an example of southern hip-hop/ethnic funk that the group calls "life music." The album is filled with spiritual/Black liberation lyrics.

Rap artist Ice-T records *Cop Killer.*

Film director John Singleton becomes the first black nominated for an Academy Award in the director category, for his movie *Boyz 'N the Hood.* The film stars the Rap artist Ice Cube.

R&B/Rock & Roll singer Little Richard's comeback includes the production of a children's album, *Shake It All About.*

Soul/Disco singer Barry White releases the album *Put Me In Your Mix.*

The Rock and Roll Hall of Fame inducts Bobby "Blue" Bland, Booker T. & the MGs, Johnny Cash, Jimi Hendrix, Isley Brothers, Sam & Dave, The Yardbirds, Elmore James, Professor Longhair, Leo Fender, Bill Graham and Doc Pomus.

Whitney Houston stars in and performs the soundtrack for the film *The Bodyguard.*

Whoopi Goldberg stars in *Sister Act,* a film that blends contemporary popular styles and gospel music styles with the traditional music of the Catholic church in its soundtrack. She also stars in the musical, anti-apartheid film *Sarafina.*

LaToya Jackson gives a triumphant performance in Paris, France at Moulin Rouge (following in the footsteps of the legendary Josephine Baker).

Pianist Awadagin Pratt becomes first African American to win the Naumberg International Piano Competition.

Composer David Baker writes *Roots II*, a five-movement suite for piano trio, based upon a wide range of sources, including work songs. It is performed by the Beaux Arts Trio at the Library of Congress in 1993 and on their CD *Spring Music*, released in 1994.

The Detroit Symphony Orchestra performs *Global Warming* at its African American Symphony Composers Forum, a work by composer Michael Abels, "conceived in the particularly hot and dry summer of 1989, when many of the recent major international political realignments were just beginning." The work has subsequently been performed by the orchestras of Cleveland, Houston, Atlanta, Baltimore, Columbus, Indianapolis, Dallas, Nashville, Phoenix, Savannah, Dayton and Toledo, and was also one of the first works of a black composer to be performed by the National Symphony of South Africa following the election of President Mandela.

The Southeast Symphony premieres *Harmonic Convergence,* a work composed by William H. Henderson.

Pianist Leon Bates premieres *Piano Concerto* (Virginia Symphony, JoAnn Faletta conducting), a work composed by Adolphus Hailstork under a commission from a consortium of five orchestras.

Classical composer Ed Bland writes *Rambunctius Serenade* for chamber orchestra, commissioned by the Afro-American Chamber Music Society.

Black nationalist Louis Farrakhan performs Mendelssohns Violin Concerto.

Frederick C. Tillis composes *A Festival Journey*, a work for solo jazz percussionist and symphony orchestra, commissioned by the Atlanta Symphony Orchestra.

Gregory Hines receives the Tony Award for Best Actor in a Musical for his performance in *Jelly's Last Jam*, the story of jazz pioneer Jelly Roll Morton, written and directed by George C. Wolfe.

Opera singer Barbara Hendricks is awarded the rank of Chevalier de al Legion dHonneur by France's President Francois Mitterand.

Anthony Davis composes the opera *Tania,* a work that he bases upon the kidnapping of Patty Hearst. The work is premiered at the American Music Theatre Festival. His music is composed in a style that challenges all boundaries, blending written music with improvised music.

Writer-director Julie Dash becomes first black woman to have a nationally distributed feature-length film, *Daughters of the Dust.*

The Anna Deavere Smith one-woman play, *Fires in the Mirror: Crown Heights, Brooklyn & Other Identities* (an examination of the August 1991 Crown Heights conflict between the Lubavitcher Jewish and Black communities) premieres at the New York Shakespeare Festival. It becomes runner-up for the Pulitzer Prize (1993), receives the Obie Award (1993), and is aired on PBS stations nationwide on *American Playhouse* (1993).

Spike Lee directs the epic film *Malcolm X.*

Poet/Playwright Derek Walcott, Boston University Professor of English, wins the Nobel Prize for Literature.

Dominique Dawes becomes the first black woman gymnast on a United States Olympic team.

Civil disturbances in Los Angeles in response to the verdicts in the Rodney King beating case (51 dead; 2,383 injured; more than 600 fires; nearly 15,000 arrests; up to $785 million in property damage). A number of works are written by composers of the classical genre as musical expressions in response to this series of events.

William Jefferson Clinton is elected president of the United States.

Dr. Mae C. Jemison becomes NASA's first black female astronaut to travel in space.

Jackie Joyner-Kersee becomes the first black woman to win back-to-back gold medals in the heptathlon competition (in the 1988 Summer Olympic Games in Seoul, South Korea, and in the 1992 Olympic Games in Barcelona, Spain).

Iku:

Choral director/conductor/composer Eva Jessye dies.

R&B singer Edward Kendricks (of The Temptations) dies.

R&B singer Mary Wells dies.

Blues singer Albert King dies of a heart attack.

 **1993**

Kuumba:

Arthur Ashe's memoir, *Days of Grace,* is published soon after his death. It contains a letter to his daughter Camera in the last chapter, articulating his dreams for her...a statement that has been subsequently used by arts advocates fighting to maintain government and community support for arts performance, creation, exhibition and education He particularly encourages his daughter:

> *To nurture an appreciation of music and the arts. When I was young, I played in my junior-high-school and high-school band for six years and developed a love of music and a persisting wonder that human beings can create and execute such wonderful melodies and harmonies. In my high-school concert each spring, we dressed in formal white jackets and bow ties and played music from Duke Ellington to Beethoven. In our collection of record albums at home you will find music from around the world, collected by me in my travels. Often, when I think of a place, music comes to mind: trumpets for Great*

> *Britain, violins for Austria and Germany, flutes for the Middle East,*
> *pianos for France,and finger pianos for West Africa; I think of drums*
> *for the American Indians, mandolins for Italy, castanets for Spain,*
> *cymbals for Japan, fiddles for our slave forebears. Each sound is like*
> *the signature of a place and its people. Each is a part of the harmony*
> *of the world* (302).

Singer Bobby McFerrin debuts as a guest conductor of the Los Angeles Philharmonic at the Hollywood Bowl. He conducts the holiday concert of the L.A. Philharmonic, performing Tchaikovsky's *Nutcracker Suite* and Beethoven's *Seventh Symphony*.

Classical composer Ed Bland writes *Grand Slam* for chamber orchestra, commissioned by the Afro-American Chamber Music Society Orchestra and dedicated to the memory of Jackie Robinson.

Conductor/composer/pianist Byron Smith founds the Spirit Chorale of Los Angeles, a professional ensemble dedicated to performing the music of the Jubilee tradition.

The Albert McNeil Jubilee Singers tour the Midwest, Germany, Austria, France, Switzerland, Luxembourg, and Toronto.

The exhibition *Beyond Category*: *The Musical Genius of Duke Ellington* opens at the Smithsonian Institution. His opera, *Queenie Pie,* is performed at the Brooklyn Academy of Music.

Jazz pianist Marcus Roberts releases the album *If I Could Be With You,* incorporating a variety of styles from the history of jazz, including gospel, ragtime, boogie-woogie, stride, swing and modern jazz.

Jazz composer/conductor/educator Gunther Schuller receives the *Down Beat* Lifetime Achievement Award.

Blues legend Ray Charles receives the Kennedy Center Honors.

Little Richard receives the lifetime achievement award from NARAS (the National Academy of Recording Arts and Sciences).

The Rock and Roll Hall of Fame inducts Ruth Brown, Cream, Creedence Clearwater Revival, The Doors, Etta James, Frankie Lymon &

the Teenagers, Van Morrison, Sly & the Family Stone, Dinah Washington, Dick Clark and Milt Gabler.

Hadda Brooks, Solomon Burke, Dave Clark, Floyd Dixon, Lowell Fulson, Erskine Hawkins, Wilson Pickett, Carla Thomas, Little Anthony and the Imperials, and Martha and the Vandellas receive Pioneer Awards from the Rhythm & Blues Foundation. James Brown receives the Lifetime Achievement Award.

Singer Michael Jackson performs a halftime extravaganza, *Heal the World* at the Super Bowl. Subsequently that year, he faces charges of child molestation.

The life of Tina Turner is depicted in the film *What's Love Got To Do With It.*

Kenny "Babyface" Edmonds releases the album *For The Cool In You.*

Boyz II Men win the Grammy award for the Best R&B Song, *End of the Road.*

Gospel singer Kirk Franklin records his debut album, *Kirk Franklin and The Family,* with its crossover hit single, "Why We Sing." The album sells one million copies over the next two years, and remains the *Billboard* No. 1 gospel album for a year. Its' crossover hit makes it to both the R&B and the pop *Billboard* charts. Franklin, who performs wearing hip-hop fashions, becomes part of the controversy over the encroachment of contemporary style into the gospel genre.

The Gospel Music Association reports that sales of gospel music recordings reaches one billion dollars. Big-name contemporary gospel music acts command fees as high as $35,000 per night.

Gospel singer Marion Williams and dancer-choreographer Arthur Mitchell receive Kennedy Center Honors.

Maya Angelou creates and performs a poem at the inauguration of president William Clinton, *On The Pulse Of Morning.* Several African American musicians perform at the inauguration concert that is produced by Quincy Jones.

Rita Dove becomes the first African American to hold the post of United States Poet Laureate.

Toni Morrison becomes the first black woman to win the Nobel Prize in Literature.

Legislation passes to establish a National African American Museum on the Mall in Washington, D.C.

Wesley Snipes stars in the film *Demolition Man.*

New Hampshire becomes the last state to approve a Martin Luther King, Jr. holiday.

Iku:

Jazz trumpeter/composer/bandleader Dizzy Gillespie dies.

Jazz singer William Clarence (Billy) Eckstine dies.

Jazz bandleader Erskine Hawkins dies.

Blues singer Albert Collins dies.

Contralto Marian Anderson dies.

Gospel composer Thomas A. Dorsey dies.

Jazz band director Sun Ra dies.

 **1994**

Kuumba:

Composer Gregory T. S. Walker writes the first rap symphony, *Dream In The Hood,* premiered by the Colorado Symphony with rappers Jeannie Madrid and Theo (Lord Of Word) Smith. Walker explains his understanding of rap: *According to the European standards, it doesn't correspond with their traditions...From the classical perspective, rap is a style that involves all phenomena that they have been trained to avoid—mechanical repetition, improvisation—finding, rather than creating or perfecting, a set of values...But in the trans-African perspective it is not so much whether rap is a subset of music, but how it is a part of life.* ("Jammin' to a Hip-Hop Classical Beat/Rap With Strings" in *Black Issues in Higher Education,* December 14, 1995, page 10.)

Classical composer Carman Moore writes *Mass for the 21st Century*, commissioned by the Lincoln Center (a work to mark the end of the 20th century and the beginning of the 21st). He describes it as a "multicultural work that is designed as a ritual in which adults turn over the stewardship of the world to the children, officially."

The Philadelphia Orchestra commissions Alvin Singleton to create a symphonic response to the Rodney King beating, *Fifty Six Blows*.

Conductor James DePreist is appointed music director of the Monte-Carlo Philharmonic.

Conductor/vocalist Boby McFerrin is appointed creative chair of the Saint Paul Chamber Orchestra.

A "cross-over" compact disc is released, *Side By Side*, with violinist Itzhak Perlman and jazz pianist Oscar Peterson.

Composer David Baker is inducted into the Down Beat Jazz Education Hall of Fame.

Jazz musician Dave Brubeck is awarded a Presidential National Medal of Arts by President Clinton.

Pianist Marcus Roberts becomes the musical director of the Lincoln Center Jazz Orchestra in New York City.

Jazz saxophonist Joshua Redman wins the *Downbeat* Jazz Artist of the Year Award, received a Grammy nomination for Best Jazz Instrumental Performance, and was chosen by the *Rolling Stone* Critics Poll as the Jazz Artist of the Year.

Jazz/pop singer Nancy Wilson releases her 55th album, *Love Nancy*.

Soul singer Aretha Franklin receives the Kennedy Center Honors.

Poet/Bluesologist/Jazz artist Gil Scott-Heron releases the album *Spirits*, including the rap song "Message To The Messengers."

Soul singer Dionne Farris makes her debut album, *Wild Seed-Wild Flower*, stretching the boundaries of soul music by combining elements of hard rock, traditional pop, folk, reggae, funk and psychedelia.

Boyz II Men release *II,* an album that sells 11.1 million copies.

The Rock and Roll Hall of Fame inducts The Animals, The Band, Duane Eddy, Grateful Dead, Elton John, John Lennon, Bob Marley, Rod Stewart, Willie Dixon, and Johnny Otis.

Singer Vanessa Williams appears on Broadway in a production of the musical, *Kiss Of The Spider Woman.*

The Kern/Hammerstein musical *Show Boat* is revived in a Broadway production directed by Harold Prince and starring Lonette McKee and Michel Bell.

Kirk Franklin wins the Gospel Music Workshop of America's Excellence Award.

Gospel groups Sounds of Blackness release the album *Africa To America: The Journey of the Drum.* The album is produced by Jimmy Jam and Terry Lewis. It features the hit single "I Believe."

Sounds of Blackness and BeBe and CeCe Winans bring gospel music to secular audiences via concert tour appearances at such places as the Greek Theater of Los Angeles.

Tramaine Hawkins releases the album *To A Higher Place.* It includes an electronically produced duet with Mahalia Jackson, "I Found The Answer." She explains that *Singing gospel music is not just a career; its a calling. Something sacred.*

The Gospel Music Industry Roundup identifies the following artists as the top songwriters of the year: Kirk Franklin, V. Michael McKay, Timothy Wright, Daryl Coley, Quincy Fielding, BeBe Winans, Marvin Winans, Margaret Douroux, Carol Antron and John P. Kee. In describing the gospel music songwriting process, V. Michael McKay suggests: *Because gospel songs are based on truth and the gospel of Jesus Christ, each song should be carefully handled. The text should be well thought out and written with integrity. Consider this, once you've written your lyrics, created your melody, and set your rhythm in preparing your song for ministry, do this one thing. Present it—imagining Jesus Christ as part of your audience. Then ask yourself, how you think he (Jesus) would feel about what he hears and sees.* (The Gospel Music Industry Round-Up, page 69.)

Hip-hop gospel music gains in popularity, including the music of such artists as A-1 Swift, Mike-E, E.T.W., and Gospel Gangstas. The music features a street beat and a Christian message.

Gospel singer Marion Williams receives a John D. and Catherine T. MacArthur Foundation genius award and a grant of $374,000. She also receives the Kennedy Center Lifetime Achievement award.

Gospel singer/composer Andrae Crouch releases the album *Mercy*. He criticizes the commercial sound of contemporary gospel music in an article in *American Visions* (Vol. 9, no. 4, page 48): *Our music is great, but a lot of the words ain't saying nothing. I feel today that our music is trying to be so sophisticated that we're losing the power of God's word. Today in gospel music you think of the people in the music, the personalities, but we have lost the word of God.*

Singer Michael Jackson marries Lisa Marie Presley, daughter of Elvis Presley.

The Education Department upholds the legality of minority scholarships created by colleges to promote diversity or to remedy past discrimination.

AIDS kills 43,566 in the United States.

Iku:

Composer/conductor Betty Jackson King dies.

Jazz drummer Connie Kay (of the Modern Jazz Quartet) dies.

Jazz vocalist Carmen McRae dies.

Entertainer Cab Calloway dies.

 **1995**

Kuumba:

The Houston Grand Opera produces *Porgy and Bess* with a co-production/touring agreement with the Cleveland Opera, Dallas Opera, Florida Grand Opera, Los Angeles Music Center Opera, Portland Opera, San Diego Opera, San Francisco Opera, Seattle Opera and The Orange

County Performing Arts Center. For the first time in history the production is stage directed by a black woman - Hope Clarke, and stars Terry Cook or Alvy Powell as Porgy, Luvenia Garner or Angela Simpson as Serena, Kimberly Jones as Clara, Jeffrey LaVar or Stacey Robinson as Crown, Larry Marshall as Sportin' Life, and Roberta Laws or Marquita Lister as Bess.

Rap artist Tupac Shakur releases the recording *Me Against the World*, a disc that moves immediately to the No. 1 spot on Billboard magazine's pop chart. During this time, the artist is in jail on New York's Rikers Island, serving two years on a sex-abuse charge.

Rap artists Aztlan Underground provide an example of cultural diversity in Rap, with the album *Decolonized EP*, including the bilingual song "My Blood Is Red":

> *Quientos anos de tu confusion/Y vives sordo y ciego en una ilusion/Pero la culpa no es tuya/Es de las culebras/Los blancs Europeos que robaron a las tierras/Y sigen controlando por todo el mundo/Me llaman 'ilegal'/Con esto me confundo/Recuerda, gringo, nuestras tierras los has robado/Entonces, gringo, tu eres el gran mojado* - meaning - *Five hundred years of confusion and you live deaf and blind in an illusion. But it's not your fault, it's their sakes. The white Europeans who stole the land and who continue to control the world. They call me 'illegal,' with this they confuse me. Remember, white boy, you stole our land. This means that you, white boy, are the real wetback.*

Rap music, particularly gangsta rap, comes under attack, described as a "violent and anti-social force" by such people as former Education Secretary William J. Bennett (*it perverts young people by glorifying immoral behavior*), conservative activist C. DeLores Tucker, head of the National Political Caucus of Black Women, and Senate Majority Leader Bob Dole who together have targeted corporate America (particularly Time Warner) for its support of this art form. As a result, Time Warner begins negotiating a way out of its $100-million share in Interscope Records, distributor of such rap stars as Snoop Doggy Dogg, Dr. Dre and Tupac Shakur. In response, Russell (Rush) Simmons, CEO of Def Jam Recordings and the "king of hip-hop entrepreneurs" as head of the largest African American owned company in the record business, issues a statement blasting the critics: *No truly in-touch person believes that the dire state of American society is the result of rap lyrics. Let's be clear, rap music is just that—music. It is an art form.*

Tha Dogg Pound's new album, *Dogg Food*, sells 278,000 copies in the first week.

Rapper Eazy E releases the album *Str8 Off Tha Streetz of Mutha-phukkin' Compton.*

Rapper Coolio releases *Gangsta's Paradise,* an album that sells 2.5 million copies. The hit track on this album is "Gangsta's Paradise," the rap song that is included in the *Dangerous Minds* film score.

West Coast hip-hop group the Watts Gangstas and the American Civil Liberties Union sue the city of Inglewood, California to stop the ban the city placed to prevent promotional advertisement for the group's album *The Real.*

Russell (Rush) Simmons produces *The Show,* a rap music documentary, and is developing plans to launch a 24-hour satellite radio network. He has established as his goal the intention *to make sure black-owned firms reap a fair portion of the profits from the hip-hop culture they invented.*

Richard (Crazy Legs) Colon and other electric boogie - breakdancers, appear in the musical *Jam On The Groove.*

Black music provides the distinctive music soundtrack for television commercials. For example, Al Jarreau sells Big Macs for MacDonalds; Aretha Franklin markets *The Wheel Of Fortune* television show; and the R&B song *Searchin'* provides the music background for a Frosted Flakes commercial.

Soul artist Stevie Wonder releases the CD *Conversation Peace.*

Soul singer Me'Shell NdegeOcello earns a Grammy Award for her album *Plantation Lullabies,* a product that stretches the boundaries of soul music by creating a hybrid of hip-hop and soul.

36-year-old singer Michael Jackson releases the two-disc album *HIStory: Past, Present & Future - Book* I (15 new songs and 15 remastered hits), marketed by a $4 million theatrical teaser, a $7 million video, and an interview appearance on TV's *Prime Time Live.* It includes Jimmy

Jam, Terry Lewis, Dallas Austin, R Kelly, Bill Bottrell and David Foster as producers, with performances with sister Janet Jackson, and rapper/basketball superstar Shaquille O'Neal. Several songs seem to be directed at the media, including *Scream, Tabloid Junkie, This Time Around*, and *2 Bad*. After national furor, Michael Jackson agrees to replace the controversial lyrics in the song *They Don't Care About Us*, deleting the *Jew me/sue me/kick me/kike me* line, language that he originally intended to use to demonstrate the ugliness of stereotyping.

Percussionist Albert William "Tootie" Heath joins the Modern Jazz Quartet. The ensemble was described by Don Heckman in a Los Angeles *Times* preview article regarding an upcoming concert: *The Modern Jazz Quartet takes the stage like a string quartet preparing to perform a cycle of Beethoven works. Dressed in dark, conservative suits or tuxedos, the four veteran players approach their instruments—piano, vibes, bass and drums— with the style and decorum, the calm, professional assuredness of classical virtuosi. The music begins, quietly at first, then urged forward by a subtle, driving swing that is simple, understated and irresistibly rhythmic. But no matter how much the music heats up—and it does—the quartet continues to retain its cool, relaxed demeanor. The magic of the modern Jazz Quartet is its talent for cranking up the fires of jazz without breaking a sweat. Forty-three years after the MJQ was formed, it has become the jazz worlds longest-lived, unerring standard of musical excellence.* (October 14, 1995) The group performs earlier in the year at a White House dinner, where President Clinton described them as *the greatest music group in history—without a saxophone.*

New York City announces plans to erect a 25-foot bronze statue of Duke Ellington at the gateway to Harlem.

Conductor/composer/arranger Quincy Jones receives the Jean Hersholt Humanitarian Award from the Academy of Motion Picture Arts and Sciences.

The Uptown String Quartet, an all black women's quartet, is in residence at Interlochen performing a style that combines jazz, blues, spirituals and ragtime on instruments that are rooted in European classical musical practice.

Jazz pianist/composer Billy Taylor releases the recording *Homage*, a disc that includes a three-part suite, *Homage*, featuring Billy Taylor with the Turtle Island String Quartet, and the nine-part *Step Into My*

Dream, a musical impression of Harlem's 125th Street, written to be performed with the David Parsons Dance Company.

Jazz pianist Ahmad Jamal releases the album *I Remember Duke, Hoagy and Strayhorn.*

The Roy Hargrove-Christian McBride-Stephen Scott Trio release the album *Parker's Mood* as a tribute to jazz saxophonist Charlie Parker.

The National Association of Recording Manufacturers announces the best-selling jazz recording, 1994-1995, to be Kenny G's *Miracles: The Holiday Album.*

Clint Eastwood establishes a jazz label, Malpaso, to be distributed through Warner Brothers.

John Biles Associate Professor at Rochester Institute of Technology has developed a music software program that lets a computer compose music for jazz solos, known as GenJam (meaning genetic jammer).

Singer Lena Horne releases the album *An Evening with Lena Horne— Live at the Supper Club.*

Singer/actress Diahann Carroll stars in *Sunset Boulevard,* playing the role of Norma Desmund.

Singer Paul Robeson is inducted into the College Football Hall of Fame.

The *Soul Train* television show celebrates its 25th anniversary.

Forbes Magazine reports the top-earning entertainers, including Boyz II Men ($17,000,000), Bill Cosby ($15,000,000), Michael Jackson ($45,000,000) and Oprah Winfrey ($74,000,000).

Hootie and the Blowfish emerge from South Carolina as a popular, mixed race mainstream pop/rock group with a multiplatinum album, *Cracked Rear View.* The African American lead singer, Darius Rucker, is described in the November 5th New York *Times* as being the musical counterpart to General Colin L. Powell—a person who *manages to be both black and separatable from blackness, able to contain his racial identity as just one aspect of his identity.* (page H36)

Public schools in Georgia hold separate high school proms for black and white students, justifying this discrimination by asserting the idea that black students and white students like different kinds of music.

The Crenshaw High School Elite Choir of Los Angeles, conducted by Iris Stevenson, performs in London for Prince Charles, in Paris at EuroDisneyland, in the city of Lyon, and in Nice at the Nice Carnival.

The Los Angeles Philharmonic performs a gala concert featuring Yvette Devereaux as conductor with choruses from Crenshaw High School, Hamilton High School Music Academy, and The FAME Freedom Choir of First A.M.E. Church of Los Angeles (with Rev. Cecil L. Murray as narrator), all in the world-premiere performance of Joe Westmoreland's *Easter Suite.*

Composer/conductor Jester Hairston is featured artist in the United States Air Force Band Guest Artist Series concert in the DAR Constitution Hall, performing with the Singing Sargeants.

The Anderson Quartet, winners of the Eastman School of Musics International Cleveland Quartet Competition, begins a guest artist residency at California State University Los Angeles. They are the first African American chamber ensemble to win a major classical music competition. The string ensemble is named in honor of contralto Marian Anderson.

Alvin Singleton composes *BluesKonzert.* The work is commissioned by a consortium of three symphony orchestras including the Detroit Symphony Orchestra, the Houston Symphony and the Kansas City Symphony.

The String Trio of New York premieres the chamber work *Sounds Without Nouns* by Anthony Davis. The piece is subsequently renamed *Happy Valley Blues,* relating the work to the area of Pennsylvania where the composer was raised. The work was commissioned by a consortium of six performing arts centers, including the Center for the Performing Arts at Penn State University and the Cerritos (California) Center for the Performing Arts. It is performed by an ensemble that consists of piano, violin, bass and guitar.

Opera singer Grace Bumbry, with her Black Music Vocal Ensemble, performs a concert of spirituals at the Salzburg Festival in Austria. She and the other singers are featured on the November 5th CBS News *Sunday Morning* show—*The singers cannot separate the faces of their grandparents from the faces of the people who created the spirituals, remembering the spirit of the spiritual made me what I am.*

Gospel singer Andrae Crouch is installed as pastor of Christ Memorial Church of God in Christ, a church founded in Pacoima, California by his father.

Singer B. B. King and actor/producer Sidney Poitier receive the Kennedy Center Honors for lifetime achievement in the performing arts.

Singer Marilyn McCoo replaces Lonette McKee as Julie in the musical *Show Boat.*

The film *Waiting To Exhale* is released, with a sound track produced by Babyface and featuring performances by Whitney Houston, CeCe Winans, Mary J. Blige, Brandy, Toni Braxton, Faith Evans, Aretha Franklin, Chaka Khan, Patti LaBelle, Chante Moore, SWV and TLC.

Keith Morrison, the Dean of the College of Creative Arts at San Francisco State University comments: *There was a time when Black people didn't have the kind of money (needed to purchase art), but today there are enough Black people with that kind of money. It is important for them to realize that their art is their legacy.*

BET (Black Entertainment Television) celebrates its 15th anniversary, having evolved into a 24-hour, 7-day-a-week organization that now generates annual revenue of over one hundred and seven million dollars.

Ebony magazine celebrates its 50th anniversary.

Essence magazine celebrates its 25th anniversary.

Black Enterprise Magazine celebrates its 25th anniversary.

The Collegium for African American Research is established—a new association of European academics who teach the culture of Black Americans.

The country moves to dismantle the accomplishments of the Great Society, including affirmative action.

The O. J. Simpson murder trial becomes a polarizing national event. It is covered by as many as 1,159 credentialed reporters, with more than 100 million viewers tuned in to see the announcement of the verdict.

The BEEM Foundation and the California Afro-American Museum produce the multimedia exhibition, *The Musical Renaissance of Black Los Angeles, 1890-1955.*

I Tell My Heart, spotlighting the work of J. Horace Pippin, becomes the first solo of an African American visual artist at the New York Metropolitan Museum.

August Wilson continues his series of plays with *Seven Guitars.*

The National Million Man March, a Holy Day of Atonement, Reconciliation, Responsibility and Absence, a day calling for atonement for unmanly behavior, a time for religious unification, voter registration and the start of a national agenda of community-building, is held on October 16th in Washington, D.C., under the leadership of Benjamin Chavis and Louis Farrakhan, with a mission statement developed by Dr. Maulana Karenga that specifies:

> *We stand in Washington conscious that its a pivotal point from which to speak to the country and the world. And we come bringing the most central views and values of our faith communities, our deepest commitments to our social justice tradition and the strategies it requires, the most instructive lessons of our history, and a profoundly urgent sense of the need for positive and productive action. In standing up and assuming responsibility in a new, renewed and expanded sense, we honor our ancestors, enrich our lives and give promise to our descendants. Moreover, through this historic work and struggle we strive to always know and introduce ourselves to history and humanity as a people who are spiritually and ethically grounded; who speak truth, do justice, respect our ancestors and elders, cherish, support and challenge our children, care for the vulnerable, relate rightfully to the environment, struggle for what is right and resist what is wrong, honor our past, willingly engage our present and self-consciously plan for and welcome our future.*

The March is celebrated in the "knowledge" Rap album *One Million*

Strong, featuring a variety of Rap artists, including Mobb Deep, Ice T, Chuck D, The RZA, The Alkaholiks, and Channel Live. Every track deals with an aspect of the black struggle.

Iku:

Composer Ulysses Kay dies of Parkinson's Disease.

Composer/ethnomusicologist John Elwood Price dies.

Composer/ethnomusicologist Gertrude Rivers Robinson dies.

Jazz composer/saxophonist Julius Arthur Hemphill dies.

Jazz drummer William R. (Cozy) Cole dies.

Composer/arranger Julian C. Work dies.

Gospel composer/conductor Doris Akers dies.

R&B singer Melvin Franklin (of The Temptations) dies.

Soul artist Junior Walker (of Junior Walker and the All Stars) dies of cancer.

Rap artist Eric Wright (Eazy-E) dies of complications from AIDS. He is eulogized in Los Angeles by Rev. Cecil Murray of First AME: *I know a little blackbird that sings. And his lyrics are, "I want you to live. I want you to be careful. I want you to slow down."*

AFRICAN AMERICAN MUSIC
BIBLIOGRAPHY

Bibliography

ARCHIVES

Atlanta Historical Society, Atlanta, Georgia

Center for Black Music Research, Columbia College, Chicago, Illinois

Center for the Study of Southern Folklore, Memphis, Tennessee

Chicago Historical Society, Chicago, Illinois

Chicago Public Library, Carter G. Woodson Branch, Vivian G. Harsh Collection of Afro-American Literature and History

Detroit Public Library (Michigan), E. Azalia Hackley Collection

Georgia State Archives, Atlanta

New York Public Library for the Performing Arts, Lincoln Center

New York Public Library, Schomburg Center for Research in Black Culture

Queens College of the City, University of New York, Benjamin S. Rosenthal Library, Louis Armstrong Archives

Rutgers University (Newark, New Jersey) Institute of Jazz Studies (including the Jazz Oral History Project)

Tulane University (New Orleans, Louisiana) William Ransom Hogan Jazz Archive

University of Chicago, Regenstein Library - Music Division, Chicago Jazz Archive

ENCYCLOPEDIAS

Case, Brian, and Stan Britt. *The Illustrated Encyclopedia of Jazz.* New York: Harmony Books, 1978.

Feather, Leonard. *Encyclopedia of Jazz.* New York: Horizon Press, 1960.

_____. *Encyclopedia of Jazz. The New Edition of the Encyclopedia of Jazz, Vol. 1.* New York: Horizon Press, 1962.

_____. *Encyclopedia of Jazz. The Encyclopedia of Jazz in the Sixties, Vol. 2.* New York: Horizon Press, 1966.

_____. *Encyclopedia of Jazz: The Encyclopedia of Jazz in the Seventies, Vol. 3.* New York: Horizon Press, 1976.

Hardy, Phil, and Dave Laing, eds. *Encyclopedia of Rock, 1955-1971.* London: Aquarius Books, 1977.

Stambler, Irwin. *Encyclopedia of Pop, Rock and Soul.* New York: St. Martin's Press, 1974.

382

Bibliography

Southern, Eileen. *Biographical Dictionary of Afro-American and African Musicians. Encyclopedia of Black Music Series.* Westport, CT: Greenwood Press, 1982.

BOOKS

Abdul, Raoul. *Blacks in Classical Music: A Personal History.* New York Dodd, Mead and Co., 1977.

Abdul, Raoul. *Famous Black Entertainers of Today.* New York : Dodd, Mead and Co., 1974.

Adler, Bill. *Rap: Portraits and Lyrics of a Generation of Black Rockers.* New York: St. Martin's Press, 1991.

Afolabi Ojo, G. J. *Yoruba Culture.* London University of Ife and University of London Press, 1966.

Albertson, Chris. *Bessie.* New York: Stein & Day, Publishers, 1972.

Allen, Walter C., and Brian Rust. *King Joe Oliver.* London and New York: Sidgwick and Jackson, 1958.

Allen, William F., Charles P. Ware, and Lucy M. Garrison. *Slave Songs of the United States.* New York: A. Simpson, 1867.

Alleyne, Mervyn C. *Roots of Jamaican Culture.* London: Pluto Press, 1988.

Anderson, Jervis. *This Was Harlem: A Cultural Portrait, 1900-1950.* New York: Farrar, Straus & Giroux, 1982.

Armstrong, Louis. *Louis Armstrong — A Self Portrait. The Interview by Richard Meryman.* New York: Eakins Press, 1971.

_____. *Satchmo: My Life in New Orleans.* New York: Prentice-Hall, 1954; Da Capo Press, 1986.

_____. *Swing That Music.* London/ New York: Longmans, Green, 1936.

Armstrong, M. F., and Helen M. Ludlow. *Hampton and Its Students.* Freeport, N.Y.: Books for Libraries Press, 1971. Originally published, 1874.

Baker, David. *Jazz Improvisation: A Comprehensive Study for All Players.* Chicago: Maher, 1969.

Baker, David, Lydia Belt and Herman Hudson. *The Black Composer Speaks.* Metuchen, NJ: The Scarecrow Press, Inc., 1978.

Baker, Houston. *Blues, Ideology, and Afro-American Literature: A Vernacular Theory.* Chicago: University of Chicago Press, 1984.

Baker, Josephine, and Jo Bouillon. *Josephine.* Paris: Laffont, 1976; Translated by Mariana Fitzpatrick. New York: Harper & Row, 1977.

383

Bibliography

Ballanta-Taylor, Nicholas. *Saint Helena Island Spirituals.* New York: Schirmer, 1925.

Balliett, Whitney. *Jelly Roll, Jabbo & Fats: 19 Portraits in Jazz.* New York: Oxford University Press, 1983.

Bane, Michael. *White Boy Singin' the Blues: The Black Roots of White Rock.* New York: Penguin Press, 1982.

Barlow, William. *Looking Up at Down: The Emergence of Blues Culture.* Philadelphia: Temple University Press, 1989.

Bascom, William R., and Melville J. Herskovits, eds. *Continuity and Change in African Cultures.* Chicago: University of Chicago Press, 1959.

Basie, Count. *Good Morning Blues: The Autobiography of Count Basie, as told to Albert Murray.* New York: Random House, 1985.

Bebey, Francis. *African Music: A People's Art.* Translated by Josephine Bennett. New York: Lawrence Hill, 1975.

Bego, Mark. *Aretha Franklin: The Queen of Soul.* New York: St. Martin's Press, Inc., 1989.

Belz, Carl. *The Story of Rock.* 2nd ed. New York: Oxford University Press, 1972.

Benjaminson, Peter. *The Story of Motown.* New York: Grove Press, 1979.

Bennett, Lerone, Jr. *Before the Mayflower: A History of the Negro in America: 1619-1962.* 4th ed. Chicago: Johnson Publishing, 1969.

Benston, Kimberly W., and Amiri Baraka (LeRoi Jones), eds. *A Collection of Critical Essays.* Englewood Cliffs, NJ: Prentice-Hall, 1978.

Berendt, Joachim-Ernst. *The Jazz Book: From New Orleans to Rock and Free Jazz.* Translated by Dan Morgenstern, Helmut Bredigkeit & Barbara Bredigkeit New York: Lawrence Hill, 1975.

Berger, Morroe, Edward Berger and James Patrick. *Benny Carter.* Metuchen, NJ: The Scarecrow Press, Inc., 1982.

Berlin, Edward A. *King of Ragtime: Scott Joplin and His Era.* New York: Oxford University Press, 1994.

_____. *Ragtime: A Musical and Cultural History.* Berkeley, CA: University of California Press, 1980.

Berry, Chuck. *Chuck Berry: The Autobiography.* New York: Harmony, 1987.

Berton, Ralph. *Remembering Bix: A Memoir of the Jazz Age.* New York: Harper and Row, 1974.

Bigard, Barney. *With Louis and the Duke: The Autobiography of a Jazz Clarinetist.* New York: Oxford University Press, 1986.

Blancq, Charles. *Sonny Rollins: The Journey of a Jazzman.* Boston: Twayne Publishers, 1983.

Blesh, Rudi. *Combo: U.S.A.: Eight Lives in Jazz.* Philadelphia : Chilton Book Co., 1971.

_____. *Shining Trumpets: A History of Jazz.* 2nd ed. New York: Alfred A. Knopf, 1958.

Blesh, Rudi, and Harriet Janis. *They All Played Ragtime: The True Story of an American Music.* 4th ed. New York: Oak Publications, 1950, 1966, 1971.

Boatner, Edward. *Spirituals Triumphant: Old and New.* Nashville: Sunday School Publishing Board, National Baptist Convention, U.S.A., 1927.

Boeckman, Charles. *And the Beat Goes On; a Survey of Pop Music in America.* Washington, D.C.: R. B. Luce, 1972.

_____. *Cool, Hot and Blue: A History of Jazz for Young People.* Washington, DC: Luce, 1968.

Bogle, Donald. *Brown Sugar: Eighty Years of Americas Black Female Superstars.* New York: Crown Publishers, Harmony Books, 1980.

Bolcom, William, and Robert Kimball. *Reminiscing with Sissle and Blake.* New York: Viking Press, 1973.

Bontemps, Arna, ed. *The Harlem Renaissance Remembered.* New York: Dodd, Mead and Co., 1972.

Boskin, Joseph. *Sambo: The Rise and Demise of an American Jester.* New York and Oxford: Oxford University Press, 1986.

Boughton, Viv. *Black Gospel.* London: Blandford Press, 1985.

Bradford, Perry. *Born With the Blues: Perry Bradford's Own Story: The True Story of the Pioneering Blues Singers and Musicians in the Early Days of Jazz.* New York: Oak Publications, 1965.

Brandel, Rose. *The Music of Central Africa: An Ethnomusicological Study.* New York: Da Capo Press, 1983.

Brawley, Benjamin. *The Negro Genius: A New Appraisal of the Achievement of the American Negro in Literature and the Fine Arts.* Reprint. New York: Biblio & Tannen, 1966.

Brooks, Edward. *The Bessie Smith Companion: A Critical Appreciation of the Recordings.* New York: Da Capo Press, 1983.

Broonzy, Big Bill, and Yannick Bruynoghe. *Big Bill Blues.* Paris: Ludd, 1987; New York: Da Capo Press, 1992.

Broughton, Viv. *Black Gospel: An Illustrated History of the Gospel Sound.* Poole, England: Blandford Press, 1985.

Brown, Charles T. *The Art of Rock and Roll.* Englewood Cliffs, N.J.: Prentice-Hall, Inc., 1983.

Brunn. H. O. *The Story of the Original Dixieland Jazz Band.* New York: Da Capo Press, 1960, 1986.

Buckley, Gail Lumet. *The Hornes - An American Family.* New York: Alfred A. Knopf, 1986.

Budds, Michael J. *Jazz in the Sixties: The Expansion of Musical Resources and Techniques.* Iowa City, IA: University of Iowa Press, 1990.

Burleigh, Harry T. *Album of Negro Spirituals.* Melville, New York: Belwin Mills, 1969. Originally published, 1917.

Burlin, Natalie Curtis. *Songs and Tales of the Dark Continent.* New York: G. Schirmer, 1920.

Burnett, James. *Billie Holiday.* New York: Hippocrene Books, 1984.

_____. *Coleman Hawkins.* New York: Hippocrene Books, 1984.

Butcher, Margaret Just. *The Negro in American Culture.* New York: New American Library, 1956.

Calloway, Cab, and Bryant Rollins. *Of Minnie the Moocher and Me.* New York: Crowell, 1976.

Calt, Stephen, and Gayle Wardlow. *King of the Delta Blues: The Life and Music of Charlie Patton.* Newton, NJ: Rock Chapel Press, 1988.

Carr, Ian. *Miles Davis.* New York: William Morrow & Co., 1982.

Cazort, Jean. *Born to Play: The Life and Career of Hazel Harrison.* Westport, Connecticut: Greenwood Press, 1983.

Chambers, Jack. *Milestones 2: The Music and Times of Miles Davis Since 1960.* Long Beach, California: Beach Tree Press, 1985.

Charles, Ray, and David Ritz. *Brother Ray: Ray Charles Own Story.* New York: The Dial Press, 1978.

Charters, Ann. *Nobody: The Story of Bert Williams.* New York: Macmillan Publishing Co., 1970.

Charters, Samuel B. *Jazz: New Orleans, 1855-1963, An Index to the Negro Musicians of New Orleans.* New York: Oak Publications, 1964.

_____. *The Bluesmen.* New York: Oak Publications, 1967.

_____. *The Country Blues.* rev. ed. New York: Da Capo Press, 1975.

_____. *The Legacy of the Blues.* New York: Da Capo Press, 1977.

_____. *The Poetry of the Blues.* New York: Avon Books, 1970.

_____. *The Roots of the Blues.* New York: Perigee Books, 1982.

Charters, Samuel, and Leonard B. Kunstadt. *Jazz: A History of the New York Scene.* Garden City, NY: Doubleday & Co., Inc., 1962.

Chilton, John. *Billies Blues: The Billie Holiday Story, 1933-1959.* Briarcliff Manor, NY: Stein & Day, Publishers, 1975.

_____. *Let the Good Times Roll: The Story of Louis Jordan and His Music.* Ann Arbor, MI: University of Michigan Press, 1994.

_____. *Who's Who of Jazz: Storyville to Swing Street.* London; New York: Chilton Book Co.; Da Capo Press, 1972; 1985.

Claghorn, Charles E. *Biographical Dictionary of Jazz.* Englewood Cliffs, NJ: Prentice-Hall, 1983.

Coker, Jerry. *Improvising Jazz.* Englewood Cliffs, NJ: Prentice-Hall, 1964.

_____. *Listening to Jazz.* Englewood Cliffs, NJ: Prentice-Hall, 1978.

Cole, Bill. *Miles Davis: A Musical Biography.* New York: William Morrow & Co., 1974.

Cole, Maria, and Lovie Robinson. *Nat King Cole, an Intimate Biography.* New York: William Morrow & Co., 1971.

Colin, Sid. *Ella: The Life and Times of Ella Fitzgerald.* London: Elm Tree Books, 1986.

Collier, Graham. *Inside Jazz.* London: Quartet, 1973.

Collier, James Lincoln. *Duke Ellington.* New York: Oxford University Press, 1987.

_____. *Louis Armstrong: An American Genius.* New York: Oxford University Press, 1983.

_____. *The Making of Jazz: A Comprehensive History.* Boston: Houghton Mifflin, 1978.

Cone, James H. *The Spirituals and the Blues: An Interpretation.* New York: The Seabury Press, 1972.

Cook, Bruce. *Listen to the Blues.* New York: Charles Scribners Sons, 1973.

Cornell, Jean Gay. *Mahalia Jackson, Queen of Gospel Song.* Champaign, IL: Garrard Publishing Co., 1974.

Costello, Mark. *Signifying Rappers.* Boston: Ecco Press, 1989.

Courlander, Harold. *Haiti Singing.* Chapel Hill, North Carolina: The University Press, 1939; New York: Cooper Square Publishers, 1973.

_____. *Negro Folk Music, USA.* New York: Columbia University Press, 1963.

_____. *A Treasury of African Folklore.* New York: Crown Publishers, 1975.

Crow, Bill. *Jazz Anecdotes.* New York. Oxford: University Press, 1990.

Cruse, Harold. *The Crisis of the Negro Intellectual: From Its Origins to the Present.* New York: William Morrow & Co., 1967.

Cuney-Hare, Maud. *Negro Musicians and Their Work.* Washington, DC: Associated Press, 1939; New York: Da Capo Press, 1974.

Curtis, Susan. *Dancing to a Black Mans Tune: A Life of Scott Joplin.* Colombia, MO: University of Missouri Press, 1994.

DAzevedo, Warren L., ed. *The Traditional Artist in African Societies.* Bloomington, IN: Indiana University Press, 1974.

Dahl, Linda. *Stormy Weather: The Music and Lives of a Century of Jazzwomen.* New York: Pantheon, 1984.

Dance, Helen. *Stormy Monday: The T-Bone Walker Story.* Baton Rouge: Louisiana State University Press, 1987.

Dance, Stanley. *The World of Count Basie.* New York: Charles Scribners Sons/Da Capo Press, 1980.

_____. *The World of Duke Ellington.* New York: Charles Scribners Sons, 1970.

_____. *The World of Earl Hines.* New York: Charles Scribners Sons, 1977.

_____. *The World of Swing.* New York: Charles Scribners Sons, 1974.

Davis, Francis. *The History of the Blues: The Roots, the Music, the People from Charley Patton to Robert Cray.* New York: Hyperion, 1995.

Davis, Miles with Quincy Troupe. *Miles: The Autobiography.* New York: Simon & Schuster, Inc., 1989; 1990.

DeLerma, Dominique-Rene. *Black Concert and Recital Music, a Provisional Repertoire List.* Bloomington, IN: The Afro-American Music Opportunities Association, 1975.

_____. *Black Music in Our Culture.* Kent, OH: Kent State University Press, 1970.

Bibliography

_____. *Reflections on Afro-American Music.* Kent, OH: Kent State University Press, 1973.

Dett, R. Nathaniel, ed. *The Dett Collection of Negro Spirituals: Originals, Settings, Anthems, Motets.* Chicago: Hall & McCreary, 1936.

_____. *Religious Folk-Songs of the Negro: As Sung at Hampton Institute.* Hampton, Virginia: Hampton Institute Press, 1927.

De Veaux, Alexis. *Don't Explain: A Song of Billie Holiday.* New York: Harper & Row, 1980.

Dixon, Robert M. W., and John Godrich. *Blues and Gospel Records, 1902-1942.* 2nd ed. London: Storyville Publications, 1969.

_____. *Recording the Blues.* New York: Stein & Day, Publishers, 1970.

Dominy, Jeannine. *Leontyne Price.* New York: Chelsea House Publishers, 1992.

Doran, James M. *Erroll Garner, the Most Happy Piano.* Metuchen, NJ: The Scarecrow Press, Inc., 1985.

Driggs, Frank and Harris Lewine. *Black Beauty, White Heat: A Pictorial History of Classic Jazz, 1920-1950.* New York: William Morrow & Co., 1982.

DuBois, William E. B. *The Souls of Black Folk. 1903.* Reprint. New York; Millwood, NY: Fawcett World Library, 1961; New York: Washington Square Press, 1970; Millwood, NY: Kraus-Thomson Organization, 1973.

Dyson, Michael Eric. *Reflecting Black: African American Cultural Criticism.* Minneapolis: University of Minnesota Press, 1993.

Elkins, Stanley M. *Slavery: A Problem in American Institutional and Intellectual Life.* Chicago: University of Chicago Press, 1959; New York: Grosset & Dunlap, 1963.

Ellington, Edward Kennedy (Duke). *Music Is My Mistress.* New York: Doubleday & Co., Inc., 1973; New York: Da Capo Press, 1976.

Ellington, Mercer, and Stanley Dance. *Duke Ellington in Person: An Intimate Memoir.* Boston: Houghton Mifflin, 1978.

Emery, Lynne Fauley. *Black Dance in the United States from 1619 to 1970.* Palo Alto, CA: National Press Books, 1972.

Epstein, Dena J. *Sinful Tunes and Spirituals. Black Folk Music to the Civil War.* Urbana and Chicago: University of Illinois Press, 1977; 1981.

Fabre, Genevieve, ed. *History and Memory in African American Culture.* New York: Oxford University Press, 1995.

Feather, Leonard. *From Satchmo to Miles.* New York: Stein & Day Publishers, 1972.

_____. *Inside Jazz.* New York: Da Capo Press, 1977.

Fennett, Gene. *Swing Out: Great Negro Dance Bands.* New York: Da Capo Press, 1970; 1993.

Ferris, William. *Blues from the Delta.* Garden City, NY: Anchor Press/ Doubleday & Co., Inc. 1979.

Finkelstein, Sidney Walter. *Jazz: A Peoples Music.* New York: Da Capo Press, 1975.

Fisher, Miles Mark. *Negro Slave Songs in the United States.* Secaucus, NJ: Citadel Press, 1978. Originally published in 1953.

Floyd, Samuel A., ed. *Black Music in the Harlem Renaissance.* Westport, Conn.: Greenwood, Press, 1990.

_____. *The Power of Black Music. Interpreting Its History from Africa to the United States.* New York: Oxford University Press, 1995.

Fox, Ted. *Showtime at the Apollo.* New York: Holt, Rinehart and Winston, 1983.

Frankl, Ron. *Charlie Parker.* New York: Chelsea House, 1993.

_____. *Duke Ellington.* New York: Chelsea House, 1988.

Frazier, E. Franklin. *The Black Bourgeoisie.* New York: Free Press, 1957.

Gammond, Peter, ed. *Duke Ellington: His Life and Music.* New York: Roy, 1958.

_____. *Scott Joplin and the Ragtime Era.* New York: St. Martin's Press, 1975.

Garland, Phyl. *The Sound of Soul.* New York: Pocket Books, 1971.

Garon, Paul. *Blues and the Poetic Spirit.* London: Eddison Press, 1975.

Gayle, Addison, Jr., ed. *The Black Aesthetic.* Garden City, New York: Doubleday, 1971.

Gelly, Dave. *Lester Young.* New York: Hippocrene Books, 1984.

Genovese, Eugene. *Roll, Jordan, Roll: The World the Slaves Made.* New York: Pantheon, 1974.

Gentry, Tony. *Dizzy Gillespie.* New York: Chelsea House, 1991.

George, Carol V. R. *Segregated Sabbaths. Richard Allen and the Rise of Independent Black Churches, 1760-1840.* New York: Oxford University Press, 1973.

George, Don. *Sweet Man: The Real Duke Ellington.* New York: G. P. Putnams Sons, 1981.

George, Nelson. *The Death of Rhythm and Blues.* New York: Pantheon Books, 1988.

Giddins, Gary. *Celebrating Bird: The Triumph of Charlie Parker.* New York: Morrow, 1987.

Gillespie, Dizzy, with Al Fraser. *To Be or Not to Bop.* New York: Doubleday & Co., Inc., 1979.

Gillette, Charlie. *The Sound of the City.* Revised and Expanded Edition. New York: Pantheon, 1983.

Gitler, Ira. *Jazz Masters of the Forties.* New York: Collier Books, 1974.

_____. *Swing to Bop.* New York: Oxford University Press, 1985.

Gleason, Ralph. *Celebrating the Duke and Louis, Bessie, Bird, Carman, Miles, Dizzy and Other Heroes.* New York: Little, Brown, 1975.

Gold, Robert. *Jazz Lexicon: An A-Z Dictionary of Jazz Terms in the Vivid Idiom of Americas Most Successful Nonconformist Minority.* New York: Alfred A. Knopf, 1964.

_____. *Jazz Talk.* Indianapolis: Bobbs-Merrill, 1975.

Goldberg, Joe. *Jazz Masters of the 50s.* New York: Macmillan Publishing Co., 1965.

Goreau, L. *Just Mahalia, Baby.* Gretna, CA: Pelican Publishing, 1975.

Gourse, Leslie. *Every Day. The Story of Joe Williams.* London: Quartet Books, 1985.

_____. *Sassy: The Life of Sarah Vaughan.* New York: Da Capo Press, 1994.

Govenar, Alan. *Meeting the Blues: The Rise of the Texas Sound.* Dallas: Taylor, 1988.

Graham, Shirley. *Paul Robeson, Citizen of the World.* New York: Messner, 1946.

Gray, John. *African Music: A Bibliographical Guide to the Traditional, Popular, Art, and Liturgical Musics of Sub-Saharan Africa.* Westport, CT: Greenwood Press, 1991.

_____. *Blacks in Classical Music.* Westport, CT: Greenwood Press, 1988.

_____. *Fire Music: A Bibliography of the New Jazz, 1959-1990.* Westport, CT: Greenwood Press, 1991.

Green, Mildred Denby. *Black Women Composers: A Genesis.* Boston: Twayne Publishers, 1983.

Bibliography

Greenfield, Eloise. *Paul Robeson.* New York: Crowell, 1975.

Gridley, Mark C. *Concise Guide to Jazz.* Englewood Cliffs, NJ: Prentice-Hall, 1992.

_____. *Jazz Styles.* Englewood Cliffs, NJ: Prentice-Hall, 1978; 2nd ed., 1985.

Groom, Bob. *The Blues Revival.* London: Studio Vista, 1971.

Guralnick, Peter. *Sweet Soul Music: Rhythm and Blues and the Southern Dream of Freedom.* New York: Harper & Row, 1986.

Gutman, Bill. *Duke: The Musical Life of Duke Ellington.* New York: Random House, Inc., 1977.

Haas, Robert Bartlett, ed. *William Grant Still and the Fusion of Cultures in American Music.* Los Angeles: Black Sparrow Press, 1972.

Hadlock, Richard. *Jazz Masters of the Twenties.* New York: Macmillan Publishing, Co., 1965.

Hager, Steve. *Hip Hop: The Illustrated History of Breakdancing, Rap Music, and Graffiti.* New York: St. Martin's Press, 1984.

Hall, Gwendolyn M. *Social Control in Slave Plantation Societies.* Baltimore: Johns Hopkins University Press, 1971.

Halliburton, Warren J. *The Picture Life of Michael Jackson.* New York: Franklin Watts, 1984.

Ham, Debra Newman, ed. *The African American Mosaic: A Library of Congress Resource Guide for the Study of Black History and Culture.* Washington, D.C.: Library of Congress, 1993.

Hamilton, Virginia. *Paul Robeson: The Life and Times of a Free Man.* New York: Harper and Row, 1974.

Hamm, Charles E., Bruno Nettl and Ronald Byrnside. *Contemporary Music Cultures.* Englewood Cliffs, NJ: Prentice-Hall, 1975.

Handy, Antoinette. *Black Women in American Bands and Orchestras.* Metuchen, NJ: The Scarecrow Press, Inc., 1981.

_____. *The International Sweethearts of Rhythm.* Metuchen, NJ: The Scarecrow Press, Inc., 1983.

Handy, William C. *Father of the Blues: An Autobiography.* New York: Macmillan Publishing Co., 1941; New York: Collier, 1970.

Haney, Lynn. *Naked at the Feast: A Biography of Josephine Baker.* New York: Dodd, Mead and Co., 1981.

Bibliography

Haralambos, Michael. *Right On: From Blues to Soul in Black America.* New York: Drake Publishers, 1975.

_____. *Soul Music.* New York: Da Capo Press, 1985.

Harris, Michael W. *The Rise of Gospel Blues: The Music of Thomas Dorsey in the Urban Church.* New York: Oxford University Press, 1992.

Harrison, Max. *Charlie Parker.* London: Cassell, 1960; New York: A. S. Barnes, 1961.

Harrisson, Daphne Duval. *Black Pearls: Blues Queens of the 1920's.* New Brunswick, NJ: Rutgers University Press, 1988.

Haskins, James. *About Michael Jackson.* Hillside, NJ: Enslow Publishers, Inc., 1985.

_____. *Black Music in America: A History Through It's People.* New York: Harper Collins, 1987.

_____. *I'm Gonna Make You Love Me: The Story of Diana Ross.* New York: Dell Publishing Co., 1980.

_____. *The Story of Stevie Wonder.* London: Granada Publishing Co., 1976.

Haskins, James, and Kathleen Benson. *Lena: A Personal and Professional Biography of Lena Horne.* New York: Stein & Day, Publishers, 1984.

_____. *Nat King Cole.* Briarcliff Manor, NY: Stein & Day, Publishers, 1984.

_____. *Scott Joplin: The Man Who Made Ragtime.* Garden City, NY: Doubleday & Co., Inc., 1978; Briarcliff Manor, NY: Stein & Day, Publishers, 1980.

Hasse, John Edward, ed. *Beyond Category: The Life and Genius of Duke Ellington.* New York: Simon & Schuster Inc., 1993.

_____. *Ragtime: Its History, Composers and Music.* New York: Schirmer Books, 1985.

Hatay, Nona. *Jimi Hendrix: The Spirit Lives On.* San Francisco: Last Gasp of San Francisco, 1983.

Haydon, Geoffrey and Dennis Marks. *Repercussions: A Celebration of African American Music.* London: Century Publishers, 1985.

Heilbut, Anthony. *The Gospel Sound: Good News and Bad Times.* New York: Simon & Schuster Inc., 1971; New York: Anchor Press/ Doubleday & Co., Inc., 1985.

Hentoff, Nat. *The Jazz Life.* New York: Dial Press, 1961.

Bibliography

_____, and Albert J. McCarthy, eds. *Jazz: New Perspectives on the History of Jazz by Twelve of the Worlds Foremost Jazz Critics and Scholars.* New York: Holt, Rinehart, and Winston, 1959; New York: Da Capo Press, 1975.

Herskovits, Melville J. *The Myth of the Negro Past.* New York: Harper & Row, 1941.

Hill, George and Spencer Moon. *Blacks in Hollywood: Five Favorable Years in Film & Television, 1987-1991.* New York: Daystar Publishing Company, 1994.

Hinton, Milt, and David G. Berger. *Bass Line.* Philadelphia: Temple University Press, 1988.

Hirsch, Paul. *The Structure of the Popular Music Industry.* Ann Arbor, MI: The Institute for Social Research, 1964.

Hirshey, Gerri. *Nowhere to Run: The Story of Soul Music.* New York: Times Books, 1984.

Hobsbawn, Eric J. *The Jazz Scene.* New York: Da Capo Press, 1975.

Hobson, Constance Tibbs and Deborra Richardson. *Ulysses Kay: A Bio-bibliography.* Westport, CT: Greenwood Press, 1994.

Hobson, Wilder. *American Jazz Music.* New York: W. W. Norton & Co., 1939.

Hodeir, Andre. *Jazz: Its Evolution and Essence.* New York: Grove Press, 1956; New York: Da Capo Press, 1975.

Holiday, Billie, with William Dufty. *Lady Sings the Blues.* New York: Doubleday & Co., Inc., 1956; New York: Penguin Books, 1984.

Holman, Michael. *Break Dancing and the New York City Breakers.* New York: Freundlich Books, 1984.

Horne, Aaron. *String Music of Black Composers.* New York: Greenwood Press, 1991.

_____. *Woodwind Music of Black Composers.* New York: Greenwood Press, 1990.

Horne, Marilyn, with Jane Scovall. *Marilyn Horne: My Life.* New York: Atheneum Publishers, 1983.

Horricks, Raymond. *Count Basie and His Orchestra. It's Music and Musicians.* London: Victor Gollancz, 1957.

_____. *Dizzy Gillespie and the Be-Bop Revolution.* New York: Hippocrene Books, 1984.

_____. *Profiles in Jazz: From Sidney Bechet to John Coltrane.* New York, London: Transaction Publishers, 1991.

Hoyt, Edwin P. Paul. *Robeson: The American Othello.* Cleveland: World, 1967.

Huggins, Nathan. *Harlem Renaissance.* New York: Oxford University Press, 1971.

Hughes, Langston, and Milton Meltzer. *Black Magic: A Pictorial History of the African American in the Performing Arts.* Englewood Cliffs, NJ, Prentice-Hall, 1967; New York: Da Capo Press, 1990.

Jackson, George Pullen. *Spiritual Folk Songs of Early America.* New York: Dover Publications, 1964.

Jackson, Mahalia, and Evan Wylie. *Movin On Up.* London: Hawthorne Books, 1966.

Jacobs, Linda. *Roberta Flack, Sound of Velvet Melting.* St. Paul, MN: EMC Corp., 1975.

James, Michael. *Dizzy Gillespie.* London: Cassell, 1959.

_____. *Miles Davis.* New York: A. S. Barnes, 1961.

Jasen, David A. *Tin Pan Alley.* New York: Donald L. Fine, 1988.

Jasen, David A., and Jay Tichenor. *Rags and Ragtime: A Musical History.* Mineola, NY: Dover Publications, 1989.

Jest, Ekkehard. *Free Jazz.* Graz: Universal, 1974.

Jewell, Derek. *Duke: A Portrait of Duke Ellington.* New York: Norton, 1977.

Johnson, James Weldon, and J. Rosamond Johnson. *The Book of American Negro Spirituals.* New York: Viking Press, 1925, 1969.

Jones, A. M.. *Studies in African Music.* London: Oxford University Press, 1956, 1959.

Jones, Hettie. *Big Star Fallin Mama: Five Women in Black Music.* New York: Viking Press, 1974.

Jones, LeRoi (Baraka, Amiri). *Black Music.* New York: William Morrow & Co., 1967.

_____. *Blues People: The Negro Experience in White America and the Music That Developed From It.* New York: William Morrow & Co., 1963, 1971.

Jones, Max, and John Chilton. *Louis: The Louis Armstrong Story.* New York: Little, Brown, 1972.

Jones, Ralph H. *Charles Albert Tindley: Prince of Preachers.* Nashville, TN: Abingdon Press, 1982.

Katz, Bernard, ed. *The Social Implications of Early Negro Music in the United States.* New York: Arno/The New York Times, 1969.

Keepnews, Orrin, and Bill Grauer, Jr. *A Pictorial History of Jazz.* 2nd ed., rev. New York: Crown, 1966.

Keil, Charles. *Urban Blues.* Chicago: University of Chicago Press, 1966.

Kennedy, Rick. *Jelly Roll, Bix and Hoagy: Gennett Studios and the Birth of Recorded Jazz.* Bloomington, IN: Indiana University Press, 1994.

Kenney, William Howland. *Chicago Jazz: A Cultural History, 1904-1930.* New York: Oxford University Press, 1993.

Kimball, Robert and William Balcom. *Reminiscing with Sissle and Blake.* New York: The Wiking Press, 1973.

Kliment, Bud. *Billie Holiday.* New York: Chelsea House, 1990.

_____. *Count Basie.* New York: Hippocrene Books, 1984.

_____. *Ella Fitzgerald.* New York: Chelsea House, 1988.

Kofsky, Frank. *Black Nationalism and the Revolution in Music.* New York: Pathfinder Press, 1970.

Kravetz, Sallie. *Ethel Ennis: The Reluctant Jazz Star.* Baltimore, MD: Hughes Enterprises, 1984.

Krehbiel, Henry Edward. *Afro-American Folksongs: A Study in Racial and National Music.* New York: Frederick Ungar Publishing Co., 1962.

Lambert, G. E. *Duke Ellington.* London: Cassell, 1959; New York: Barnes, 1961.

Larkin, Rochelle. *Soul Music.* New York: Lancer Books, 1970.

Laufe, Abe. *Broadway's Greatest Musicals.* New York: Funk and Wagnalls, 1969.

Layne, Maude Wanzer. *The Negros Contribution to Music.* Philadelphia: Theodore Presser, 1942.

Lee, Edward. *Jazz: An Introduction.* London: Kahn & Averill, 1972.

Leonard, Neil. *Jazz and the White Americans. The Acceptance of a New Art Form.* Chicago: University of Chicago Press, 1962.

Lester, James. *Too Marvelous for Words: The Life and Genius of Art Tatum.* New York: Oxford University Press, 1994.

Levine, Lawrence W. *Black Culture and Black Consciousness: Afro-American Folk Thought from Slavery to Freedom.* New York: Oxford University Press, 1977.

Levy, Eugene. *James Weldon Johnson: Black Leader, Black Voice.* Chicago: University of Chicago Press, 1973.

Lewis, David Levering. *The Portable Harlem Renaissance Reader.* New York: Penguin Publishers, 1994.

_____. *When Harlem Was in Vogue.* New York: Alfred A. Knopf, 1981.

Lichtenstein, Grace, and Laura Dankner. *Musical Gumbo: The Music of New Orleans.* New York: W. W. Norton & Co., 1993.

Lieb, Sandra. *Mother of the Blues: A Study of Ma Rainey.* Amherst, MA: University of Massachusetts Press, 1981.

Litweiler, John. *The Freedom Principle: Jazz After 1958.* New York: William Morrow & Co., 1984.

Locke, Alain. *The Negro and His Music.* New York: Arno/The New York Times (reissue of a 1936 edition), 1969.

Lomax, Alan. *Mister Jelly Roll: The Fortunes of Jelly Roll Morton, New Orleans Creole and Inventor of Jazz.* New York: Duell, Sloane and Pearce, 1950; 2nd ed. Berkeley: University of California Press, 1973.

_____. *The Land Where the Blues Began.* New York: Pantheon Books, 1993.

Lomax, John A. and Alan Lomax. *American Ballads and Folk Songs.* New York: Macmillan Publishing Co., 1934.

Lott, Eric. *Love & Theft: Blackface Minstrelsy and the American Working Class.* New York: Oxford University Press, 1993.

Lovell, John. *Black Song: The Forge and the Flame.* New York: Paragon House Publishers, 1972, 1986.

Lovinggood, Penman. *Famous Modern Negro Musicians.* 2nd ed. New York: Da Capo Press, 1978. Originally published, 1921.

Machlin, Paul S. *Stride: The Music of Fats Waller.* Boston: Twayne Publishers, 1985.

Major, Clarence. *Dictionary of Afro-American Slang.* New York: International, 1970.

Mapp, Edward. *Blacks in American Films: Today and Yesterday.* Metuchen, NJ: The Scarecrow Press, Inc., 1972.

Marquis, Donald M. *In Search of Buddy Bolden: First Man of Jazz.* New York: Da Capo Press, 1980.

Marsh, J. B. T. *The Story of the Jubilee Singers.* New York: Negro University Press, 1969.

Bibliography

Maultsby, Portia K. *Afro-American Religious Music: A Study in Musical Diversity.* New York: Wittenberg University, 1986.

McCarthy, Albert J. *Louis Armstrong.* New York: A. S. Barnes, 1961.

McDearmon, Kay. *Mahalia.* New York: Dodd, Mead and Co., 1976.

McEwen, Joe. *Sam Cooke: The Man Who Invented Soul.* New York: Chappell Music, 1977.

McKay, Claude. *Harlem: Negro Metropolis.* New York: Dutton, 1940.

McKee, Margaret, and Fred Chisenhall. *Beale Black and Blue: Life and Music on Black Americas Main Street.* Baton Rouge, LA: Louisiana State University Press, 1981.

Meeker, David. *Jazz in the Movies: A Guide to Jazz Musicians, 1917-1977.* New Rochelle, NY: Arlington House, 1977.

Millar, Bill. *The Coasters.* London: W. H. Allen, 1975.

_____. *The Drifters.* London: Studio Vista, 1971.

Mingus, Charles. *Beneath the Underdog.* New York: Knopf, 1971.

Moore, Carman. *Somebody's Angel Child: The Story of Bessie Smith.* New York: T. Y. Crowell, 1969.

Moore, MacDonald Smith. *Yankee Blues: Musical Culture and American Identity.* Bloomington, IN: Indiana University Press, 1985.

Morgan, Thomas L., and William Barlow. *From Cakewalks to Concert Hall: An Illustrated History of African American Popular Music From 1895 to 1930.* Washington, DC: Elliott & Clark, 1992.

Morgenstern, Dan, and Ole Brask. *Jazz People.* Englewood Cliffs, NJ; New York: Prentice-Hall; Harry N. Abrams, 1976.

Morgun, Alun. *Count Basie.* New York: Hippocrene Books, 1984.

Morris, Aldon. *The Origins of the Civil Rights Movement.* New York: The Free Press, 1984.

Morton, David C., with Charles K. Wolfe. *Deford Bailey: A Black Star in Early Country Music.* Knoxville: University of Tennessee Press, 1991.

Mulhern, Tom, ed. *Bass Heroes. Styles, Stories and Secrets of 30 Great Bass Players.* San Francisco: GPI Books, Miller Freeman, Inc. 1993.

Murray, Albert. *Stomping the Blues.* New York: Vintage Books, 1982.

_____. *The Hero and the Blues.* Columbia, MO: University of Missouri Press, 1973.

Nanry, Charles. *American Music—From Storyville to Woodstock*. New Brunswick, NJ: Transaction, 1972.

Neff, Robert and Anthony Connor. *Blues*. Boston: David R. Godine, 1975.

Nelson, Havelock, and Michael A. Gonzales. *Bring the Noise: A Guide to Rap Music and Hip Hop Culture*. New York: Crown, 1991.

Nettl, Bruno. *Folk and Traditional Music of the Western Continents*. Englewood Cliffs, NJ: Prentice-Hall, 1965.

Nettl, Bruno. *Folk Music in the United States: An Introduction*. Detroit: Wayne State University Press, 3rd ed., 1976.

Newmark, Mark. *Entrepreneurs of Profit and Pride: From Black Appeal to Radio Soul*. New York: Praeger, 1988.

The New National Baptist Hymnal. Nashville: National Baptist Publishing Board, 1982.

Nicholson, Stuart. *Ella Fitzgerald: A Biography of the First Lady of Jazz*. New York: Scribner and Sons, 1994.

Nketia, J. H. Kwabena. *Folk Songs of Ghana*. Legon: University of Ghana, 1963.

_____. *The Music of Africa*. New York: W. W. Norton & Co., 1974.

O'Meally, Robert. *Lady Day: The Many Faces of Billie Holiday*. New York: Arcade Publishing, 1991.

Oakley, Giles. *The Devil's Music*. London: P. Ariel Books, 1983.

Obrecht, Jas, ed. *Blues Guitar: The Men Who Made the Music*. San Francisco: GPI Books, 1990.

Odum, Howard W., and Guy B. Johnson. *The Negro and His Songs: A Study of Typical Negro Songs in the South*. Chapel Hill: Univ. of North Carolina Press, 1925.

Oliver, Paul. *Blues Fell This Morning: The Meaning of the Blues*. London: Cassell, 1960; New York: Horizon Press, 1983.

_____. *Blues Off the Record*. Turnbridge Wells: Baton Press, 1985.

_____. *Conversations with the Blues*. New York: Horizon Press, 1983.

_____. *Savannah Syncopators*. New York: Stein & Day, Publishers, 1970.

_____. *Screening the Blues*. London: Cassell, 1968.

_____. *Songsters and Saints: Vocal Traditions on Race Records*. Cambridge, England: Cambridge University Press, 1984.

_____. *The Story of the Blues*. Philadelphia: Chilton Book Co., 1969.

Oliver, Paul, Max Harrison, and William Bolcom. *The New Grove Gospel, Blues and Jazz*. New York: W. W. Norton & Co., 1980, 1986.

Ostransky, Leroy. *The Anatomy of Jazz*. Seattle, WA: University of Washington Press, 1960; Westport, CT: Greenwood Press, 1963.

_____. *Understanding Jazz*. Englewood Cliffs, NJ: Prentice-Hall/ Spectrum Books, 1977.

Palmer, Richard. *Oscar Peterson*. New York: Hippocrene Books, 1984.

Panassie, Hugues. *Louis Armstrong*. New York: Scribners & Sons, 1971.

_____. *The Real Jazz*. London: Smith and Durrell, 1942; Westport, CT: Greenwood Press, 1973.

Papich, Stephen. *Remembering Josephine: A Biography of Josephine Baker*. New York/ Indianapolis: Bobbs-Merrill, 1976.

Parrish, Lydia. *Slave Songs of the Georgia Sea Islands*. Hatboro, PA: Folklore Associates, 1942, 1965. Reprint

Patterson, Willis, comp. *Anthology of Art Songs by Black American Composers*. New York: Edward B. Marks Music, 1977.

Payne, Bishop Daniel E. *History of the African Methodist Episcopal Church*. New York: Johnson Reprint Corporation, 1968. Originally published in 1891

Petrie, Gavin, ed. *Black Music*. London; New York: Hamlyn, 1974.

Pike, Gustavus D. *The Singing Campaign For Ten Thousand Pounds*. Rev. ed. New York: American Missionary Association, 1974. Originally published, 1875.

Pleasants, Henry. *The Agony of Modern Music*. New York: Simon & Schuster Inc., 1955.

_____. *The Great American Popular Singers*. New York: Simon & Schuster Inc., 1974

Ploski, Harry A. and Ernest Kaiser. *The Negro Almanac*. Boston: The Bellwether Company, 1971

Porter, Lewis. *Lester Young*. Boston: G.K. Hall & Co., 1985

Porter, Lewis, Michael Ullman with Edward Hazell. *Jazz From Its Origins to the Present*. Englewood Cliffs, New Jersey: Prentice Hall, 1993.

Pratt, Ray. *Rhythm and Resistance: The Political Uses of American Popular Music*. Washington, DC: Smithsonian Institution Press, 1994.

Priestley, Brian. *Charlie Parker*. New York: Hippocrene Books, 1984.

Rattenbury, Ken. *Duke Ellington: Jazz Composer.* New Haven, Conn.: Yale University Press, 1990.

Reagon, Bernice Johnson, ed. *Black-American Culture and Scholarship: Contemporary Issues.* Washington, DC: Smithsonian Institution Press, 1986.

_____, ed. *Well Understand It Better By and By.* Washington, DC: Smithsonian Institution Press, 1992.

Reese, Krista. *Chuck Berry: Mr. Rock 'n' Roll.* London: Proteus Books, 1982.

Reisner, Robert George. *Bird: The Legend of Charlie Parker.* New York: Citadel Press, 1961; New York: Da Capo Press, 1975.

_____. *The Jazz Titans.* Garden City, NY: Doubleday & Co., Inc., 1960.

_____. *The Literature of Jazz, a Preliminary Bibliography.* New York: New York Public Library, 1954.

Ricks, George Robinson. *Some Aspects of the Religious Music of the United States Negro: An Ethnomusicological Study with Emphasis on the Gospel Tradition.* New York: Arno Press, 1977.

Ritz, David. *Divided Soul: The Life of Marvin Gaye.* New York: McGraw-Hill, 1985.

Roach, Hildred. *Black American Music: Past and Present.* Boston: Crescendo Publishing, 1973; Melbourne, FL: Krieger Publishing Co., 2nd ed., 1992.

Roberts, John Storm. *Black Music of Two Worlds.* New York: William Morrow & Co., 1974.

Robeson, Eslanda Goode. *Paul Robeson, Negro.* London: Victor Gollancz, Ltd., 1930.

Robeson, Paul. *Here I Stand.* New York: Othello Associates, 1957.

Robeson, Susan. *The Whole World In His Hands: A Pictorial Biography of Paul Robeson.* New York: Citadel Press - Carol Publishing Group, 1981, 1990.

Rooney, James. *Bossmen: Bill Monroe and Muddy Waters.* New York: Da Capo Press, 1991.

Rose, Al. *Eubie Blake.* New York: Schirmer Books, 1979.

_____. *I Remember Jazz.* Louisiana: Louisiana State University Press, 1987.

_____. *Storyville, New Orleans: Being an Authentic, Illustrated Account of the Notorious Red-Light District.* Alabama: University of Alabama, 1974.

Rose, Tricia. *Black Noise: Rap Music and Black Culture in Contemporary America.* Hanover, NH: Wesleyan University Press, 1994.

Rose, Tricia, and Andrew Ross, eds. *Microphone Fiends: Youth Music and Youth Culture.* New York: Routledge, 1994.

Rowe, Mike. *Chicago Blues.* New York: Da Capo Press, 1981.

Rublowsky, John. *Black Music in America.* New York: Basic Books, 1971.

Russell, Ross. *Bird Lives! The High Life and Hard Times of Charlie (Yardbird) Parker.* New York: Charterhouse, 1973.

_____. *Jazz Style in Kansas City and the Southwest.* Berkeley, Los Angeles: University of California Press, 1971.

Russell, Tony. *Blacks, Whites and Blues.* New York: Stein & Day, Publishers, 1970.

Russo, William. *Jazz Composition and Orchestration.* Chicago: University of Chicago Press, 1968.

Rust, Brian. *The Dance Bands.* New Rochelle, NY: Arlington House, 1974.

Sampson, Harry T. *Blacks in Blackface: A Source Book on Early Black Musical Shows.* Metuchen, NJ, London: The Scarecrow Press, Inc., 1980.

Sargeant, Winthrop. *Jazz: A History.* New York: McGraw-Hill, 1964; New York: Da Capo Press, 3rd ed., 1975.

Sawyer, Charles. *The Arrival of B. B. King: The Authorized Biography.* New York: Doubleday & Co., Inc., 1980.

Scarborough, Dorothy. *On the Trail of Negro Folksongs.* Cambridge, MA: Harvard University Press, 1925.

Schafer, William J., and Johannes Riedel. *The Art of Ragtime: Form and Meaning of an Original Black American Art.* Baton Rouge, LA: Louisiana State University Press, 1973.

Schwerin, Jules. *Got To Tell It: Mahalia Jackson, Queen of Gospel.* New York: Oxford University Press, 1992.

Schiffman, Jack. *Uptown: The Story of Harlems Apollo Theatre.* New York: Cowles Book Company, 1971.

Schleman, Hilton R. *Rhythm on Record: A Who's Who and Register of Recorded Dance Music, 1906-1936.* London: Melody Maker, 1936.

Schuller, Gunther. *Early Jazz: It's Roots and Musical Development.* New York: Oxford University Press, 1968.

_____. *The Swing Era.* New York: Oxford University Press, 1989.

Selfridge, John. *John Coltrane.* New York: Chelsea House, 1994.

Seton, Marie. *Paul Robeson.* London: Dobson Press, 1958.

Shapiro, Nat, and Nat Hentoff. *Hear Me Talkin to Ya: The Story of Jazz by the Men Who Made It.* New York: Dover Publications, 1955.

_____. *The Jazz Makers.* New York: Rinehart, 1957; Westport, CT: Greenwood Press, 1975.

Shaw, Arnold. *Black Popular Music in America.* New York: Schirmer Books, 1986.

_____. *Fifty Second Street: The Street of Jazz.* New York: Da Capo Press, 1977.

_____. *Honkers and Shouters: The Golden Years of Rhythm and Blues.* New York: Macmillan Publishing Co., 1978.

_____. *The Rockin 50's: The Decade that Transformed the Pop Music Scene.* New York: Hawthorn Books, Inc., 1974.

_____. *The World of Soul.* New York: Cowles Book Co., 1970.

Sidran, Ben. *Black Talk.* New York: Holt, Rinehart and Winston, 1971.

Simon, George T. *The Big Bands.* rev. ed. New York: Macmillan Publishing Co., 1975.

Simpkins, C. O. *Coltrane.* Baltimore: Black Classic Press, 1989.

Small, Christopher. *Music of the Common Tongue: Survival and Celebration in Afro-American Music.* New York: Riverrun Press, 1987.

Smith, Ruth A. *The Life and Works of Thomas A. Dorsey.* Chicago: Thomas A. Dorsey, 1935.

Smith, Willie The Lion. *Music On My Mind.* New York: Da Capo Press, 1978.

Songs of Zion. Nashville: Abingdon, 1981.

Sonnier, Austin. *A Guide to the Blues: History, Who's Who, Research Sources.* Westport, CT: Greenwood Press, 1994.

Southall, Geneva. *Blind Tom: The Post-Civil War Enslavement of a Black Musical Genius.* Minneapolis: Challenge Productions, Inc., 1980.

Southern, Eileen. *The Music of Black Americans: A History.* rev. ed. New York: W. W. Norton & Co., 1971, 1982.

_____, ed. *Readings in Black American Music.* New York: W. W. Norton & Co., 1972.

Southern, Eileen, and Josephine Wright, comps. *African American Traditions in Song, Sermon, Tale, and Dance, 1600s-1920: An Annotated Bibliography of Literature, Collections, and Artworks.* Westport, Conn.: Greenwood Press, 1990.

Bibliography

Spellman, A. B. *Black Music: Four Lives in the Bebop Business*. New York: Pantheon, 1966; New York: Schocken, reprint, 1970.

Spencer, Jon Michael. *Black Hymnody: A Hymnological History of the African American Church*. Knoxville: University of Tennessee Press, 1992.

Standifer, James, and Barbara Reeder. *Source Book of African and Afro-American Materials for Music Educators*. Washington, DC: Contemporary Music Project, 1972.

Stearns, Marshall W. *Jazz Dance: The Story of American Vernacular Dance*. New York: Macmillan Publishing Co., 1968.

_____. *The Story of Jazz*. New York: Oxford University Press, 1956, 1970.

Stewart, Rex. *Jazz Masters of the Thirties*. Roots of Jazz Series. New York: Da Capo Press, 1980.

Stewart-Baxter, Derrick. *Ma Rainey and the Classic Blues Singers*. New York: Stein & Day, Publishers, 1970.

Sudhalter, R. M., P. R. Evans, and W. D. Myatt. *Bix: Man and Legend*. New York: Schirmer Books, 1974.

Summerfield, Maurice J. *The Jazz Guitar: Gateshead, Tyne and Wear*. England: Ashley Mark Publishing Company, 1978.

Tanenhaus, Sam. *Louis Armstrong*. New York: Chelsea House, 1989.

Tanner, Paul O. W., and Maurice Gerow. *A Study of Jazz*. Dubuque, IA: William C. Brown, 1973.

Taraborelli, J. Randy, with Darryl Minger and Reginald Wilson. *Diana Ross*. Garden City: Doubleday & Co., Inc., 1985.

Taylor, Billy. *Jazz Piano: A Jazz History*. Dubuque, IA: William C. Brown Co., 1982.

_____. *How to Play Bebop Piano*. New York: Chas. H. Hansen, 1974.

Thomas, J. C. *Chasin' the Trane: The Music and Mystique of John Coltrane*. New York: Da Capo Press, 1976.

Thompson, June Taylor. *Samuel Coleridge-Taylor: The Development of His Compositional Style*. Metuchen, NJ: The Scarecrow Press, Inc., 1994.

Thurman, Howard. *Deep River: Reflections on the Religious Insights of Certain of the Negro Spirituals*. New York: Harper, 1955.

Tirro, Frank. *Jazz: A History*. New York: W. W. Norton & Co., 1977.

Titon, Jeff Todd. *Early Downhome Blues: A Musical and Cultural Analysis*. Urbana, IL: The University of Illinois Press, 1977, 1985.

Tobias, Tobi. *Marian Anderson.* New York: T. Y. Crowell Company, 1972.

Toll, Robert C. *Blacking Up: The Minstrel Show in Nineteenth Century America.* New York: Oxford University Press, 1974.

Tortolano, William. *Samuel Coleridge-Taylor: Anglo-Black Composer. 1875-1912.* Metuchen, N.J.: Scarecrow Press, 1977.

Traguth, Fred. *Modern Jazz Dance.* Englewood Cliffs, NJ: Prentice-Hall, 1983.

Trotter, James. *Music and Some Highly Musical People.* Boston; New York: Johnson Reprint Corporation, 1878; 1968.

Tucker, Mark. *Ellington: The Early Years.* Urbana, IL: The University of Illinois Press, 1991.

_____, ed. *The Duke Ellington Reader.* New York: Oxford University Press, 1993.

Turner, Tina, and Kurt Loder. *I, Tina, My Life Story.* New York: William Morrow & Co., 1986.

Ulanov, Barry. *A History of Jazz In America.* New York: Da Capo Press, 1972.

_____. *Duke Ellington.* New York: Creative Age Press, 1946.

_____. *Handbook of Jazz.* New York: Viking Press, 1957.

Vulliamy, Graham. *Jazz and Blues.* Boston: Routledge & Kegan, 1982.

Waldo, Terry. *This Is Ragtime.* New York: Da Capo Press, 1991 (unabridged republication of original 1976 edition).

Walker, Wyatt Tee. *Somebody's Calling My Name: Black Sacred Music and Social Change.* Valley Forge, PA: Judson Press, 1979.

Walker-Hill, Helen. *Piano Music by Black Women Composers.* New York: Greenwood Press, 1992.

Waller, Maurice, and Anthony Calabrese. *Fats Waller.* New York: Schirmer Books (Macmillan Publishing Co.), 1977.

Walton, Ortiz. *Music: Black, White and Blue.* New York. William Morrow & Co., 1972.

Warner, Jay. *The Billboard Book of American Singing Groups. A History, 1940-1990.* New York: Watson-Guptill Publications, 1992.

Waters, Ethel, and Charles Samuels. *His Eye Is on the Sparrow.* New York: Doubleday & Co., Inc., 1950.

Watkins, William, and Eric Franklin. *Breakdance.* Chicago: Contemporary Books, 1984.

White, Charles. *The Life and Times of Little Richard: The Quasar of Rock.* New York: Crown Publishers, Harmony Books, 1984.

White, Evelyn Davidson, comp. *Choral Music by Afro-American Composers.* Metuchen, NJ: The Scarecrow Press, Inc., 1981.

White, John. *Billie Holiday: Her Life and Times.* New York: Universe, 1987.

Whiteman, Paul, with Mary Margaret McBride. *Jazz.* New York: Arno Press, 1975.

Wilcox, Donald E., with Buddy Guy. *Damn Right I've Got the Blues.* San Francisco: Woodford Press, 1993.

Wilder, Alec. *American Popular Song.* New York: Oxford University Press, 1972.

Williams, Martin. *Jazz Masters in Transition, 1957-1969.* New York: Macmillan Publishing Co.; Da Capo Press 1970; 1980.

_____. *Jazz Masters of New Orleans.* New York: Macmillan Publishing Co., 1967.

_____. *Jazz Panorama.* New York: The Crowell-Collier Publishing Co., 1962.

_____. *Jelly Roll Morton.* New York: A. S. Barnes, 1963.

_____. *King Oliver.* New York: A. S. Barnes, 1961.

_____. *The Art of Jazz. Essays on the Nature and Development of Jazz.* New York: Oxford University Press, 1959.

_____. *The Jazz Tradition.* New York: Oxford University Press, 1970.

_____. *Where's the Melody?* New York: Pantheon Books, 1969.

Williams, Ora. *American Black Women in the Arts and Social Sciences: A Bibliographic Survey.* Metuchen, NJ: The Scarecrow Press, Inc., 1973, 1981, 1994.

Wilmer, Valerie. *Jazz People.* Indianapolis: Bobbs-Merrill, 1971.

Wilson, John S. *Jazz: The Transition Years, 1940-1960.* New York: Appleton, Century, Crofts, 1966.

Witmark, Isadore. *The Story of the House of Witmark: From Ragtime to Swing Time.* New York: L. Furman, 1939.

Wolfe, Charles, and Kip Lornell. *The Life and Legend of Leadbelly.* New York: Harper Collins, 1992.

Wolfe, Rinna Evelyn. *The Calvin Simmons Story, or Don't Call Me Maestro.* Berkeley, California: Muse Wood Press, 1994.

Wolff, Daniel, with S. R. Crain, Clifton White and G. David Tenenbaum. *You Send Me: The Life and Times of Sam Cooke*. New York: William Morrow & Co., 1995.

Woll, Allen. *Black Musical Theatre: From Coontown to Dreamgirls*. New York: Da Capo Press, 1991.

Work, John W. *American Negro Songs*. New York: Howell, Soskin & Co., 1940.

SELECTED DISSERTATIONS

Adkins, Aldrich Wendell. *The Development of Black Art Song*. D.M.A., University of Texas at Austin, 1971.

Berliner, Paul Franklin. *The Soul of Mbira: An Ethnography of the Mbira Among the People of Rhodesia*. Ph.D., Wesleyan University, 1954.

Black, Donald Fisher. *The Life and Work of Eva Jessye and Her Contributions to American Music*. University of Michigan, 1987. Ann Arbor: University Microfilms.

Boyer, Horace Clarence. *An Analysis of Black Church Music, with Examples Drawn from Services in Rochester*. New York. Ph.D., Music, University of Rochester, 1973.

Caldwell, Hansonia. *Black Idioms in Opera as Reflected in the Works of Six Afro-American Composers*. Los Angeles, California: University of Southern California, 1974.

Davis, Nathan Tate. *Charlie Parker's Kansas City Environment and its Effect on His Later Life*. Ph.D., Wesleyan University, 1974.

Ennett, Dorothy. *An Analysis and Comparison of Selected Piano Sonatas by Three Contemporary Black Composers: George Walker, Howard Swanson, and Roque Cordero*. Ph.D., Performance, New York University, 1973.

Garcia, William Burres. *The Life and Choral Music of John Wesley Work III (1901-1967)*. Ph.D., Choral Literature, University of Iowa, 1973.

George, Zelma Watson. *A Guide to Negro Music: An Annotated Bibliography of Negro Folk Music and Art Music by Negro Composers or Based on Negro Thematic Material*. New York University, 1953.

Harris, Carl. *A Study of Characteristic Stylistic Trends Found in the Choral Works of a Selected Group of Afro-American Composers and Arrangers*. D.M.A., Performance, University of Missouri, Kansas City, 1973.

Jackson, Raymond. *The Evolution of Piano Music as Seen in Works of Four Black Composers (R. Nathaniel Dett, Florence Price, Howard Swanson, George Walker)*. D.M.A., Piano, The Julliard School of Music, 1973.

Kamin, Jonathan Liff. *Rhythm and Blues in White America: Rock and Roll as Acculturation and Perceptual Learning*. Ph.D., Princeton University, 1975.

McBrier, Vivian Flagg. *The Life and Works of Robert Nathaniel Dett.* Catholic University of America, 1967. Ann Arbor: University Microfilms (No. 67-17142).

Reed, Addison Walker. *The Life and Works of Scott Joplin.* Ph.D., Musicology, University of North Carolina, 1973.

Reisser, Marsha J. *Compositional Techniques and Afro-American Musical Traits in Selected Published Works by Howard Swanson.* Ph.D., University of Wisconsin. Ann Arbor: University Microfilms, 1982.

Riis, Thomas Laurence. *Black Musical Theatre in New York, 1890-1915.* The University of Michigan, 1981.

Schlosser, Anatol. *Paul Robeson, His Career in the Theater, Motion Pictures, and on the Concert Stage.* New York University.

Stewart, Milton. *Structural Development in the Jazz Improvisational Technique of Clifford Brown.* Ph.D., Musicology, University of Michigan, 1973.

Thompson, Leon Everette. *A Historical and Stylistic Analysis of the Music of William Grant Still and a Thematic Catalogue of His Works.* University of Southern California, 1966.

Turkson, Adolphus. *Effutu Asafo Music: A Study of a Traditional Music of Ghana with Special Reference to the Role of Tone Language in Choral Music Involving Structural and Harmonic Analysis.* Ph.D., Musicology, Northwestern University, 1972.

JOURNALS AND MAGAZINES

Allegro, The Monthly Journal of New York's Local 802. American Federation of Musicians.

Annual Review of Jazz Studies (Transaction Books: Rutgers University; New Brunswick, N.J. 08903)

Bebop and Beyond (Los Angeles)

Black Music Research Journal (Center for Black Music Research, Columbia College Chicago)

Black Perspective in Music (The Foundation for Research in the Afro-American Creative Arts, Inc.)

Blues Revue Quarterly (Rt. 2, Box 18; West Union, West Virginia 26456)

Cadence (Cadence Building; Redwood, New York 13679)

CBMR Digest (Center for Black Music Research, Columbia College Chicago)

Coda (Box 87 Station J; Toronto, Ontario; M4J4X8 Canada)

Bibliography

Crescendo (122 Wardour Street; London W1V3LA; England)

Current Biography Yearbook

Down Beat (222 W. Adams Street; Chicago, Illinois 60606)

The Duke Ellington Society Newsletter (published monthly - Duke Ellington Society, PO Box 31, Church Street Station, New York, New York 10008-0031)

Guitar Player Magazine (Saratoga, California)

Institute for Studies in American Music Newsletter (Brooklyn College, City University of New York)

Jazz Educators Journal (The National Association of Jazz Educators; Box 724; Manhattan, Kansas 66502)

Jazz Journal International (35 Great Russell Street; London WC1B3PP; England)

Jazz Letter (PO Box 240; Ojai, California 93023)

Jazz Research Papers (The National Association of Jazz Educators; Box 724, Manhattan, Kansas 66502)

Jazz Times (8055 13th Street, Suite 301; Silver Spring, Maryland 20910)

Jazziz (PO Box 8309; Gainesville, Florida 32605-8309)

Jazzletter (Ojai, California - edited by Gene Lee)

Journal of American Folk-Lore (American Folk-Lore Society)

Living Blues, A Journal of the African American Blues Tradition (Circulation Department; University of Mississippi; University, Mississippi 38677)

The Wire (Units G & H; 115 Cleveland Street; London W1P5PN; England)

AFRICAN AMERICAN MUSIC
INDEX

413

414

Index

Index

428

AFRICAN AMERICAN MUSIC
ARTIST/RECORDING INDEX

Index

Index